WILD BLUE

STORIES OF SURVIVAL
FROM AIR AND SPACE

WILD BLUE

STORIES OF SURVIVAL FROM AIR AND SPACE

EDITED BY DAVID FISHER AND WILLIAM GARVEY
ADRENALINE SERIES EDITOR CLINT WILLIS

(adrenaline) ™

Thunder's Mouth Press/
Balliett & Fitzgerald Inc.

New York

First Edition

Compilation copyright © 2000 by David Fisher and William Garvey
Introductions copyright © 2000 by David Fisher and William Garvey

Adrenaline ™ and the Adrenaline™ logo are trademarks of
Balliett & Fitzgerald, Inc. New York, NY.

An Adrenaline™ Book

Published by
Thunder's Mouth Press
841 Broadway, 4th Floor
New York, NY 10003

and

Balliett & Fitzgerald Inc.
66 West Broadway, Suite 602
New York, NY 10007

Distributed by Publishers Group West

Series Editor: Clint Willis

Book design: Sue Canavan

frontispiece photo: © Corbis/Bettmann

Manufactured in the United States of America

ISBN: 1-56025-251-0

Library of Congress Cataloging-in-Publication Data

Wild blue: stories of survival from air and space / edited by David Fisher and
William Garvey; series editor Clint Willis, —1st ed.
     p. cm
"An Adrenaline book"—T.p. verso.
ISBN 1-56025-251-0
1. Aircraft accidents—Prevention—Anecdotes. 2.Airplanes—Piloting—
Anecdotes. 3. Near misses (Aeronautics)—Anecdotes. 4. Near-death experi-
ences—Anecdotes. I. Fisher, David, 1946–II. Garvey, William. III. Willis,
Clint.

TL553.5.W55 2000
629.132'5214—dc21   99-045737

For Tamara and the four kidlings, story lovers all.

—Bill Garvey

Laura, Jesse and Beau, who have taught me a new way to fly.

—David Fisher

c o n t e n t s

p h o t o g r a p h s

introduction

Though not yet a century old, flying has become commonplace. We're sometimes lulled into the notion that it's reasonable or even natural for human beings to sail above the clouds in winged vessels made of cloth and metal.

But there's nothing natural about people flying, and on some level we all know it; that's why so many of us are at least a little afraid to get on an airplane. The sky can be a hostile place, deceptive and dangerous; it's a trap as well as a temple. The air throughout most of the atmosphere is too thin and too cold to support life, and even at treetop level, gravity's power is deadly. Flight takes us to places where we're alien, unfit to live. William Rankin exits from a crippled F8U Crusader at around 47,000 feet; as he plummets through space, unable to see or even breathe, Rankin finds himself at the mercy of a maelstrom that defies measurement—an environment that more than rivals the earth's poles or the summit of Everest for sheer brutality.

Enter that environment in a fast-moving, complex machine that carries large amounts of explosive fuel, and your margin for error can thin to velum. A switch is forgotten, a directive misunderstood, a tube overstressed, a maneuver poorly performed—even such minor glitches can be fatal in the context of flight.

But like Everest or Antarctica, the sky and the space that surrounds it exercise a curious power over some of us. That power derives in part from the unpredictability at the heart of any real adventure. Ernest Gann expects that his night flight on a DC-2 from Nashville to New York will be routine; instead, he comes close to dying because the wrong airports are closed when the weather turns bad. Gann might not call his experience fun, but in a way it was.

The literature of aviation has evolved with flying itself; like the sea, the sky has attracted adventurers with sure hands and poets' hearts who find in flight experience and metaphor that serve us all. Antoine de Saint-Exupéry takes us with him into the heart of a Patagonian gale; Slim Lindbergh, still an unknown, launches us off a barnstormer's wing; teenager Rinker Buck sends us whabanging onto a tumbleweed strip near the Pecos. For some reason, they all want us along for the ride—at least the ride taken in retrospect. Their wish to share the intensity of their experience is impressive as well as flattering; the stories that result are illuminating as well as exciting.

Some of these stories are about dying or killing or both. Roald Dahl and his comrades climb into their 12 Hurricanes to engage 200 Messerschmitts over Athens during World War II. Marshall Harrison directs air strikes in Vietnam from his jungle spotter aircraft. These men's machines were tools of destruction; the men in them were men, acutely aware of their mortality and the astonishing power their machines bestowed upon them—an intoxicating mix for the fliers and for us.

Many of the pilots who wrote or figure in the stories and selections in this book took terrible risks in pursuit of their vocation. Martha Gellhorn's visit to an RAF hospital burn ward reminds us that such risks have consequences. The pilots themselves—from Chuck Yeager (cool) to Sherman Baldwin (worried) to William Lishman (too happy to care)—remind us that there are many ways to face such risks, just as there are many ways to live; and that some ways are more joyful than others—more alive at any rate. The aviator's world is one of astonishing beauty: flying on a clear night over the North Atlantic with brilliant stars above and shimmering icebergs gliding below like galleons; skimming across a regiment of mesas under a cloudless sky toward a vast desert lake, cool, empty and inviting; wheeling and soaring in and out of clouds.

Building these machines and flying them, men and women during the past century have drawn upon their intelligence and courage and craftmanship. The appeal and the interest lie partly in that—in the work itself. Here is Beryl Markham writing of her love of flight:

> "No human pursuit achieves dignity until it can be called work, and when you can experience a physical loneliness for the tools of your trade, you see that the other things— the experiments, the irrelevant vocations, the vanities you used to hold—were false to you."

Markham set aside her fears to make an Atlantic crossing for reasons that for all her eloquence she can't fully explain; her heart's desire almost killed her—not a bad way to almost go. Sculptor William Lishman wanted to fly with birds and found a glider to attempt it; one day he got his wish:

> "The air was full of ducks—in front, below, above, behind, some in ragged chevrons, some in amorphous clusters, wings flashing in the early light . . . I winged along, just another bird in the autumnal squadron headed for the marshes to the northwest, my attention focused on a duck off to my left holding perfect formation about four feet off my wingtip, just as if I had always been his wingmate. . . ."

It's not that Gann and Yeager and the rest are not afraid. It's that flying is worth it.

—William Garvey and David Fisher

from Going Solo
by Roald Dahl

Before writing his famous children's books, Roald Dahl (1916–1990) served as a British fighter pilot in World War II. After surviving a crash in Libya, Dahl was ordered to fly one of the new Hurricane fighters to Greece to join a small group of hopelessly outnumbered RAF pilots. Dahl had never flown in combat; worse, he'd never flown a modern fighter plane at all.

So this was Greece. And what a different place from the hot and sandy Egypt I had left behind me some five hours before. Over here it was springtime and the sky a milky blue and the air just pleasantly warm. A gentle breeze was blowing in from the sea beyond Piraeus and when I turned my head and looked inland I saw only a couple of miles away a range of massive craggy mountains as bare as bones. The aerodrome I had landed on was no more than a grassy field and wild flowers were blossoming blue and yellow and red in their millions all around me.

The two airmen who had helped to lift my cramped body out of the cockpit of the Hurricane had been most sympathetic. I leant against the wing of the plane and waited for the cramp to go out of my legs.

'A bit scrunched up in there, were you?' one of the airmen said.

'A bit,' I said. 'Yes.'

'You oughtn't to be flyin' fighters a chap of your height,' he said. 'What you want is a ruddy great bomber where you can stretch your legs out.'

'Yes,' I said. 'You're right.'

This airman was a Corporal. He had taken my parachute out of the cockpit and now he brought it over and placed it on the ground beside me. He stayed with me and it was clear that he wanted to do some more talking. 'I don't see the point of it, 'he went on. 'You bring a brand-new kite, an *absolutely spanking brand-new kite* straight from the factory and you bring it all the way from ruddy Egypt to this god-forsaken place and what's goin' to 'appen to it?'

'What?' I said.

'It's come even *further* than from Egypt!' he cried. 'It's come all the way from *England*, that's where it's come from! It's come all the way from England to Egypt and then all the way across the Med to this soddin' country and all for what? What's goin' to 'appen to it?'

'What *is* going to happen to it?' I asked him. I was a bit taken aback by this sudden outburst.

'I'll tell you what's goin' to 'appen to it,' the Corporal said, working himself up. 'Crash bang wallop! Shot down in flames! Explodin' in the air! Ground-strafed by the One-O-Nines right 'ere where we're standin' this very moment! Why, this kite won't last one week in this place! None of 'em do!'

'Don't say that,' I told him.

'I 'as to say it,' he said, 'because it's the truth.'

'But why such prophecies of doom?' I asked him. 'Who is going to do this to us?'

'The Krauts, of course!' he cried. 'Krauts is *pourin'* in 'ere like ruddy ants! They've got *one thousand planes* just the other side of those mountains there and what've we got?'

'All right then,' I said. 'What *have* we got?' I was interested to find out.

'It's pitiful what we've got,' the Corporal said.

'Tell me,' I said.

'What we've got is exactly what you can see on this ruddy field!' he said. '*Fourteen 'urricanes!* No it isn't. It's gone up to fifteen now you've brought this one out!'

I refused to believe him. Surely it wasn't possible that fifteen Hurricanes were all we had left in the whole of Greece.

'Are you absolutely sure of this?' I asked him, aghast.

'Am I lyin'?' he said, turning to the second airman. 'Please tell this officer whether I am lyin' or whether it's the truth.'

'It's the gospel truth,' the second airman said.

'What about bombers?' I said.

'There's about four clapped-out Blenheims over there at Menidi,' the Corporal said, 'and that's the lot. *Four Blenheims and fifteen 'urricanes* is the entire ruddy RAF in the 'ole of Greece.'

'Good Lord,' I said.

'Give it another week,' he went on, 'and every one of us'll be pushed into the sea and swimmin' for 'ome!'

'I hope you're wrong.'

'There's five 'undred Kraut fighters and five 'undred Kraut bombers just around the corner,' he went on, 'and what've we got to put up against them? We've got a miserable fifteen 'urricanes and I'm mighty glad I'm not the one that's flyin' 'em! If you'd 'ad any sense at all, matey, you'd've stayed right where you were back in old Egypt.'

I could see he was nervous and I couldn't blame him. The ground-crew in a squadron, the fitters and riggers, were virtually non-combatants. They were never meant to be in the front line and because of that they were unarmed and had never been taught how to fight or defend themselves. In a situation like this, it was easier to be a pilot than one of the ground-crew. The chances of survival might be a good deal slimmer for the pilot, but he had a splendid weapon to fight with.

The Corporal, as I could tell by the grease on his hands, was a fitter. His job was to look after the big Rolls-Royce Merlin engines in the Hurricanes and there was little doubt that he loved them dearly. 'This is a brand-new kite,' he said, laying a greasy hand on the metal wing and stroking it gently. 'It's took somebody *thousands of hours* to build it. And now those silly sods behind their desks back in Cairo 'ave sent it out 'ere where it ain't goin' to last two minutes.'

'Where's the Ops Room?' I asked him.

He pointed to a small wooden hut on the other side of the landing field. Alongside the hut there was a cluster of about thirty tents. I slung my parachute over my shoulder and started to make my way across the field to the hut.

To some extent I was aware of the military mess I had flown in to. I knew that a small British Expeditionary Force, backed up by an equally small air force, had been sent to Greece from Egypt a few months earlier to hold back the Italian invaders, and so long as it was only the Italians they were up against, they had been able to cope. But once the Germans decided to take over, the situation immediately became hopeless. The problem confronting the British now was how to extricate their army from Greece before all the troops were either killed or captured. It was Dunkirk all over again. But it was not receiving the publicity that Dunkirk had received because it was a military bloomer that was best covered up. I guessed that everything the Corporal had just told me was more or less true, but curiously enough none of it worried me in the slightest. I was young enough and starry-eyed enough to look upon this Grecian escapade as nothing more than a grand adventure. The thought that I might never get out of the country alive didn't occur to me. It should have done, and looking back on it now I am surprised that it didn't. Had I paused for a moment and calculated the odds against survival, I would have found that they were about fifty to one and that's enough to give anyone the shakes.

I pushed open the door of the Ops Room hut and went in. There were three men in there, the Squadron-Leader himself and a Flight-Lieutenant and a wireless-operator Sergeant with ear-phones on. I had never met any of them before. Officially, I had been a member of 80 Squadron for more than six months, but up until now I had not succeeded in getting anywhere near it. The last time I had tried, I had finished up on a bonfire in the Western Desert. The Squadron-Leader had a black moustache and a Distinguished Flying Cross ribbon on his chest. He also had a frowning worried look on his face. 'Oh, hello,' he said. 'We've been expecting you for some time.'

'I'm sorry I'm late,' I said.

'Six months late,' he said. 'You can find yourself a bunk in one of the tents. You'll start flying tomorrow like the rest of them.'

I could see that the man was preoccupied and wished to get rid of me, but I hesitated. It was quite a shock to be dismissed as casually as this. It had been a truly great struggle for me to get back on my feet and join the squadron at last, and I had expected at least a brief 'I'm glad you made it,' or 'I hope you're feeling better.' But this, as I suddenly realized, was a different ball game altogether. This was a place where pilots were disappearing like flies. What difference did an extra one make when you only had fourteen? None whatsoever. What the Squadron-Leader wanted was *a hundred* extra planes and pilots, not one.

I went out of the Ops Rooms hut still carrying my parachute over my shoulder. In the other hand I carried a brown paper-bag that contained all the belongings I had been able to bring with me, a toothbrush, a half-finished tube of toothpaste, a razor, a tube of shaving soap, a spare khaki shirt, a blue cardigan, a pair of pyjamas, my Log Book and my beloved camera. Ever since I was fourteen I had been an enthusiastic photographer, starting in 1930 with an old double-extension plate camera and doing my own developing and enlarging. Now I had a Zeiss Super Ikonta with an f 6.3 Tessar lens.

Out in the Middle East, both in Egypt and in Greece, unless it was winter we dressed in nothing but a khaki shirt and khaki shorts and stockings, and even when we flew we seldom bothered to put on a sweater. The paper-bag I was now carrying, as well as the Log Book and the camera, had been tucked under my legs on the flight over and there had been no room for anything else.

I was to share a tent with another pilot and when I ducked my head low and went in, my companion was sitting on his camp-bed and threading a piece of string into one of his shoes because the shoe-lace had broken. He had a long but friendly face and he introduced himself as David Coke, pronounced Cook. I learnt much later that David Coke came from a very noble family, and today, had he not been killed in his Hurricane later on, he would have been none other than the Earl of

Leicester owning one of the most enormous and beautiful stately homes in England, although anyone acting less like a future Earl I have never met. He was warm-hearted and brave and generous, and over the next few weeks we were to become close friends. I sat down on my own camp-bed and began to ask him a few questions.

'Are things out here really as dicey as I've been told?' I asked him.

'It's absolutely hopeless,' he said, 'but we're plugging on. The German fighters will be within range of us any moment now, and then we'll be outnumbered by about fifty to one. If they don't get us in the air, they'll wipe us out on the ground.'

'Look,' I said, 'I have never been in action in my life. I haven't the foggiest idea what to do if I meet one of them.'

David Coke stared at me as though he were seeing a ghost. He could hardly have looked more startled if I had suddenly announced that I had never been up in an aeroplane before. 'You don't mean to say,' he gasped, 'that you've come out to this place of all places with absolutely no experience whatsoever!'

'I'm afraid so,' I said. 'But I expect they'll put me to fly with one of the old hands who'll show me the ropes.'

'You're going to be unlucky,' he said. 'Out here we go up in ones. It hasn't occurred to them that it's better to fly in pairs. I'm afraid you'll be all on your own right from the start. But seriously, have you never even been in a squadron before in your life?'

'Never,' I said.

'Does the CO know this?' he asked me.

'I don't expect he's stopped to think about it,' I said. 'He simply told me I'd start flying tomorrow like all the others.'

'But where on earth have you come from then?' he asked. 'They'd never send a totally inexperienced pilot to a place like this.'

I told him briefly what had been happening to me over the last six months.

'Oh Christ!' he said. 'What a place to start! How many hours do you have on Hurricanes?'

'About seven,' I said.

'Oh, my God!' he cried. 'That means you hardly know how to fly the thing!'

'I don't really,' I said. 'I can do take-offs and landings but I've never exactly tried throwing it around in the air.'

He sat there still not quite able to believe what I was saying.

'Have you been here long?' I asked him.

'Not very,' he said. 'I was in the Battle of Britain before I came here. That was bad enough, but it was peanuts compared to this crazy place. We have no radar here at all and precious little RT. You can only talk to the ground when you are sitting right on top of the aerodrome. And you can't talk to each other at all when you're in the air. There is virtually no communication. The Greeks are our radar. We have a Greek peasant sitting on the top of every mountain for miles around, and when he spots a bunch of German planes he calls up the Ops Room here on a field telephone. That's our radar.'

'Does it work?'

'Now and again it does,' he said. 'But most of our spotters don't know a Messerschmitt from a baby-carriage.' He had managed to thread the string through all the eyes in his shoe and now he started to put the shoe back on his foot.

'Have the Germans really got a thousand planes in Greece?' I asked him.

'It seems likely,' he said. 'Yes, I think they have. You see, Greece is only a beginning for them. After they've taken Greece, they intend to push on south and take Crete as well. I'm sure of that.'

We sat on our camp-beds thinking about the future. I could see that it was going to be a pretty hairy one.

Then David Coke said, 'As you don't seem to know anything at all, I'd better try to help you. What would you like to know?'

'Well, first of all,' I said, 'what do I do when I meet a One-O-Nine?'

'You try to get on his tail,' he said. 'You try to turn in a tighter circle than him. If you let him get on to your tail, you've had it. A Messerschmitt has cannon in its wings. We've only got bullets, and they aren't even incendiaries. They're just ordinary bullets. The Hun has cannon-shells that explode when they hit you. Our bullets just make little holes in the fuselage. So you've got to hit him smack in the engine to bring him down. He can hit you anywhere at all and the cannon-shell will explode and blow you up.'

I tried to digest what he was saying.

'One other thing,' he said, 'never, absolutely never, take your eyes off your rear-view mirror for more than a few seconds. They come up behind you and they come very fast.'

'I'll try to remember that,' I said. 'What do I do if I meet a bomber? What's the best way to attack him?'

'The bombers you will meet will be mostly Ju 88s,' he said. 'The Ju 88 is a very good aircraft. It is just about as fast as you are and it's got a rear-gunner and a front-gunner. The gunners on a Ju 88 use incendiary tracer bullets and they aim their guns like they're aiming a hosepipe. They can see where their bullets are going all the time and that makes them pretty deadly. So if you are attacking a Ju 88 from astern, make quite sure you get well below him so the rear-gunner can't hit you. But you won't shoot him down that way. You have to go for one of his engines. And when you are doing that, remember to allow plenty of deflection. Aim well in front of him. Get the nose of his engine on the outer ring of your reflector sight.'

I hardly knew what he was talking about, but I nodded and said, 'Right. I'll try to do that.'

'Oh my God,' he said. 'I can't teach you how to shoot down Germans in one easy lesson. I just wish I could take you up with me tomorrow so I could look after you a bit.'

'Can't you?' I said eagerly. 'We could ask the CO.'

'Not a hope,' he said. 'We always go up singly. Except when we do a sweep, then we all go up together in formation.'

He paused and ran his fingers through his pale-brown hair. 'The trouble here', he said, 'is that the CO doesn't talk much to his pilots. He doesn't even fly with them. He must have flown once because he's got a DFC, but I've never seen him get into a Hurricane. In the Battle of Britain the Squadron-Leader always flew with his squadron. And he gave lots of advice and help to his new pilots. In England you always went up in pairs and a new boy always went up with an experienced man. And in the Battle of Britain we had radar and we had RT that jolly well worked. We could talk to the ground and we could talk to each other all the time in the air. But not here. The big thing to remember here is that you are totally on your own. No one is going to help you, not even the CO. In the Battle of Britain', he added, 'the new boys were very carefully looked after.'

'Has flying finished for the day?' I asked him.

'Yes,' he said. 'It'll be getting dark soon. In fact it's about time for supper. I'll take you along.'

The officers' mess was a tent large enough to contain two long tres-tle tables, one with food on it and the other where we sat down to eat. The food was tinned beef stew and lumps of bread, and there were bot-tles of Greek retsina wine to go with it. The Greeks have a trick of dis-guising a poor quality wine by adding pine resin to it, the idea being that the taste of the resin is not quite so appalling as the taste of the wine. We drank retsina because that was all there was. The other pilots in the squadron, all experienced young men who had nearly been killed many times, treated me just as casually as the Squadron-Leader had. Formalities did not exist in this place. Pilots came and pilots went. The others hardly noticed my presence. No real friendships existed. The way David Coke had treated me was exceptional, but then he was an exceptional person. I realized that nobody else was about to take a beginner like me under his wing. Each man was wrapped up in a cocoon of his own problems, and the sheer effort of trying to stay alive and at the same time doing your duty was concentrating the minds of everyone around me. They were all very quiet. There was no larking about. There were just a few muttered remarks about the pilots who had not come back that day. Nothing else.

There was a notice-board nailed to one of the tent poles in the mess and on it was pinned a single typed sheet with the names of the pilots who were to go on patrol the next morning as well as the times of their take-offs. I learnt from David Coke that a patrol meant stooging around directly above the airfield and waiting for the ground controller to call you up and direct you to a precise area where German planes had been spotted by one of the Greek comedians on top of his mountain. The take-off time against my name was 10 a.m.

When I woke up the next morning, all I could think about was my ten o'clock take-off time and the fact that I would almost certainly be meeting the Luftwaffe in some form or another and entirely on my own for the first time. Such thoughts as these tend to loosen the bowels and I asked David Coke where I could find the latrines. He told me roughly where they were and I wandered off to find them.

I had been in some fairly primitive lavatories in East Africa, but the 80 Squadron latrines at Elevsis beat the lot. A wide trench six feet deep and sixteen feet long had been dug in the ground. Down the whole length of this trench a round pole had been suspended about four feet above the ground, and I watched in horror as an airman who had got there before me lowered his trousers and attempted to sit on the pole. The trench was so wide that he could hardly reach the pole with his hands. But when he did, he had to turn around and do a sort of backwards leap in the hope of his bottom landing squarely on the pole. Having managed this, but only just, he had to grip the pole with both hands to keep his balance. He lost his balance and over he went backwards into the awful pit. I pulled him out and he hurried away I know not where to try to wash himself. I refused to risk it. I wandered away and found a place behind an olive tree where the wild flowers grew all around me.

At exactly ten o'clock I was strapped into my Hurricane ready for take-off. Several others had gone off singly before me during the past half-hour and had disappeared into the blue Grecian sky. I took off and climbed to 5,000 feet and started circling above the flying field while somebody in the Ops Room tried to contact me on his amazingly inefficient apparatus. My code-name was Blue Four.

Through a storm of static a far-away voice kept saying in my earphones, 'Blue Four, can you hear me? Can you hear me?' And I kept replying, 'Yes, but only just.'

'Await orders,' the faint voice said. 'Listen out.'

I cruised around admiring the blue sea to the south and the great mountains to the north, and I was just beginning to think to myself that this was a very nice way to fight a war when the static erupted again and the voice said, 'Blue Four, are you receiving me?'

'Yes,' I said, 'but speak louder please.'

'Bandits over shipping at Khalkis,' the voice said. 'Vector 035 forty miles angels eight.'

'Received,' I said. 'I'm on my way.'

The translation of this simple message, which even I could understand, told me that if I set a course on my compass of thirty-five degrees and flew for a distance of forty miles, I would then, with a bit of luck, intercept the enemy at 8,000 feet, where he was trying to sink ships off a place called Khalkis, wherever that might be.

I set my course and opened the throttle and hoped I was doing everything right. I checked my ground speed and calculated that it would take me between ten and eleven minutes to travel forty miles to this place called Khalkis. I cleared the top of the mountain range with 500 feet to spare, and as I went over it I saw a single solitary goat, brown and white, wandering on the bare rock. 'Hello goat,' I said aloud into my oxygen mask, 'I'll bet you don't know the Germans are going to have you for supper before you're very much older.'

To which, as I realized as soon as I'd said it, the goat might very well have answered, 'And the same to you, my boy. You're no better off than I am.'

Then I saw below me in the distance a kind of waterway or fjord and a little cluster of houses on the shore. Khalkis, I thought. It must be Khalkis. There was one large cargo ship in the waterway and as I was looking at it I saw an enormous fountain of spray erupting high in the air close to the ship. I had never seen a bomb exploding in the water before, but I had seen plenty of photographs of it happening. I looked up into the sky above the ship, but I could see nothing there. I kept staring. I figured that if a bomb had been dropped, someone must be up there dropping it. Two more mighty cascades of water leapt up around the ship. Then suddenly I spotted the bombers. I saw the small black dots wheeling and circling in the sky high above the ship. It gave me quite a shock. It was my first-ever sight of the enemy from my own plane. Quickly I turned the brass ring of my firing-button from 'safe' to 'fire'. I switched on my reflector-sight and a pale red circle of light with two crossbars appeared suspended in the air in front of my face. I headed straight for the little dots.

Half a minute later, the dots had resolved themselves into black twin-engine bombers. They were Ju 88s. I counted six of them. I glanced above and around them but I could see no fighters protecting them. I remember being absolutely cool and unafraid. My one wish was to do my job properly and not to make a hash of it.

There are three men in a Ju 88, which gives it three pairs of eyes. So six Ju 88s have no less than eighteen pairs of eyes scanning the sky. Had I been more experienced, I would have realized this much earlier on and before going any closer I would have swung round so that the sun was behind me. I would also have climbed very fast to get well above them before attacking. I did neither of these things. I simply went straight for them at the same height as they were and with the strong Grecian sun right in my own eyes.

They spotted me while I was still half a mile away and suddenly all six bombers banked away steeply and dived straight for a great mass of mountains behind Khalkis.

I had been warned never to push my throttle 'through the gate' except in a real emergency. Going 'through the gate' meant that the big Rolls-Royce engine would produce absolute maximum revs, and three minutes was the limit of time it could tolerate such stress. OK, I thought, this is an emergency. I rammed the throttle right 'through the gate'. The engine roared and the Hurricane leapt forward. I began to catch up fast on the bombers. They had now gone into a line-abreast formation which, as I was soon to discover, allowed all six of their rear-gunners to fire at me simultaneously.

The mountains behind Khalkis are wild and black and very rugged and the Germans went right in among them flying well below the summits. I followed, and sometimes we flew so close to the cliffs I could see the startled vultures taking off as we roared past. I was still gaining on them, and when I was about 200 yards behind them, all six rear-gunners in the Ju 88s began shooting at me. As David Coke had warned, they were using tracer and out of each one of the six rear turrets came a brilliant shaft of orange-red flame. Six different shafts of bright orange-red came arcing towards me from six different turrets. They were like very thin streams of coloured water from six different hosepipes. I found them fascinating to watch. The deadly orange-red streams seemed to start out quite slowly from the turrets and I could see them bending in the air as they came towards me and then suddenly they were flashing past my cockpit like fireworks.

I was just beginning to realize that I had got myself into the worst possible position for an attacking fighter to be in when suddenly the passage between the mountains on either side narrowed and the Ju 88s were forced to go into line astern. This meant that only the last one in the line could shoot at me. That was better. Now there was only a single stream of orange-red bullets coming towards me. David Coke had said, 'Go for one of his engines.' I went a little closer and by jiggling my plane this way and that I managed to get the starboard engine of the bomber into my reflector-sight. I aimed a bit ahead of the engine and pressed the button. The Hurricane gave a small shudder as the eight Brownings in the wings all opened up together, and a second later I saw a huge piece of his metal engine-cowling the size of a dinner-tray go flying up into the air. Good heavens, I thought, I've hit him! I've actually hit him! Then black smoke came pouring out of his engine and very slowly, almost in slow motion, the bomber winged over to starboard and began to lose height. I throttled back. He was well below me now. I could see him clearly by squinting down out of my cockpit. He wasn't diving and he wasn't spinning either. He was turning slowly over and over like a leaf, the black smoke pouring out from the starboard engine. Then I saw one . . . two . . . three people jump out of the fuselage and go tumbling earthwards with legs and arms outstretched in grotesque attitudes, and a moment later one . . . two . . . three parachutes billowed open and began floating gently down between the cliffs towards the narrow valley below.

I watched spellbound. I couldn't believe that I had actually shot down a German bomber. But I was immensely relieved to see the parachutes.

I opened the throttle again and began to climb up above the mountains. The five remaining Ju 88s had disappeared. I looked around me and all I could see were craggy peaks in every direction. I set a course due south and fifteen minutes later I was landing at Elevsis. I parked my Hurricane and clambered out. I had been away for exactly one hour. It seemed like ten minutes. I walked slowly all the way round my Hurricane looking for damage. Miraculously the fuselage seemed to be completely unscathed. The only mark those six rear-gunners had been able to make on a sitting-duck like me was a single neat round hole in one of the blades of my wooden propeller. I shouldered my parachute and walked across to the Ops Rooms hut. I was feeling pretty good.

As before, the Squadron-Leader was in the hut and so was the wireless-operator Sergeant with the ear-phones on his head. The Squadron-Leader looked up at me and frowned. 'How did you get on?' he asked.

'I got one Ju 88,' I said, trying to keep the pride and satisfaction out of my voice.

'Are you sure?' he asked. 'Did you see it hit the ground?'

'No,' I said. 'But I saw the crew jump out and open their parachutes.'

'OK,' he said. 'That sounds definite enough.'

'I'm afraid there's a bullet hole in my prop,' I said.

'Oh well,' he said. 'You'd better tell the rigger to patch it up as best he can.'

That was the end of our interview. I expected more, a pat on the ᵇ or a 'Jolly good show' and a smile, but as I've said before ᵇ things on his mind including Pilot Officer Holᵐ thirty minutes before me and hadn't come bᵃ come back.

David Coke had also been flying that mᵣ ting on his camp-bed doing notʰⁱ

'Never do that again,' he said. 'Never sit on the tails of six Ju 88s and expect to get away with it because next time you won't.'

'What happened to you?' I asked him.

'I got one One-O-Nine,' he said. He said it as calmly as if he were telling me he'd caught a fish in the river across the road. 'It's going to be very dangerous out there from now on,' he added. 'The One-O-Nines and the One-One-O's are swarming like wasps. You'd better be very careful next time.'

'I'll try,' I said. 'I'll do my best.'

The next morning I was ordered to go on patrol at six o'clock. I took off dead on time and climbed in a tight circle to 5,000 feet over the airfield. The sun had just cleared the horizon and I could see the Parthenon glowing white and wonderful on the famous hill above Athens. My radio crackled almost at once and the voice from the Ops Room gave me precisely the same instructions it had given me the day before. I was to proceed to Khalkis where the enemy was again bombing the shipping. Five Hurricanes had taken off before me that morning and I had watched them all being sent away one by one in different directions. The enemy was all around us now and we were having to spread ourselves extremely thin. Khalkis, it seemed, was reserved for me.

I had learnt the night before from someone in the Ops Room that the big cargo vessel lying off Khalkis was an ammunition ship. It was loaded to the brim with high explosives and the Germans had found out about it. The brave Greeks, who were trying their best to offload the bullets and bombs and whatever other fireworks there were on board, knew that it only needed one direct hit to blow everything sky-high, including the town of Khalkis and most of its inhabitants.

I arrived over Khalkis at 6:15 a.m. The big cargo ship was still there and there was now a lighter alongside it. A derrick was hoisting a large crate up from the ship's forward hold and, lowering it into the lighter. I searched the sky for enemy planes but I couldn't see any. A man on the deck of the ship looked up and waved his cap at me. I slid back the roof of my cockpit and waved back at him.

I am writing this forty-five years afterwards, but I still retain an absolutely clear picture of Khalkis and how it looked from a few thousand feet up on a bright-blue early April morning. The little town with its sparkling white houses and red-tiled roofs stood on the edge of the waterway, and behind the town I could see the jagged grey-black mountains where I had chased the Ju 88s the day before. Inland, I could see a wide valley and there were green fields in the valley and among the fields there were splashes of the most brilliant yellow I had ever seen. The whole landscape looked as though it had been painted on to the surface of the earth by Vincent Van Gogh. On all sides and wherever I looked there was this dazzling panorama of beauty, and for a moment or two I was so overwhelmed by it all that I didn't see the big Ju 88 screaming up at me from below until he was almost touching the underbelly of my plane. He was climbing right up at me with the tracer pouring like yellow fire out of his blunt perspex nose and in that thousandth of a second I actually saw the German front-gunner crouching over his gun and gripping it with both hands as he squeezed the trigger. I saw his brown helmet and his pale face with no goggles over the eyes and he was wearing some sort of a black flying-suit. I yanked my stick back so hard the Hurricane shot vertically upwards like a rocket. The violent change of direction blacked me out completely, and when my sight returned my plane was at the top of a vertical climb and standing on its tail with almost no forward movement at all. My engine was spluttering and beginning to vibrate. I've been hit, I thought, I've been hit in the engine. I rammed the stick hard forward and prayed she would respond. By some miracle, the aircraft dropped its nose and the engine began to pick up and within a few seconds the marvellous machine was flying straight and level once again.

But where was the German?

I looked down and spotted him about 1,000 feet below me. His wings were silhouetted against the blue water of the bay, and I could hardly believe it but he was actually ignoring me completely and was beginning to make his bombing run over the ammunition ship! I opened the throttle and dived after him. In eight seconds I was on him, but I was diving so steeply and so fast that when the great grey-green bomber came into my sights, I was only able to get in a very short burst and then I was past him and yanking back hard on the stick to stop myself from diving on into the water.

I had made a mess of it. For the second time running I had gone barging in to the attack without pausing for just a fraction of a second to work out the best way of doing things. I roared upwards again and banked round sharply to have another go at him. He was still heading for the ship. But then something quite startling happened. I saw his nose drop suddenly downwards and he went plunging head first in an absolutely straight vertical line into the blue waters of Khalkis Bay. He hit the water not far from the ship and there was a tremendous white splash and then the waves closed over him and he was gone.

How on earth did I manage that? I wondered. The only explanation I could think of was that a lucky bullet must have hit the pilot so that he slumped over his stick and pushed it forward and down she went. I could see several Greek seamen on the deck of the ship waving their caps at me and I waved back at them. That is how stupid I was. I quite literally sat there in my cockpit waving away at the Greek seamen below, forgetting that I was in a hostile sky that could be seething with German aircraft. When I stopped waving and looked around me, I saw something that made me jump. There were aeroplanes everywhere. They were diving and climbing and turning and banking wherever I looked, and they all had black and white crosses on their bodies and black swastikas on their tails. I knew right away what they were. They were the dreaded little German Messerschmitt 109 fighters. I had never seen one before but I knew darn well what they looked like. I swear there must have been thirty or forty of them within a few hundred yards of me. It was like having a swarm of wasps around your head and quite honestly I did not know what to do next. It would have been suicide to stay and fight, and in any event my duty was to save my plane at all costs. The Germans had hundreds of fighters. We had only a few left.

I shoved the stick forward and opened the throttle and dived flat out for the ground. I had a feeling that if I could fly very low and very dangerously over the treetops and hedges then the German pilots might not be prepared to take the same risk.

When I levelled out from the dive I was doing about 300 miles an hour and flying some twenty feet above the ground. That is below rooftop level and is a fairly hairy thing to do at such a speed. But I was in a hairy situation. I was flying up the yellow Van Gogh valley now and a swift glance in my rear-view mirror showed a bunch of 109s right on my tail. I went lower. I went so low I actually had to leapfrog over the small olive trees that were scattered around everywhere. Then I took a huge but calculated risk and went lower still, almost brushing the grass in the fields. I knew the Germans couldn't hit me unless they came down to my height, and even if they did, the concentration required to fly a plane very fast at almost ground level was so great they would hardly be able to shoot straight at the same time. You may not believe it but I can remember having literally to lift my plane just a tiny fraction to clear a stone wall, and once there was a herd of brown cows in front of me and I'm not sure I didn't clip some of their horns with my propeller as I skimmed over them.

Suddenly the Messerschmitts had had enough. In the mirror I saw them pull away one after the other, and oh the relief of being able to climb up to a safer height and to go whistling back over the mountains to Elevsis.

The bad news I brought with me to the squadron was that the German fighter planes were now within range of us. In their hundreds they could reach our airfield any time they liked.

The next three days, 17, 18 and 19 April 1941, are a little blurred in my memory. The fourth day, 20 April, is not blurred at all. My Log Book records that from Elevsis aerodrome

on 17 April I went up three times

on 18 April I went up twice
on 19 April I went up three times
on 20 April I went up four times.

Each one of those sorties meant running across the airfield to wherever the Hurricane was parked (often 200 yards away), strapping in, starting up, taking off, flying to a particular area, engaging the enemy, getting home again, landing, reporting to the Ops Room and then making sure the aircraft was refuelled and rearmed immediately so as to be ready for another take-off.

Twelve separate sorties against the enemy in four days is a fairly hectic pace by any standards, and each one of us knew that every time a sortie was made, somebody was probably going to get killed, either the Hun or the man in the Hurricane. I used to figure that the betting on every flight was about even money against my coming back, but in reality it wasn't even money at all. When you are outnumbered by at least ten to one on nearly every occasion, then a bookmaker, had there been one on the aerodrome, would probably have been willing to lay something like five to one against your return on each trip.

Like all the others, I was always sent up alone. I wished I could sometimes have had a friendly wing-tip alongside me, and more importantly, a second pair of eyes to help me watch the sky behind and above. But we didn't have enough aircraft for luxuries of that sort.

Sometimes I was over Piraeus harbour, chasing the Ju 88s that were bombing the shipping there. Sometimes I was around the Lamia area, trying to deter the Luftwaffe from blasting away at our retreating army, although how anyone could think that a single Hurricane was going to make any difference out there was beyond me. Once or twice, I met the bombers over Athens itself, where they usually came along in groups of twelve at a time. On three occasions my Hurricane was badly shot up, but the riggers in 80 Squadron were magicians at patching up holes in the fuselage or mending a broken spar. We were so frantically busy during these four days that individual victories were hardly noticed or counted. And unlike the fighter aircraft back in Britain, we had no camera-guns to tell us whether we had hit anything or not. We seemed to spend our entire time running out to the aircraft, scrambling, dashing off to some place or other, chasing the Hun, pressing the firing-button, landing back at Elevsis and going up again.

My Log Book records that on 17 April we lost Flight-Sergeant Cottingham and Flight-Sergeant Rivelon and both their aircraft.

On 18 April Pilot Officer Oofy Still went out and did not return. I remember Oofy Still as a smiling young man with freckles and red hair.

That left us with twelve Hurricanes and twelve pilots with which to cover the whole of Greece from 19 April onwards.

As I have said, 17, 18 and 19 April seem to be all jumbled up together in my memory, and no single incident has remained vividly with me. But 20 April was quite different. I went up four separate times on 20 April, but it was the first of these sorties that I will never forget. It stands out like a sheet of flame in my memory.

On that day, somebody behind a desk in Athens or Cairo had decided that for once our entire force of Hurricanes, all twelve of us, should go up together. The inhabitants of Athens, so it seemed, were getting jumpy and it was assumed that the sight of us all flying overhead would boost their morale. Had I been an inhabitant of Athens at that time, with a German army of over 100,000 advancing swiftly on the city, not to mention a Luftwaffe of about 1,000 planes all within bombing distance, I would have been pretty jumpy myself, and the sight of twelve lonely Hurricanes flying overhead would have done little to boost my morale.

However, on 20 April, on a golden springtime morning at ten o'clock, all twelve of us took off one after the other and got into a tight formation over Elevsis airfield. Then we headed for Athens, which was no more than four minutes' flying time away.

I had never flown a Hurricane in formation before. Even in training I had only done formation flying once in a little Tiger Moth. It is not a particularly tricky business if you have had plenty of practice, but if you are new to the game and if you are required to fly within a few feet of your neighbour's wing-tip, it is a dicey experience. You keep your position by jiggling the throttle back and forth the whole time and by being extremely delicate on the rudder bar and the stick. It is not so bad when everyone is flying straight and level, but when the entire formation is doing steep turns all the time, it becomes very difficult for a fellow as inexperienced as I was.

Round and round Athens we went, and I was so busy trying to prevent my starboard wing-tip from scraping against the plane next to me that this time I was in no mood to admire the grand view of the Parthenon or any of the other famous relics below me. Our formation was being led by Flight-Lieutenant Pat Pattle. Now Pat Pattle was a legend in the RAF. At least he was a legend around Egypt and the Western Desert and in the mountains of Greece. He was far and away the greatest fighter ace the Middle East was ever to see, with an astronomical number of victories to his credit. It was even said that he had shot down more planes than any of the famous and glamorized Battle of Britain aces, and this was probably true. I myself had never spoken to him and I am sure he hadn't the faintest idea who I was. I wasn't anybody. I was just a new face in a squadron whose pilots took very little notice of each other anyway. But I had observed the famous Flight-Lieutenant Pattle in the mess tent several times. He was a very small man and very soft-spoken, and he possessed the deeply wrinkled doleful face of a cat who knew that all nine of its lives had already been used up.

On that morning of 20 April, Flight-Lieutenant Pattle, the ace of aces, who was leading our formation of twelve Hurricanes over Athens, was evidently assuming that we could all fly as brilliantly as he could, and he led us one hell of a dance around the skies above the city. We were flying at about 9,000 feet and we were doing our very best to show the people of Athens how powerful and noisy and brave we were, when suddenly the whole sky around us seemed to explode with German fighters. They came down on us from high above, not only 109s but also the twin-engined 110s. Watchers on the ground say that there cannot have been fewer than 200 of them around us that morning. We broke formation and now it was every man for himself. What has become known as the Battle of Athens began.

I find it almost impossible to describe vividly what happened during the next half-hour. I don't think any fighter pilot has ever managed to convey what it is like to be up there in a long-lasting dog-fight. You are in a small metal cockpit where just about everything is made of riveted aluminum. There is a plexiglass hood over your head and a sloping bullet-proof windscreen in front of you. Your right hand is on the stick and your right thumb is on the brass firing-button on the top loop of the stick. Your left hand is on the throttle and your two feet are on the rudder-bar. Your body is attached by shoulder-straps and belt to the parachute you are sitting on, and a second pair of shoulder-straps and a belt are holding you rigidly in the cockpit. You can turn your head and you can move your arms and legs, but the rest of your body is strapped so tightly into the tiny cockpit that you cannot move. Between your face and the windscreen, the round orange-red circle of the reflector-sight glows brightly.

Some people do not realize that although a Hurricane had eight guns in its wings, those guns were all immobile. You did not aim the guns, you aimed the plane. The guns themselves were carefully sighted and tested beforehand on the ground so that the bullets from each gun would converge at a point about 150 yards ahead. Thus, using your reflector-sight, you aimed the plane at the target and pressed the button. To aim accurately in this way requires skilful flying, especially as you are usually in a steep turn and going very fast when the moment comes.

Over Athens on that morning, I can remember seeing our tight little formation of Hurricanes all peeling away and disappearing among the swarms of enemy aircraft, and from then on, wherever I looked I saw an endless blur of enemy fighters whizzing towards me from every side. They came from above and they came from behind and they made frontal attacks from dead ahead, and I threw my Hurricane around as best I could and whenever a Hun came into my sights, I pressed the button. It was truly the most breathless and in a way the most exhilarating time I have ever had in my life. I caught glimpses of planes with black smoke pouring from their engines. I saw planes with pieces of metal flying off their fuselages. I saw the bright-red flashes coming from the wings of the Messerschmitts as they fired their guns, and once I saw a man whose Hurricane was in flames climb calmly out on to a wing and jump off. I stayed with them until I had no ammunition left in my guns. I had done a lot of shooting, but whether I had shot anyone down or had even hit any of them I could not say. I did not dare to pause for even a fraction of a second to observe results. The sky was so full of aircraft that half my time was spent in actually avoiding collisions. I am quite sure that the German planes must have often got in each other's way because there were so many of them, and that, together with the fact that there were so few of us, probably saved quite a number of our skins.

When I finally had to break away and dive for home, I knew my Hurricane had been hit. The controls were very soggy and there was no response at all to the rudder. But you can turn a plane after a fashion with the ailerons alone, and that is how I managed to steer the plane back. Thank heavens the undercarriage came down when I engaged the lever, and I landed more or less safely at Elevsis. I taxied to a parking place, switched off the engine and slid back the hood. I sat there for at least one minute, taking deep gasping breaths. I was quite literally over-whelmed by the feeling that I had been into the very bowels of the fiery furnace and had managed to claw my way out. All around me now the sun was shining and wild flowers were blossoming in the grass of the airfield, and I thought how fortunate I was to be seeing the good earth again. Two airmen, a fitter and a rigger, came trotting up to my machine. I watched them as they walked slowly all the way round it. Then the rigger, a balding middle-aged man, looked up at me and said, 'Blimey mate, this kite's got so many 'oles in it, it looks like it's made out of chicken-wire!'

I undid my straps and eased myself upright in the cockpit. 'Do your best with it,' I said. 'I'll be needing it again very soon.'

I remember walking over to the little wooden Operations Room to report my return and as I made my way slowly across the grass of the landing field I suddenly realized that the whole of my body and all my clothes were dripping with sweat. The weather was warm in Greece at that time of year and we wore only khaki shorts and khaki shirt and stockings even when we flew, but now those shorts and shirt and stockings had all changed colour and were quite black with wetness. So was my hair when I removed my helmet. I had never sweated like that before in my life, even after a game of squash or rugger. The water was pouring off me and dripping to the ground. At the door of the Ops Room three or four other pilots were standing around and I noticed that each one of them was as wet as I was. I put a cigarette between my lips and struck a match. Then I found that my hand was shaking so much I couldn't put the flame to the end of the cigarette. The doctor, who was standing nearby, came up and lit it for me. I looked at my hands again. It was ridiculous the way they were shaking. It was embarrassing. I looked at the other pilots. They were all holding cigarettes and their hands were all shaking as much as mine were. But I was feeling pretty good. I had stayed up there for thirty minutes and they hadn't got me.

They got five of our twelve Hurricanes in that battle. One of our pilots baled out and was saved. Four were killed. Among the dead was the great Pat Pattle, all his lucky lives used up at last. And Flight-Lieutenant Timber Woods, the second most experienced pilot in the squadron, was also among those killed. Greek observers on the ground as well as our own people on the airstrip saw the five Hurricanes going down in smoke, but they also saw something else. They saw twenty-two Messerschmitts shot down during that battle, although none of us ever knew who got what.

So we now had seven half-serviceable Hurricanes left in Greece, and with these we were expected to give air cover to the entire British Expeditionary Force which was about to be evacuated along the coast. The whole thing was a ridiculous farce.

I wandered over to my tent. There was a canvas washbasin outside the tent, one of those folding things that stand on three wooden legs, and David Coke was bending over it, sloshing water on his face. He was naked except for a small towel round his waist and his skin was very white.

'So you made it,' he said, not looking up.

'So did you,' I said.

'It was a bloody miracle,' he said. 'I'm shaking all over. What happens next?'

'I think we're going to get killed,' I said.

'So do I,' he said. 'You can have the basin in a moment. I left a bit of water in the jug just in case you happened to come back.'

from The Man Who Rode the Thunder
by William H. Rankin

William H. Rankin (born 1920) in 1959 became famous as the man who fell through a thunderstorm. His 40-minute free fall from the stratosphere into the storm was even more terrifying. Rankin parted company with his plane at around 47,000 feet above sea level—nearly 18,000 feet higher than Mt. Everest's summit.

Over New York, the weather was immaculate, not a cloud in the sky. From our altitude, the great metropolis was an impressive, strangely miniature sight. We could see the entire city, from its northern border at Yonkers to the tip of Manhattan. You get the feeling that this enormous mass of mortar and concrete and black-ribboned streets must have taken centuries to build; you even feel its importance as part of America. Yet, paradoxically, from nearly nine miles up, it looks like such a simple, quiet place, everything neat and well organized. It is geometry glorified.

Soon we were over Atlantic City, where the sky began to get a bit hazy, with scattered and broken clouds. As we approached Norfolk, Virginia, I noticed that the entire area was covered with the dark, massive, rolling clouds of a thunderstorm. I looked at my wristwatch; it was now a few minutes before six p.m. In about half an hour, we should be touching down at Beaufort. I looked at the storm again. It appeared to be slightly higher than the 40,000-foot maximum the aerologist had reported at South Weymouth. I began thinking that we might have to climb a bit to be sure we'd pass over the top.

· As I started my climb, I noticed that I was passing through the thin, wispy tops of the storm at 45,000 feet and therefore decided to continue climbing. At 48,000 feet, now well above the tops, I levelled off again, and soon Herb was abeam of me, about 500 feet off, not too tight, not too loose, a nice comfortable formation for a routine, uneventful flight.

We had just passed over the Norfolk *Tacan*, an electronic navigation check point, where we picked up a range and bearing signal, and I was making an easy right hand turn to take up the next heading for Cherry Point, on a course of about 250 degrees. As I was checking my navigation frequency, I noticed that I appeared to be slowing down a bit, so I nosed over slightly to pick up speed. Assuming at least another half hour of flying time, I reached down to crank out my rudder pedals a little more; I wanted to stretch my legs, feel comfortable. Then I started to ease into a cruise climb again, having noticed that at 44,000 feet I could see the tops of the clouds ahead. I had planned to go back to 48,000 feet, and I was just passing the 47,000-foot mark, still climbing, when suddenly I heard a thump and a rumbling sound behind and under me.

I quickly scanned my instruments. I was at .82 mach, and nothing appeared to be wrong. My rpm instrument indicated no loss of power. But still I sensed that something was about to happen. I had flown too many hours in an F8U not to recognize that the "thump" and "rumble" were abnormal sounds. I glanced out to my right, noticing that Herb was at my two o'clock position, slightly down. I was about to call Herb to let him know that I was anticipating trouble, when I heard the thump and the rumbling sound again. Suddenly, the fire warning light flashed on.

There are a number of warning lights in the F8U, each one serious; but the fire warning light, about the size of a quarter, is the one that unnerves pilots most. It flashes on in a bright, traffic-light red, silhouetting four black letters: FIRE. It is connected to an electronic sensing system which warns that somewhere in the plane there is excessive heat where there should not be, and there may soon be a fire, or a fire may already have started. Usually, it means trouble somewhere in the engine system, in which case the warning light is tantamount to an order: DON'T WASTE TIME. EJECT!

Once before I had experienced a fire warning light, in the F9F-2; but it had turned out to be a false alarm. In fact, most pilots had considered the F9F fire sensing system so ultra-sensitive that we'd disconnect it to avoid continual scares. I knew several pilots who had ejected instantly from the F9F upon getting the fire warning flash, only to learn ruefully that there had been no fire. But in the F8U, the fire sensing system is extremely efficient and when the light flashes it is critical.

There were a number of emergency actions I could take, but my life might depend on picking the right one—my diagnosis had to be rapid as well as accurate. Instinctively, I took the first emergency measure immediately—cut back on power!

As I came back on the throttle, I pressed my microphone button, placed conveniently on the throttle, and called Herb.

"Tiger Two, this is Tiger One. I'm having engine trouble. Stand by. I might have to eject." At the moment, I wasn't certain I'd have to go out, but, in case I did, I wanted to be sure that Herb would see me and make the necessary reports to effect my rescue—or recover my body.

Herb replied instantly. "Roger, Tiger One. If you have to go, let me know." That was my last communication with Herb.

Quickly, I scanned the instrument panel in front of me. Retarding the throttle apparently had been effective. The fire warning light had gone out. Momentarily, I felt a great sense of relief. But then my rpm indicator started to unwind rapidly, frighteningly. In a matter of five or six seconds, the rpm indicator went from about ninety per cent to zero! I had never seen it happen that fast.

I have had jet flameouts, in which the rpm indicator runs down, but gradually. When it happened, I'd dive down to a denser atmosphere to get a re-light, each time successfully. But in this case I quickly had to rule out an emergency dive for a re-light because the symptom, the rapid rpm unwind, did not fit a diagnosis of flameout.

Still scanning the instruments, I was convinced that I was having a one-in-a-million kind of emergency, "engine seizure." Something, some awful friction, perhaps because of loss of oil, had caused the excessive heat, had caused the engine to "freeze"; no engine, no power, no radio. The sudden disappearance of the characteristic crackling noises in my radio headset gave me, for a moment, an awesome feeling of loneliness; nobody to talk to, not even to hear me cry, "I'm going out."

But in a crippled high-performance, high-altitude aircraft, sweeping up past 47,000 feet, only a few thousand feet from the dividing line between earth's atmosphere and true space, you don't waste precious time on personal thoughts. In air so "thin" that scientists maintained it would cause the blood in an unprotected human body, literally, to boil, you don't feel an urge to clasp your hands in prayer. You're much too busy fighting for your life.

At this moment, my life depended on an accurate diagnosis, and thinking about the engine seizure was bad enough. I had experienced engine seizure only experimentally in an F8U, when oil was deliberately drained from an engine on a static-stand test. Although the engine had been going at maximum power, after the oil was gone the engine "seized," froze solid, in seven seconds!

Without an engine, I'd need not only electrical power, but hydraulic power to control the plane. The control stick on the F8U is irreversibly linked to the hydraulic system. Moving at supersonic, even subsonic speeds, the forces on the surfaces are so great that not even a Hercules could exert sufficient pressure on the control stick to guide the plane. Hydraulic pressure is essential; without it, you might as well think of yourself as riding an uncontrollable rocket. One, you know, that is apt to "tuck" and carry you down at fatal supersonic speeds; or suddenly whip into such a ferocious spin that the g forces will hold you pinned to your seat, your arms practically plastered to the bulkhead. A spin in an F8U is a particularly grim possibility because you sit at the extreme forward tip of the fuselage, where the spin achieves ultimate violence.

With the engine dead, my next action was automatic—pull out the auxiliary power package, which is an air-driven turbine. Built into the side of the airplane, it flops down from a long-piano-hinged pocket and the force of the rushing air turns the turbine, generating power. The power package also actuates an emergency hydraulic pump, enabling you to maintain control.

I reached over to the left side of the cockpit, grabbed a small T-shaped handle (something like the handbrake in an auto) and pulled to release the auxiliary package. The handle moved the prescribed distance—but nothing happened. There had been, in my lifetime of flying, several instances in which I had to pull out my emergency power package, and it had never failed. I had gotten to know its characteristic *thump* as it flopped out the side of the plane and hit the slipstream, causing a slight, familiar yaw. But now I felt nothing, no thump, no yaw. Perhaps it *had* flopped out; perhaps I was too preoccupied to bear the thump, feel the yaw. But my ammeter showed no indication of power. Nor did any of my other instruments show signs of power; nor was there any indication of hydraulic pressure. Previously, I had seen power come on instantly from the emergency package. Perhaps I hadn't pulled hard enough.

Quickly, I reached over to pull the handle again, hopefully, with greater force. But the handle came completely out of the wall! It couldn't be! I didn't want to believe my eyes. But there it was, the handle in my hand. I let it drop to the deck.

A chilling feeling of helplessness crept over me. This complex leviathan of flaming flight, now dead and cold, a coffin of steel, was still carrying me upward in a climb, was making a mockery of all my years of training. There was nothing more I could do. I could not even dive to a lower, safer level for ejection.

But I could not remain much longer. Still climbing and still subsonic, I was in a highly favorable position for ejection. Yet at any moment one of two things might happen in the climb: running out of airspeed, the plane might stall and fall off into a wild spin; or it might suddenly tuck and go down at supersonic speed. In a flash, the thought of the civilian test pilot who had ejected at supersonic speed and had become, in effect, a living vegetable, whipped through my mind. I thought also of those few occasions when, in an F8U, I had fallen into mild spins and could recall vividly how strong the g forces had been. I had been almost unable to lift my arms to maneuver out of those spins. No, I could risk neither an ejection at supersonic speed, nor from a wildly spinning airplane.

Meanwhile, as I had later learned, Herb had been trying to contact me on the radio. Unable to do so, he called the Norfolk control center, said, "Emergency in the area; pilot has ejected," and gave the necessary information.

Now it was my moment of decision, the most harrowing decision of my life. I had never heard or known of anyone having ejected at this altitude, at any speed, supersonic or subsonic, with or without a pressure suit or some protective clothing. The temperature outside was close to 70 below zero, and I had on only a summer-weight flying suit, gloves, helmet, Marine field shoes. Perhaps I would survive frostbite without permanent injury, but what about "explosive" decompression at almost ten miles up? And what about that thunderstorm directly below me? If it could be hazardous for an airplane in flight, what would it do to a mere human? And a dozen other "what abouts . . . ?" crowded into my mind.

From the time I had heard the first indication of trouble until this moment, no more than twenty seconds had elapsed, although it seemed as if I had been acting and thinking for hours. I took one final look at the instruments and made the decision—EJECT!

I was not panicky. Mentally, I was fully prepared to eject. By training, by experience, by instinct, I knew exactly what to do and did it rapidly but deliberately.

I positioned myself in the seat, feet firmly on the deck, back erect, shoulders squared and tugged at my torso harness for reassurance. Then I reached up behind me, gripped the ejection seat handles and pulled hard. The curtain came down before my eyes; I expected to feel a tremendous blast of air as the canopy tore away. But I didn't feel anything, nor did the curtain pause at the point where I'd have to reach back for the lever that would bypass the canopy arming mechanism. With the curtain coming down smoothly, I was not going to stop. All I could think of in that brief moment was, "Oh, my God! Here I go through the canopy." And then I simultaneously heard and felt the ejection seat fire, almost as though a huge bull elephant had kicked me in the rear and made an explosive snort at the same time. It gave me a peculiar sense of relief because I knew I was going out. The ejection seat, at least, was not defective. As I shot up and out of the plane, I remembered a strange, ripping sensation, as if part of my body or flight suit had caught on a jagged edge of something solid and was being dragged through a row of sharp, uneven teeth. I wasn't sure whether this meant I was being shot through the unopened canopy, but later I discovered little stab wounds in my shoulders, indicating that I probably did go through the canopy.

As I rose from the shelter of the cockpit I hit a tremendous, wall-like blast of air, and the ejection curtain was ripped from my hands, the cable pulling the ejection seat away. My body was suddenly a freezing, expanding mass of pain. In that first moment alone in space I had the feeling that I had reached the end, that I would not survive.

My first shock was the incredibly cold air. I had gone abruptly from a comfortable cockpit temperature of 75° F. to almost *minus* 70° F., the sudden frigidity enormously compounded by the "chill factor"—cold plus the force of wind, precisely the difference between feeling cold winter air on your face when there's no wind, and feeling the same air when there's a tremendous wind. But up there the "wind" condition—my body shooting through the air at several hundred miles per hour—was unbelievably cold. I felt as though I were a chunk of beef being tossed into a cavernous deep freeze. Almost instantly all exposed parts of my body—around the face, neck, wrists, bands, and ankles—began to sting from the cold. It felt as if I were on fire. Then, seconds later, the burning sensation turned to a blessed numbness.

Meanwhile, the pain of "explosive" decompression was unbearable. I could feel my abdomen distending, stretching, stretching, stretching, until I thought it would burst. My eyes felt as though they were being ripped from their sockets, my head as if it were splitting into several parts, my ears bursting inside, and throughout my entire body there were severe cramps.

At first, there was no sensation of falling, only of zooming through the air. I knew my dark tinted visor had blown away because as I spun through the air the brilliance of the sun came through the thin atmosphere in blinding white flashes. Then, as I apparently had fallen to the level of the clouds' fleecy white tops, still spinning, everything about me seemed like a kaleidoscope of rotating brilliant colors. Against a purplish void, the sun went by in streaks of blurred reddish-orange, like an elongated fireball, between glimpses of undulating milky-white fields that were the cloud tops.

My first sensation of falling came just before I reached the thick layer of clouds. Then it seemed as if I had jumped from a high fence and a white wall was speeding toward me. Otherwise, I was not too conscious of falling.

I was preoccupied with the pain of decompression. It was nature's cruelest torture, the screw and rack of space, the body crusher, the body stretcher, each second another turn of the screw, another wrench of the rack, another interminable shot of pain. Once I caught a horrified glimpse of my stomach, swollen as though I were in well advanced pregnancy. I had never known such savage pain. I was convinced I would not survive; no human could.

But after perhaps no more than fifteen or twenty seconds had elapsed, just as I had begun to enter the soft white tops of the clouds, I was suddenly overwhelmed with a feeling of elation, gratitude. I was conscious; *in spite of everything I was conscious!*

Hang on, I thought. *Hang on! You might make it yet. You're thinking.*

You're conscious. You know what's going on. Just ride out this free fall and you've got it made.

I became conscious of my body tumbling, spinning, and cartwheeling through space. I spun like a pinwheel, my limbs trying to go in every possible direction at once. I spun on the vertical, diagonal and horizontal axis. I felt the enormous pulling, stretching effects of g forces. I was a huge stiff blob of helplessness! I recognized that my body was literally spread-eagled and the force was so great I could not move my hands or legs. Several times I tried to bring my arms in to my body but it was like pulling on a stone wall. The effect of the g forces on my arms and legs must have been to multiply their weight many times.

But now I was desperate to get my arms in—something was beating against my face, relentlessly, painfully. It was my oxygen mask. *My oxygen mask! God, I had almost forgotten.* In spite of the painful pounding, I was now strangely pleased, knowing that I had *not* lost my oxygen mask. It served to remind me that I was not getting oxygen. I had just left an airplane where I had been on 100 per cent oxygen and perhaps enough had remained in my blood to sustain me for a while, but not for long. I'd need that oxygen soon to avoid almost certain unconsciousness, possibly serious brain damage. I knew also that I was freefalling and must continue the free fall until my 'chute would open automatically at 10,000 feet. But what if something went wrong and the 'chute did not open and I were unconscious at the moment, unable to pull the D-ring to save myself? *I must get that oxygen mask! It's still flapping wildly against my face. It might come off. Get it.*

I continued struggling, to pull in my hands, but to no avail. I was still a human centrifuge, and the strain on my arms seemed to increase until I felt as though my arms were being torn from their sockets. Now, no part of my body seemed free of pain; but merely thinking about it gave me a peculiar feeling of satisfaction because it reminded me that I was still conscious. Maintaining consciousness had now become my consuming desire. Repeatedly, I thought, *Keep it up. That's fine. Keep going. Fine, fine, fine. You're still conscious. It won't be long now. You'll be falling into denser air. More oxygen, less decompression, less pain. Keep going.*

Suddenly, as I entered what appeared to be a dense overcast of grey and white clouds, I was able to pull in my right hand, then my left hand. I was winning. I grabbed the oxygen mask with my right hand, held it to my face, and held the top of my helmet with my left hand. Meanwhile, the strain seemed to ease on my legs and they started flailing about, like rubber. But I didn't care. I was mainly concerned about keeping that oxygen mask on my face. I had held my helmet, although at the moment I was not concerned about losing it, because the strap had been straining so sharply, tightly against my neck it felt as if I were in a hangman's noose. Holding the helmet seemed to ease the strain.

In denser atmosphere, I was beginning to feel a little better, more confident, almost certain I'd survive. I was enormously pleased with myself for remaining conscious. I would be able to report in detail what had happened. It would be good news to high-altitude aviators: *We can survive effects of decompression at 47,000 feet, perhaps much higher, perhaps 50,000 feet. But I'll report only 47,000 feet because that was the last altimeter setting I had seen before ejecting. Yet I'm certain I was higher because after I had looked at the altimeter the plane continued climbing. Other instruments demanded my attention. I'm thankful I can remember them, the settings, the positions, the readings, the rapidly unwinding rpm, the oil pressure . . . the oil pressure? What WAS the oil pressure?*

Paradoxically, for a few moments I seemed to forget about my falling, tumbling, twisting, my numbness, pain, and cold. I could not seem to picture the oil pressure gauge in my mind and it distressed me. It seemed to be the only instrument I could not remember. (Till this day, the oil pressure reading is the only thing I cannot recall. Psychiatrists tell me that years from now it may suddenly come back to me.) Abruptly, however, I stopped thinking about the instruments. I had suddenly, inexplicably felt a powerful urge to open my parachute.

I was still in a free fall. I knew I had to continue the free fall. But I just didn't seem to trust the idea of it; perhaps I had lost confidence in another automatic savior, the barometric sensing device that would respond to heavier air at 10,000 feet and open the 'chute for me. I don't remember why I felt as if I had to open the 'chute. I know only that it was an almost overwhelming temptation. I let go of my helmet and reached for the D-ring. But fortunately just as I started clawing at the D-ring, I realized it was the wrong thing to do. *That's a damned stupid thing to do,* I thought. *Do you want to freeze to death, going down slowly in an opened 'chute? And what about your oxygen? That emergency supply won't last more than five minutes, perhaps only three minutes. Just enough to get you through the free fall. Free fall, Bill, free fall. . . .*

I took my hand away from the D-ring and continued holding my helmet. *That's good. Keep your hands busy. Hold your oxygen mask, your helmet.* It was then I felt something streaming down my face, around my neck, and suddenly freezing. I took my right hand away from the mask for a moment and noticed that it was covered with blood. I wasn't quite certain where the blood had been coming from. Perhaps the pounding mask had broken my nose. Perhaps I was bleeding from the eyes and ears, as well as the nose. As I was to learn later, I did not have a broken nose, but I had bled from the eyes, ears, nose and mouth as a result of ruptures caused by the "explosive" decompression.

Now, I was in heavier air and starting to feel more comfortable. But the overcast had become so dense that without reference to even a patch of sky, I had almost lost all sensation of movement. I felt as if I were suspended in a soft, milk-white substance and falling as though in some huge amorphous easy chair, my feet in the air. Only the sound of air rushing past me—and the flailing, loose oxygen hose—gave me a feeling of movement. The sight of the loose oxygen hose reminded me that earlier I had done something foolish.

After I had managed to get the oxygen mask to my face, I saw the loose hose, now below me, now above me, as I tumbled. I thought the hose connecting my mask to the emergency oxygen container had become disconnected, especially after I had caught a glimpse of the coupling. I struggled to grasp the hose and succeeded in doing so, only to realize that it was a different hose, the one that had been ripped away from the main oxygen supply in the airplane. I had been confused by the identical couplings. But in the process of reaching for the hose and then releasing it, I noticed my right glove ballooning from the force of air and felt, mistakenly, that the glove would only get in my way. I had already lost my left glove and forgot that my left hand had instantly frozen numb. I simply held my right hand out for a moment, and the force of air ripped it from my hand; not until I saw the glove sailing rapidly off into the murky overcast did I realize it was a stupid thing to do. Now my right hand would freeze—and it did, within seconds.

As I continued falling, I was amazed suddenly to realize how much thinking I had been able to do. With the effects of decompression diminishing, although the pain was still great throughout my body, I recognized that numbness had become an analgesic, helping me to tolerate the pain. But as the overcast grew darker, having lost reference even to the flailing oxygen hose, I felt as if I were in a complete void; I could no longer tell whether I was spinning, rolling, tumbling, or cartwheeling; whether I was on my back, stomach or falling feet first. Again, I felt a strong urge to open my 'chute and it was at this moment I began to think of the passage of time.

I made several attempts to look at my watch. Although I could not be certain, it seemed to indicate four or five minutes after six p.m. In the overcast the luminous dial was barely visible. Then I started thinking about my rate of fall. Undoubtedly, I had slowed to terminal velocity downward, seconds after I had ejected, and was now falling at an average rate of about 10,000 feet per minute. But I was not exactly calculating with slide-rule precision. As a matter of fact, at one point I had confused the terminal velocity of my free-falling body with the rate of descent of a jet, about 4,000 feet a minute, coming down through overcast for a landing; and the result shook me for a moment. *What the hell's going on here,* I thought. *Come on, boy, get hold of yourself. You're not a jet, you're a pilot, you're free-falling. Get those rates squared away in your mind.*

But having made the rough, quick calculations with the proper rate of fall, the confidence I had built up in survival almost vanished. Since

I had left my airplane at exactly six p.m. and at approximately 47,000 feet, and now it was several minutes past six, or so it seemed, why hadn't my 'chute opened? Had I sped past the 10,000-foot mark? In this overcast, unable to see anything, what if I were only several hundred feet from the ground and about to crash into it? I knew my 'chute had not opened because I had not felt the characteristic violent jerk.

Once more I felt a tremendous desire to open my 'chute. But now my trained instincts were in control. I could think more clearly. I knew my timing was not precise. I knew I should have more confidence in the automatic 'chute opener. I decided to wait a little longer, fifteen seconds, perhaps half a minute, maybe a minute. I would judge according to circumstances; and just then my confidence was somewhat restored by a feeling that my body had been struck by little rocks. I remembered the thunderstorm and realized that those "little rocks" were perhaps hail, drops of rain carried to the freezing level by the storm's updrafts, quickly frozen, then falling as hail. *The freezing level for rain? It must be at least 10,000 feet or more. Good. Keep free-falling, keep going, keep conscious.*

I tried to see what was going on but I felt a peculiar sensation in my eyeballs, as though they were freezing. It was the same tingling sensation I had felt earlier just before the exposed parts of my body turned numb. I closed my eyes and kept them closed, although it also occurred to me that perhaps it was the moisture of the clouds that was freezing in my eyes, not my eyes' fluids.

I started thinking about the 'chute again and came to the conclusion that perhaps it should have opened. I was certain that I was now in denser, more comfortable air. I was still quite cold but the little straining effects of gas seeking to escape from my body under continuing decompression seemed to disappear. I felt now the risk of crashing into the ground in an unopened 'chute was greater than the risk of freezing to death, or being for a while without oxygen. I reached for the D-ring and was about to pull it when suddenly my body lurched violently— my feet had gone through a floor in midair and wanted to keep going while the rest of my body could not. My 'chute had opened! Almost at the same time the oxygen mask collapsed against my face. *Uncanny, perfect timing,* I thought. The emergency supply of oxygen was designed to sustain me during a free fall, after which my 'chute would open at a level where I would no longer be concerned about oxygen and the supply would give out, and it did.

Still, I wanted to be certain about it. The violent opening of a 'chute was no novel experience to me. I remembered my bailout in Korea. But this had been a tremendous, far more violent sensation than anything I had felt before. I knew I had been falling at a rate in excess of 100 miles per hour and had suddenly decelerated to perhaps 10 miles per hour and at the moment of such a shocking deceleration I had felt greater violence—but I wanted to see the 'chute with my own eyes, and I could not. When I looked up it was much darker than I had anticipated. I could not see the beautiful, joyous, reassuring sight of the "silk." However, I could see, and feel, my parachute risers, taut, straight up. *The 'chute must have opened,* I thought. *There are the risers, nice and straight, straining against my body, on my torso harness.* But in the thick overcast, without references, I could not tell the position of my body, nor how fast I was falling. Suppose I had a streamer, a partially opened 'chute? Or suppose I had a damaged 'chute? A missing panel or two? Was I floating, or still rocketing toward earth? I reached up and felt the risers. They felt nice and firm. Good. I rocked the risers. Now I felt better. I was confident I had a good 'chute. Rocking the risers did it; it was the same "feel" as when I had rocked the risers coming down in the 'chute in Korea.

Again, a rough calculation. *I'm at the 10,000-foot level. Descending at the rate of about 1,000 feet per minute, give or take a couple of hundred feet. I should be down in about ten minutes. That's great. All's well now. I've got a good 'chute. I'm comfortable. I'm conscious. I've survived.*

I felt good, I felt wonderful. I was even buoyant, elated. Now I could relax a bit. I could take off the oxygen mask, and did. When the oxygen mask fell away, a small pool of blood spilled into my hand. Apparently, the violent opening of the 'chute had started my nosebleed again. At the same time, I noticed a huge deep cut just above the knuckle of the little finger on my right band. The finger itself was dangling at an odd angle. *Must have gashed it,* I thought, *when I ejected. Guess I did go through the canopy. Good time now to take inventory.* I looked all about me, checking my hands, feet, helmet, flight suit, boots, life jacket. Except for a slightly tattered flight suit, everything seemed to be intact. *Wonderful,* I thought. *Just great. If I hit the ground, I'll be able to walk away—that is, if I don't break a leg or otherwise get hurt upon landing. I'm lucky. I've known many aviators who had lost their shoes ejecting at even lower speeds and lower altitudes. And if I should hit the water, well, I've got my life jacket, and I'm a good swimmer.*

I realized now I was deliberately keeping myself busy, checking myself, the 'chute's risers, even rationalizing my horrifying misfortune, my agonizing decompression, my aches and pains, by equating it all with the astonishing good fortune I'd had to survive, to be floating gently down, safely, in relative comfort. With time to spare, I had also become somewhat more conscious of all the aches and pains and felt as if my body had been wrung out, and the internal organs and the bones and the flesh were painfully reshaping. My face felt terribly raw and swollen, my hands icily numb and very stiff. I looked at my dangling finger again. The cut was really deep; I could see what was either the tendon or the bone.

Perhaps no more than a minute had elapsed when I suddenly began to feel a slight turbulence in the air, and it reminded me that I had left the plane above a thunderstorm. But the turbulence wasn't too bad. It rocked me a bit, sometimes lifted me, giving me a slight feeling of zero g, rising in an updraft, momentarily halting, then falling again. But it wasn't bad at all. It gave me something to think about, taking my mind off my fiercely aching gashed finger. What I forgot to think about was that in a thunderstorm, where the barometric pressure is usually lower than normal, my 'chute might have opened not at the 10,000-foot level, but at 15,000 feet, or higher, where the 'chute's barometric sensing device could have been "fooled" and might have opened prematurely.

But now I was no longer gravely concerned about anything, except where and how I would land in the 'chute, hopeful I would not land in water or in one of the many swampy areas along North Carolina's coast. Although in the vicinity of Norfolk when I had ejected, I knew that, from more than nine miles up, I could be swept many miles from Norfolk, and might not land in Virginia at all.

Nonetheless, I was most pleased with the thought that I had seemed to maintain consciousness all the way down. True, there were moments when I thought I'd pass out from the severe pain of decompression, but I could not recall any time I might have passed out. I could not recall any moment when I had to ask myself, *What happened? Where am I?*

I knew my body had been subjected to tremendous shock and had accordingly responded by shooting huge doses of adrenalin into my blood, helping me survive the shock, helping me fight for survival, helping me to think rationally. On the ground, I'd probably suffer from postshock depression and weakness; I might even be helpless for a while; but why worry about it now? Under the circumstances, over-joyed to be alive and going down safely, consciously, even the increas-ing turbulence of the air meant nothing. It was all over now, I thought, the ordeal had ended.

But it hadn't. I was about to plunge into the center of the storm.

My entry into the throat of the storm came—as almost always the storm itself comes on earth—gradually.

The first reminder that I had fallen into a thunderstorm was the rel-atively mild turbulence I had felt just prior to and immediately after my 'chute had opened, although after the 'chute had opened the tur-bulence felt somewhat stronger—perhaps not quite strong enough, however, to think of it as turbulence, as violent churning. I thought of it as updrafts. It was as though I had been suddenly taken up in an ele-vator, two or three rapid rides in succession, each ride a brief but speedy one, ending suddenly, with the strange feeling of negative g, then a feeling of weightlessness. But when the "updrafts" increased in frequency and strength, I knew it was the turbulence of the storm, the powerful, massive blasts of air which have inspired scientists to describe thunderstorms as, "in effect, a large heat engine," having "strong updrafts and downdrafts thermally driven by differences in air temperature," and in which "engine" it would not be unusual for a large body, such as an airplane or a human being, to be shot up at the rate of 100 feet per second.

After the first few shocks of turbulence, virtually straight up-and-down actions, I felt a queasiness in my stomach. For me it was a strange feeling because, in spite of literally thousands of hours in the air, in all sorts of airplanes, under all sorts of weather, combat and training conditions, I had never suffered motion sickness. Still, I was neither disturbed nor frightened. I had been through much worse in an airplane, wherein my principal concern had been not drifting safely down in a parachute, not a little discomfort, as now, but wrestling the turbulence for control of a big, complex machine.

But my mind changed rapidly after I was hit by the first real shock from nature's "heat engine." It came with incredible suddenness and fury. It hit me like a tidal wave of air, a massive blast, as though forged under tremendous compression, aimed and fired at me with the savagery of a cannon. I was jarred from head to toe. Every bone in my body must have rattled, and I went soaring up and up and up as though there would be no end to its force. As I came down again, I saw that I was in an angry ocean of boiling clouds, blacks and grays and whites, spilling over each other, into each other, digesting each other.

I became a veritable molecule trapped in the thermal pattern of heat engine. I was buffeted in all directions—up, down, sideways, clockwise, counterclockwise, over and over; I tumbled, spun, and zoomed, straight up, straight down, and I was rattled violently, as though a monstrous cat had caught me by the neck, and was determined to shake me until I had gasped my last breath. I felt all the painful and weird sensations of the g forces—positive, negative and zero. I was pushed up, pushed down, stretched, slammed, and pounded. I was a bag of flesh and bones crashing into a concrete floor, an empty human shell soaring, a lifeless form strangely suspended in air. During moments of zero g, I could recall the times when map cases, note paper, and pencils had floated in the cockpits of my jet planes, and now I felt as though I were as helpless as those inanimate objects. The rapid changes between positive, negative and zero g were sickening. I know I vomited time after time. It was maddening, and I felt as if I were not only fighting for my life, but my sanity as well.

At one point, after I had been literally shot up like a bullet leaving a gun, I found myself looking down into a long, black tunnel, a nightmarish corridor in space. Sometimes, I didn't want to see what was going on. I kept my eyes shut, tight. This was not turbulence. This was nature's bedlam, an ugly black cage of screaming, violent, fanatical lunatics, having a game with me, tossing me about, beating me with big flat sticks, roaring at me, screeching, trying to crush me or rip me with their bands. One sensation I'll never forget: I remember it as the "accordion," being squeezed simultaneously from top and bottom.

Several times—I could not believe it at first—I felt as though I had been looping around my parachute, like a pendulum. But it was no gentle to-and-fro swing. I went up, out, around and down as if on a speeding centrifuge. I could feel blood rushing to my feet, then my head. Practically, I would not have known whether I was upside down, or otherwise oblique, except that I could "sense" it by the centrifugal force on my body.

There were times when I simply would not believe that my parachute could withstand the strain. Something had to give, the risers, the shrouds, perhaps the buckles on my torso harness. Once or twice, perhaps more often, my 'chute seemed to lose its precious "billow" and I thought it was a miracle that I did not go streaming toward earth with a long, narrow white tail, my collapsed 'chute. I had quick visions of myself crashing into the earth, a helpless mass of flesh and bones wrapped in a white shroud.

This punishment, I thought, is overwhelming. I'll never survive. No one could survive it. What supreme irony—to come out alive from "explosive" decompression, to maintain consciousness all the way down, only to be bat-

tered to death by a thunderstorm. When they find my body, they'll never know how I died. The pathologist might say that I died of shock, or that "explosive" decompression had been too much for my heart. What a pity I shall not be there to say, "No, no, no. The 'explosive' decompression was bad, painful. But it did not kill me. The frostbite was agony, but it did not kill me. It was the raging storm that tore the life from me."

There were times during my decompression pains when I did not feel too confident about survival. But they were not strong feelings of despair. Stronger were the feelings that I'd pass out and not remember what had happened to me, not remember the details which the flight surgeons and the aeromedical experts might like to learn about. Now, however, I was absolutely certain that I was having my last thoughts on earth. I no longer wondered whether I would die, but how I would die.

However, I was not quite prepared to give up the fight. Sometimes I found myself grasping the risers of my 'chute, as if this would help me hang on to life itself. At one point I crossed my arms over my chest, as though I were trying to hang on to myself.

During the turbulence I clung to hope because I felt I had become or might become a part of the storm's pattern, blasts of air shooting up, then down, but not always straight down. Some air would spill over the top of each rising current, out and then down, as in the shape of a broad mushroom. I might spill over with the air and if that were the case, sooner or later, I'd be released from the vortex and float down. In the process, I might be swept across dozens of miles of land, perhaps hundreds of miles. I might end up in Pennsylvania or New Jersey or over the ocean!—wherever the storm itself might weaken or die and eventually disgorge me. But I didn't care where it would happen, so long as it released me.

Before long, however, I found that the storm had allies with whom I had to do battle, physically and mentally: thunder, lightning, hail and rain.

The first clap of thunder came as a deafening explosion, followed by a blinding flash of lightning, then a rolling, roaring sound which seemed to vibrate every fibre of my body. The lightning was so close, so brilliant that even after I had instinctively closed my eyes I got the sensation of "seeing" a deep red outside. Then the thunder and lightning combination continued, relentlessly.

Throughout the time I spent in the storm, the booming claps of thunder were not auditory sensations; they were unbearable physical experiences—every bone and muscle responded quiveringly to the crash. I didn't *hear* the thunder, I *felt* it.

I felt that if it had not been for my helmet, the tight, cushioning fit over my ears, the explosions of thunder would have shattered my eardrums irreparably. It was my only feeling of solace, of joy and gratitude—that I had been a stickler on the rules of the game and had always tightened my helmet to avoid losing it in the event of an emergency ejection. I was grateful for it when I fell through the frigid, subzero temperatures, having given me at least partial protection; I was grateful for it when I thought I had gone through the canopy, and when it protected my skull against the blast of air after I had been shot out of the plane. But now it was a downright blessing to have its cushioning effects against my ears and later its protection against pounding hail.

I used to think of lightning as long, slender, jagged streaks of electricity; but no more. The real thing is different. I saw lightning all around me, over, above, everywhere, and I saw it in every shape imaginable. But when very close it appeared mainly as a huge, bluish sheet, several feet thick, sometimes sticking close to me in pairs, like the blades of a scissor, and I had the distinct feeling that I was being sliced in two.

As the huge bolts of lightning streaked past me, I thought of the phenomenon we call St. Elmo's fire, the static electricity that dances along the wingtips of an airplane in flight, especially an airplane that might have just passed through a storm. I have seen St. Elmo's fire leap from wingtip to wingtip, and I have seen planes seriously damaged by it. I once saw an airplane with huge, gaping holes in its metallic skin, burned through by St. Elmo's fire. I began to wonder whether it was possible for St. Elmo's fire to dance off a human form, one that had been tossed so violently and at such high speeds through a storm that it might have been building up its own enormous reservoir of static electricity. I was no expert on lightning, but I had always assumed that lightning did not strike unless it were attracted to another body of an opposite charge and that the earth, being such a body, was a constant attraction for lightning; and that lightning would do no harm unless it went through you into the ground. I was not grounded in the air, of course, but it had been raining and everything seemed so wet, so drenched I felt almost certain that the saturated air would have been ground enough for the lightning to pass through me. Many times lightning struck so close I thought, indeed, it had passed through me. I cannot be sure it did not.

What concerned me most was the possibility of lightning striking my 'chute and melting it as rapidly as a tiny ball of cellophane might disappear in a roaring fire. Theoretically, this would have been a rare, if not impossible, occurrence; or so I thought. Where was the contact between the 'chute and the ground, to attract the lightning and to make it possible for the lightning to cause damage? Well, I had seen huge shots of lightning seemingly jumping from one part of the clouds to another, like immense spark plugs firing in the dark. What was there to prevent lightning from going through my 'chute during one such charge, or to prevent the 'chute itself from attracting lightning? Had I known at the time lightning has been seen striking down huge balloons, such as the one ten stories high, hailed as the world's largest balloon, launched by a Naval Air Station in Georgia, I would have been utterly terrified— if it were possible to have been more terrified in that fiery, exploding chaos we have so politely labelled thunderstorm.

After each flash of lightning, everything turned completely black. I was lost in a pool of ink. During the intense brilliant light, when bolts shot by, the clouds seemed to boil around me, sending up huge vaporous balls of grayish cotton. Even when I kept my eyes closed the lightning had a blinding effect.

Invariably, lightning struck in uncanny synchronization with claps of thunder, followed by a rolling explosion which literally shook my teeth; I could feel the vibrations on my teeth as though a giant tuning fork had been struck against them and held there. The lightning-thunder combinations seemed to come at least once or twice each minute. I wondered whether anything like this had been taking place on earth below, whether it was as black down there as up here. It was not, of course, although later I learned that this storm was one of the most violent ever recorded on the East Coast.

I think actually it was the combination, the one-two jabs of lightning and thunder, that filled me most with the fear that I'd never survive the ordeal. At one point, I saw such an eerie effect that I thought I had already died. I had been looking up in the direction of my 'chute, when a bolt of lightning struck, illuminating the huge interior of the 'chute's billow as though it were a strange white-domed cathedral, and the effect seemed to linger on the retinas of my eyes. For a moment, I had the distinct feeling that I was sailing into a softly lit church and at any moment I might hear the subdued strains of an organ and a mournful voice in prayer—and I thought I had died. *Maybe this is it,* I thought. *This is the way it all begins after death. You're dead, Bill. It's all over. Now you'll have peace.*

If this was my moment or two of irrationality in the storm, I don't know and may never know. I do know that I distinctly encouraged myself to have hope, to fight back. Yet there were times when I felt I might die of sheer exhaustion because it seemed as if either the storm might never end, or I was going to be swept along with it on its insane journey up the coast for as long as that journey might take—hours, days. This feeling was most intense when I decided to look at my watch and glimpsed the time during a flash of lightning. At first I thought what a wonderful thing it was not to have lost my watch all through ejection, decompression, blasts of air, and now this; and, then, what a silly thing, looking at the time! But when I saw that it was twenty minutes past six, I thought: *My God, you should have been on the ground at least ten minutes ago! You are really trapped. You are really in the pattern of the storm and a part of it, a speck of human dust, up-over-and-down, up-over-and-down and that's the way it's going to be. But how long? For how long?*

I don't remember whether I had looked at my watch again after that, although I seem to recall vaguely that I did, perhaps several times.

Nonetheless, I was preoccupied with more than turbulence and thunder and lightning (such mild words). It had been raining torrentially all through the storm, but sometimes the rain was so dense and came in such swift, drenching sheets, I thought I would drown in midair. It was as though I were under a swimming pool, and I had held my breath several times, fearful of drowning. If I had not run out of oxygen, I would have held the mask over my face as protection against drowning. Sometimes, I was tempted to put on the mask, thinking that I'd rather suffocate to death than drown.

How silly, I thought. *They're going to find you hanging from some tree, in your parachute harness, limp, lifeless, your lungs filled with water, wondering how on earth did you drown!* Sometimes, I found myself gasping for air as if I actually were drowning.

Occasionally, I'd look up to try and see what was happening to my parachute. I was concerned about the 'chute collapsing or losing some of its panels, which might cause it to collapse or practically cause me to fall so rapidly the impact might kill me. And during one such observation, I saw and felt what I shall perhaps never witness again (unless in a thunderstorm). A sudden and violent blast of air, coming from the long dark narrow corridor in the storm, apparently hitting me with greater force and just prior to hitting my 'chute, sent me careening up into the 'chute itself.

At least I am convinced this is what happened, for I could feel the clammy silk draped over me like a large wet sheet. The 'chute was collapsed over me and I felt sure I had become tangled in the lines and was doubtful that the 'chute would ever blossom again properly. *When they find my body they'll say my 'chute never opened, but they'll be wrong again.* A few moments later, however, there was a mild jerk on my body harness and once again I had good, taut, risers. The impossible had happened.

Seeing the 'chute intact was a source of encouragement to me. *If this damn thing can survive,* I thought, *so can I.*

The moment I had most felt that I had become a part of the pattern of the storm was when the hail struck. From all-weather flight studies, I knew that hail formed in a storm as a result of drops of rain being caught in the turbulence of the storm's drafts, being shot up to higher, colder levels, freezing, solidifying, then falling, then being caught and shot up again, refreezing and solidifying and growing in size, until they would spill over and come down to earth, melting as they reached warmer air.

From the way I had been pelted by relentless showers of hail, I think that if most hail did not melt prior to striking the earth it would number among nature's most calamitous phenomena. Even now, as I understand, hailstorms are a serious agricultural problem in America, frequently ruining as much as $100,000,000 worth of crops a year.

Experts tell me that unbelievably large chunks of hail have been known to strike the earth, such as the time during a thunderstorm over Potter, Nebraska, in 1928, when hailstones as large as seventeen inches in circumference, weighing well over a pound, were officially recorded.

A U.S. Weather Bureau official once said, "A violent hailstorm has to be experienced to be believed." I could believe it.

During my bouts with hailstones in the storm, I felt as though I were being pounded by a symphony of hammers, drumming at every part of my body. Sometimes, hitting my helmet, the hail gave me the feeling it was raining baseballs. I don't know how large the hailstones were because I cannot recall seeing them. I was afraid to open my eyes during those seemingly interminable moments when hail struck. Later, from the mass of black-and-blue welts covering my body no calipers were needed to know that the hailstones were large—and hard. It was also during periods of hail strikes that I thanked the Lord for having my helmet. I am certain that without a helmet I would have suffered severe head injuries, at least concussion, quite probably a fractured skull.

Luckily, during lulls in the storm, lulls lasting perhaps ten to thirty seconds each, my mind remained active, thinking about what I would do upon finally landing. I continually reminded myself that, when breaking out of the overcast, I should be sure to get the lay of the land. If coming down over water, make a mental note about wind direction, wind force, and the direction of the shoreline. If coming down over land, note the terrain, its character, whether wooded, possibly swampy; look for signs of civilization—houses, farms, roads.

Remaining mentally active, I think, prevented me from losing my mind, at the very least from panicking. I was terrified, but not petrified. I knew that in spite of some severe moments when I felt as if I might pass out, I had been conscious all the time. I cannot, of course, be certain of continual consciousness under such circumstances, but one of my most vivid recollections is never at any time during the entire descent, from moment of ejection through the storm, did I feel as if I had been "out of this world," as in a daze.

Meanwhile, my thoughts stimulated by the pattern of hail formation, I was mainly concerned about how long I would be trapped in the storm's pattern. My most frightening thought came when I remembered our gunnery training in Guantanamo, where tropical thunderstorms were almost a daily affair, and some of the thunderheads seemed to remain over one area for days and weeks at a time, building up day by day before unleashing their elements over land. There had been one thunderhead that had remained almost stationary over the bay for so long, and with such seeming permanence of station, that we used to refer to it as the "duty storm," always there like a duty officer at headquarters. We'd fly around it and over it by instinct, as though it were an immovable traffic island in the sky. I wondered, fearfully, whether I might not have been caught in a "duty storm," which are also common during the summer months over Norfolk's waters.

I think that's when I gave up trying to look at my watch. I had reconciled myself to a hard, long battle and continued to fight it, armed with hope and mental activity. I thought of myself as being on a strange ferris wheel of nature, and sooner or later the turbulence would have to run out of energy, releasing me gradually toward earth.

Eventually, I realized that the air was getting smoother, and the rain was falling more gently. Looking up, I could see my white 'chute clearly against the gray clouds. I could sense that I was near the earth, and I knew that below the storm I would probably have only two or three hundred feet of ceiling. Suddenly a patch of green flashed through a break in the clouds.

from The Right Stuff
by Tom Wolfe

The most memorable character in Tom Wolfe's (born 1931) paean to the first astronauts was never a spaceman—and didn't think much of those who were. But Chuck Yeager could make an airplane do things that bordered on the impossible. That made him the right man to break the sound barrier, a feat many people thought was just that: impossible.

Anyone who travels very much on airlines in the United States soon gets to know the voice of *the airline pilot* . . . coming over the intercom . . . with a particular drawl, a particular folksiness, a particular down-home calmness that is so exaggerated it begins to parody itself (nevertheless!—it's reassuring) . . . the voice that tells you, as the airliner is caught in thunderheads and goes bolting up and down a thousand feet at a single gulp, to check your seat belts because "it might get a little choppy" . . . the voice that tells you (on a flight from Phoenix preparing for its final approach into Kennedy Airport, New York, just after dawn): "Now, folks, uh . . . this is the captain . . . ummmm . . . We've got a little ol' red light up here on the control panel that's tryin' to tell us that the *landin'* gears're not . . . uh . . . *lock*in' into position when we lower 'em . . . Now . . . I don't believe that little ol' red light knows what it's *talkin'* about—I believe it's that little ol' red *light* that iddn' workin' right" . . . faint chuckle, long pause, as if to say, *I'm not even sure all this is really worth going* *into—still, it may amuse you . . .* "But . . . I guess to play it by the rules, we oughta *hum*or that little ol' light . . . so we're gonna take her down to about, oh, two or three hundred feet over the runway at Kennedy, and the folks down there on the ground are gonna see if they caint give us a *vis*ual inspection of those ol' landin' gears"—with which he is obviously on intimate ol'-buddy terms, as with every other working part of this mighty ship—"and if I'm right . . . they're gonna tell us everything is copa*cet*ic all the way aroun' an' we'll jes take her on in". . . and, after a couple of low passes over the field, the voice returns: "Well, folks, those folks down there on the ground—it must be too early for 'em or somethin'—I 'spect they still got the *sleep*ers in their eyes . . . 'cause they say they caint tell if those ol' landin' gears are all the way down or not . . . But, you know, up here in the cockpit we're convinced they're all the way down, so we're jes gonna take her on in . . . And oh" . . . (*I almost forgot*) . . . "while we take a little swing out over the ocean an' empty some of that surplus fuel we're not gonna be needin' anymore—that's what you might be seein' comin' out of the wings—our lovely little ladies . . . if they'll be so kind . . . they're gonna go up and down the aisles and show you how we do what we call 'assumin' the position'" . . . another faint chuckle (*We do this so often, and it's so much fun, we even have a funny little name for it*) . . . and the stewardesses, a bit grimmer, by the looks of them, than *that voice*, start telling the passengers to take their glasses off and take the ballpoint pens and other sharp objects out of their pockets, and they show them *the position*, with the head lowered . . . while down on the field at Kennedy the little yellow emergency trucks start roaring across the field—and even though in your pounding heart and your sweating palms and your broiling brainpan you *know* this is a critical moment in your life, you still can't quite bring yourself to be*lieve* it, because if it were . . . how could *the captain*, the man who knows the actual situation most intimately . . . how could he keep on drawlin' and chucklin' and driftin' and lollygaggin' in that particular voice of his—

Well!—who doesn't know that voice! And who can forget it!—even after he is proved right and the emergency is over.

That particular voice may sound vaguely Southern or Southwestern, but it is specifically Appalachian in origin. It originated in the mountains of West Virginia, in the coal country, in Lincoln County, so far up in the hollows that, as the saying went, "they had to pipe in daylight." In the late 1940's and early 1950's this up-hollow voice drifted down from on high, from over the high desert of California, down, down, down, from the upper reaches of the Brotherhood into all phases of American aviation. It was amazing. It was *Pygmalion* in reverse. Military pilots and then, soon, airline pilots, pilots from Maine and Massachusetts and the Dakotas and Oregon and everywhere else, began to talk in that poker-hollow West Virginia drawl, or as close to it as they could bend their native accents. It was the drawl of the most righteous of all the possessors of the right stuff: Chuck Yeager.

Yeager had started out as the equivalent, in the Second World War, of the legendary Frank Luke of the 27th Aero Squadron in the First. Which is to say, he was the boondocker, the boy from the back country, with only a high-school education, no credentials, no cachet or polish of any sort, who took off the feed-store overalls and put on a uniform and climbed into an airplane and lit up the skies over Europe.

Yeager grew up in Hamlin, West Virginia, a town on the Mud River not far from Nitro, Hurricane Whirlwind, Salt Rock, Mud, Sod, Crum, Leet, Dollie, Ruth, and Alum Creek. His father was a gas driller (drilling for natural gas in the coalfields), his older brother was a gas driller, and he would have been a gas driller had he not enlisted in the Army Air Force in 1941 at the age of eighteen. In 1943, at twenty, he became a flight officer, i.e., a non-com who was allowed to fly, and went to England to fly fighter planes over France and Germany. Even in the tumult of the war Yeager was somewhat puzzling to a lot of other pilots. He was a short, wiry, but muscular little guy with dark curly hair and a tough-looking face that seemed (to strangers) to be saying: "You best not be lookin' me in the eye, you peckerwood, or I'll put four more holes in your nose." But that wasn't what was puzzling. What was puzzling was the way Yeager talked. He seemed to talk with some older forms of English elocution, syntax, and conjugation that had been preserved up-hollow in the Appalachians. There were people up there who never said they disapproved of anything, they said: "I don't hold with it." In the present tense they were willing to *help* out, like anyone else; but in the past tense they only *holped*. "H'it weren't nothin' I hold with, but I holped him out with it, anyways."

In his first eight missions, at the age of twenty, Yeager shot down two German fighters. On his ninth he was shot down over German-occupied French territory, suffering flak wounds; he bailed out, was picked up by the French underground, which smuggled him across the Pyrenees into Spain disguised as a peasant. In Spain he was jailed briefly, then released, whereupon be made it back to England and returned to combat during the Allied invasion of France. On October 12, 1944, Yeager took on and shot down five German fighter planes in succession. On November 6, flying a propeller-driven P-51 Mustang, he shot down one of the new jet fighters the Germans had developed, the Messerschmitt-262, and damaged two more, and on November 20 he shot down four FW-190s. It was a true Frank Luke-style display of warrior fury and personal prowess. By the end of the war he had thirteen and a half kills. He was twenty-two years old.

In 1946 and 1947 Yeager was trained as a test pilot at Wright Field in Dayton. He amazed his instructors with his ability at stunt-team flying, not to mention the unofficial business of hassling. That plus his up-hollow drawl had everybody saying, "He's a natural-born stick 'n' rudder man." Nevertheless, there was something extraordinary about it when a man so young, with so little experience in flight test, was selected to go to Muroc Field in California for the X-1 project.

Muroc was up in the high elevations of the Mojave Desert. It looked like some fossil landscape that had long since been left behind by the rest of terrestrial evolution. It was full of huge dry lake beds, the biggest being Rogers Lake. Other than sagebrush the only vegetation was Joshua trees, twisted freaks of the plant world that looked like a cross between cactus and Japanese bonsai. They had a dark petrified green color and horribly crippled branches. At dusk the Joshua trees stood out in silhouette on the fossil wasteland like some arthritic nightmare.

In the summer the temperature went up to 110 degrees as a matter of course, and the dry lake beds were covered in sand, and there would be windstorms and sandstorms right out of a Foreign Legion movie. At night it would drop to near freezing, and in December it would start raining, and the dry lakes would fill up with a few inches of water, and some sort of putrid prehistoric shrimps would work their way up from out of the ooze, and sea gulls would come flying in a hundred miles or more from the ocean, over the mountains, to gobble up these squirming little throwbacks. A person had to see it to believe it: flocks of sea gulls wheeling around in the air out in the middle of the high desert in the dead of winter and grazing on antediluvian crustaceans in the primordial ooze.

When the wind blew the few inches of water back and forth across the lake beds, they became absolutely smooth and level. And when the water evaporated in the spring, and the sun baked the ground hard, the lake beds became the greatest natural landing fields ever discovered, and also the biggest, with miles of room for error. That was highly desirable, given the nature of the enterprise at Muroc.

Besides the wind, sand, tumbleweed, and Joshua trees, there was nothing at Muroc except for two quonset-style hangars, side by side, a couple of gasoline pumps, a single concrete runway, a few tarpaper shacks, and some tents. The officers stayed in the shacks marked "barracks," and lesser souls stayed in the tents and froze all night and fried all day. Every road into the property had a guardhouse on it manned by soldiers. The enterprise the Army had undertaken in this godforsaken place was the development of supersonic jet and rocket planes.

At the end of the war the Army had discovered that the Germans not only had the world's first jet fighter but also a rocket plane that had gone 596 miles an hour in tests. Just after the war a British jet, the Gloster Meteor, jumped the official world speed record from 469 to 606 in a single day. The next great plateau would be Mach 1, the speed of sound, and the Army Air Force considered it crucial to achieve it first.

The speed of sound, Mach 1, was known (thanks to the work of the physicist Ernst Mach) to vary at different altitudes, temperatures, and wind speeds. On a calm 60-degree day at sea level it was about 760 miles an hour, while at 40,000 feet, where the temperature would be at least sixty below, it was about 660 miles an hour. Evil and baffling things happened in the transonic zone, which began at about .7 Mach. Wind tunnels choked out at such velocities. Pilots who approached the speed of sound in dives reported that the controls would lock or "freeze" or even alter their normal functions. Pilots had crashed and died because they couldn't budge the stick. Just last year Geoffrey de Havilland, son of the famous British aircraft designer and builder, had tried to take one of his father's DH 108s to Mach 1. The ship started buffeting and then disintegrated, and he was killed. This led engineers to speculate that the g-forces became infinite at Mach 1, causing the aircraft to implode. They started talking about "the sonic wall" and "the sound barrier."

So this was the task that a handful of pilots, engineers, and mechanics had at Muroc. The place was utterly primitive, nothing but bare bones, bleached tarpaulins, and corrugated tin rippling in the heat with caloric waves; and for an ambitious young pilot it was perfect. Muroc seemed like an outpost on the dome of the world, open only to a righteous few, closed off to the rest of humanity, including even the Army Air Force brass of command control, which was at Wright Field. The commanding officer at Muroc was only a colonel, and his superiors at Wright did not relish junkets to the Muroc rat shacks in the first place. But to pilots this prehistoric throwback of an airfield became . . . shrimp heaven! the rat-shack plains of Olympus!

Low Rent Septic Tank Perfection . . . yes; and not excluding those traditional essentials for the blissful hot young pilot: Flying & Drinking and Drinking & Driving.

Just beyond the base, to the southwest, there was a rickety windblown 1930's-style establishment called Pancho's Fly Inn, owned, run, and bartended by a woman named Pancho Barnes. Pancho Barnes wore tight white sweaters and tight pants, after the mode of Barbara Stanwyck in *Double Indemnity*. She was only forty-one when Yeager arrived at Muroc, but her face was so weatherbeaten, had so many hard miles on it, that she looked older, especially to the young pilots at the base. She also shocked the pants off them with her vulcanized tongue. Everybody she didn't like was an old bastard or a sonofabitch. People she liked were old bastards and sonsabitches, too. "I tol' 'at ol' bastard to get 'is ass on over here and I'd g'im a drink." But Pancho Barnes was anything but Low Rent. She was the granddaughter of the man who designed the old Mount Lowe cable-car system, Thaddeus S. C. Lowe. Her maiden name was Florence Leontine Lowe. She was brought up in San Marino, which adjoined Pasadena and was one of Los Angeles' wealthiest suburbs, and her first husband—she was married four times—was the pastor of the Pasadena Episcopal Church, the Rev. C. Rankin Barnes. Mrs. Barnes seemed to have few of the conventional community interests of a Pasadena matron. In the late 1920's, by boat and plane, she ran guns for Mexican revolutionaries and picked up the nickname Pancho. In 1930 she broke Amelia Earhart's airspeed record for women. Then she barnstormed around the country as the featured performer of "Pancho Barnes's Mystery Circus of the Air." She always greeted her public in jodhpurs and riding boots, a flight jacket, a white scarf, and a white sweater that showed off her terrific Barbara Stanwyck chest. Pancho's desert Fly Inn had an airstrip, a swimming pool, a dude ranch corral, plenty of acreage for horseback riding, a big old guest house for the lodgers, and a connecting building that was the bar and restaurant. In the barroom the floors, the tables, the chairs, the walls, the beams, the bar were of the sort known as extremely weatherbeaten, and the screen doors kept banging. Nobody putting together such a place for a movie about flying in the old days would ever dare make it as dilapidated and generally go-to-hell as it actually was. Behind the bar were many pictures of airplanes and pilots, lavishly autographed and inscribed, badly framed and crookedly hung. There was an old piano that had been dried out and cracked to the point of hopeless desiccation. On a good night a huddle of drunken aviators could be heard trying to bang, slosh, and navigate their way through old Cole Porter tunes. On average nights the tunes were not that good to start with. When the screen door banged and a man walked through the door into the saloon, every eye in the place checked him out. If he wasn't known as somebody who had something to do with flying at Muroc, he would be eyed like some lame goddamned mouse-shit sheepherder from *Shane*.

The plane the Air Force wanted to break the sound barrier with was called the X-1. The Bell Aircraft Corporation had built it under an Army contract. The core of the ship was a rocket of the type first developed by a young Navy inventor, Robert Truax, during the war. The fuselage was shaped like a 50-caliber bullet—an object that was known to go supersonic smoothly. Military pilots seldom drew major test assignments; they went to highly paid civilians working for the aircraft corporations. The prime pilot for the X-1 was a man whom Bell regarded as the best of the breed. This man looked like a movie star. He looked like a pilot from out of *Hell's Angels*. And on top of everything else there was his name: Slick Goodlin.

The idea in testing the X-1 was to nurse it carefully into the transonic zone, up to seven-tenths, eight-tenths, nine-tenths the speed of sound (.7 Mach, .8 Mach, .9 Mach) before attempting the speed of sound itself, Mach 1, even though Bell and the Army already knew the X-1 had the rocket power to go to Mach 1 and beyond, if there *was* any *beyond*. The consensus of aviators and engineers, after Geoffrey de Havilland's death, was that the speed of sound was an absolute, like the firmness of the earth. The sound barrier was a farm you could buy in the sky. So Slick Goodlin began to probe the transonic zone in the X-1, going up to .8 Mach. Every time he came down he'd have a riveting tale to tell. The buffeting, it was so fierce—and the listeners, their imaginations aflame, could practically see poor Geoffrey de Havilland disintegrating in midair. And the goddamned aerodynamics—and the listeners got a picture of a man in ballroom pumps skidding across a sheet of ice, pursued by bears. A controversy arose over just how much bonus Slick Goodlin should receive for assaulting the dread Mach 1 itself. Bonuses for contract test pilots were not unusual; but the figure of $150,000 was now bruited about. The Army balked, and Yeager got the job. He took it for $283 a month, or $3,396 a year; which is to say, his regular Army captain's pay.

The only trouble they had with Yeager was in holding him back. On his first powered flight in the X-1 he immediately executed an unauthorized zero-g roll with a full load of rocket fuel, then stood the ship on its tail and went up to .85 Mach in a vertical climb, also unauthorized. On subsequent flights, at speeds between .85 Mach and .9 Mach, Yeager ran into most known airfoil problems—loss of elevator, aileron, and rudder control, heavy trim pressures, Dutch rolls, pitching and buffeting, the lot—yet was convinced, after edging over .9 Mach, that this would all get better, not worse, as you reached Mach 1. The attempt to push beyond Mach 1—"breaking" the sound barrier"—was set for October 14, 1947. Not being an engineer, Yeager didn't believe the "barrier" existed.

October 14 was a Tuesday. On Sunday evening, October 12, Chuck Yeager dropped in at Pancho's, along with his wife. She was a brunette named Glennis, whom he had met in California while he was in training, and she was such a number, so striking, he had the inscription "Glamorous Glennis" written on the nose of his P-51 in Europe and, just a few weeks back, on the X-1 itself. Yeager didn't go to Pancho's and knock back a few because two days later the big test was coming up. Nor did he knock back a few because it was the weekend. No, he knocked back a few because night had come and he was a pilot at Muroc. In keeping with the military tradition of Flying & Drinking, that was what you did, for no other reason than that the sun had gone down. You went to Pancho's and knocked back a few and listened to the screen doors banging and to other aviators torturing the piano and the nation's repertoire of Familiar Favorites and to lonesome mouse-turd strangers wandering in through the banging doors and to Pancho classifying the whole bunch of them as old bastards and miserable peckerwoods. That was what you did if you were a pilot at Muroc and the sun went down.

So about eleven Yeager got the idea that it would be a hell of a kick if he and Glennis saddled up a couple of Pancho's dude-ranch horses and went for a romp, a little rat race, in the moonlight. This was in keeping with the military tradition of Flying & Drinking and Drinking & Driving, except that this was prehistoric Muroc and you rode horses. So Yeager and his wife set off on a little proficiency run at full gallop through the desert in the moonlight amid the arthritic silhouettes of the Joshua trees. Then they start racing back to the corral, with Yeager in the lead and heading for the gateway. Given the prevailing condi-tions, it being nighttime, at Pancho's, and his head being filled with a black sandstorm of many badly bawled songs and vulcanized oaths, he sees too late that the gate has been closed. Like many a hard-driving midnight pilot before him, he does not realize that he is not equally gifted in the control of all forms of locomotion. He and the horse hit the gate, and he goes flying off and lands on his right side. His side hurts like hell.

The next day, Monday, his side still hurts like hell. It hurts every time he moves. It hurts every time he breathes deep. It hurts every time he moves his right arm. He knows that if he goes to a doctor at Muroc or says anything to anybody even remotely connected with his superiors, he will be scrubbed from the flight on Tuesday. They might even go so far as to put some other miserable peckerwood in his place. So he gets on his motorcycle, an old junker that Pancho had given him, and rides over to see a doctor in the town of Rosamond, near where he lives. Every time the goddamned motorcycle hits a pebble in the road, his side hurts like a sonofabitch. The doctor in Rosamond informs him he has two broken ribs and he tapes them up and tells him that if he'll just keep his right arm immobilized for a couple of weeks and avoid any physical exertion or sudden movements, he should be all right.

Yeager gets up before daybreak on Tuesday morning—which is sup-posed to be the day he tries to break the sound barrier—and his ribs still hurt like a sonofabitch. He gets his wife to drive him over to the field, and he has to keep his right arm pinned down to his side to keep his ribs from hurting so much. At dawn, on the day of a flight, you could hear the X-1 screaming long before you got there. The fuel for the

X-1 was alcohol and liquid oxygen, oxygen converted from a gas to a liquid by lowering its temperature to 297 degrees below zero. And when the lox, as it was called, rolled out of the hoses and into the belly of the X-1, it started boiling off and the X-1 started steaming and screaming like a teakettle. There's quite a crowd on hand, by Muroc standards . . . perhaps nine or ten souls. They're still fueling the X-1 with the lox, and the beast is wailing.

The X-1 looked like a fat orange swallow with white markings. But it was really just a length of pipe with four rocket chambers in it. It had a tiny cockpit and a needle nose, two little straight blades (only three and a half inches thick at the thickest part) for wings, and a tail assembly set up high to avoid the "sonic wash" from the wings. Even though his side was throbbing and his right arm felt practically useless, Yeager figured he could grit his teeth and get through the flight—except for one specific move he had to make. In the rocket launches, the X-1, which held only two and a half minutes' worth of fuel, was carried up to twenty-six thousand feet underneath the wings of a B-29. At seven thousand feet, Yeager was to climb down a ladder from the bomb bay of the B-29 to the open doorway of the X-1, hook up to the oxygen system and the radio microphone and earphones, and put his crash helmet on and prepare for the launch, which would come at twenty-five thousand feet. This helmet was a homemade number. There had never been any such thing as a crash helmet before. Throughout the war pilots had used the old skin-tight leather helmet-and-goggles. But the X-1 had a way of throwing the pilot around so violently that there was danger of getting knocked out against the walls of the cockpit. So Yeager had bought a big leather football helmet—there were no plastic ones at the time—and he butchered it with a hunting knife until he carved the right kind of holes in it, so that it would fit down over his regular flying helmet and the earphones and the oxygen rig. Anyway, then his flight engineer, Jack Ridley, would climb down the ladder, out in the breeze, and shove into place the cockpit door, which had to be lowered out of the belly of the B-29 on a chain. Then Yeager had to push a handle to lock the door airtight. Since the X-1's cockpit was minute, you had to push the handle with your right hand. It took quite a shove. There was no way you could move into position to get enough leverage with your left hand.

Out in the hangar Yeager makes a few test shoves on the sly, and the pain is so incredible he realizes that there is no way a man with two broken ribs is going to get the door closed. It is time to confide in somebody, and the logical man is Jack Ridley. Ridley is not only the flight engineer but a pilot himself and a good old boy from Oklahoma to boot. He will understand about Flying & Drinking and Drinking & Driving through the goddamned Joshua trees. So Yeager takes Ridley off to the side in the tin hangar and says: Jack, I got me a little ol' problem here. Over at Pancho's the other night I sorta . . . dinged my goddamned ribs. Ridley says, Whattya mean . . . *dinged?* Yeager says, Well, I guess you might say I damned near like to . . . *broke* a coupla the sonsabitches. Whereupon Yeager sketches out the problem he foresees.

Not for nothing is Ridley the engineer on this project. He has an inspiration. He tells a janitor named Sam to cut him about nine inches off a broom handle. When nobody's looking, he slips the broomstick into the cockpit of the X-1 and gives Yeager a little advice and counsel.

So with that added bit of supersonic flight gear Yeager went aloft.

At seven thousand feet he climbed down the ladder into the X-1's cockpit, clipped on his hoses and lines, and managed to pull the pumpkin football helmet over his head. Then Ridley came down the ladder and lowered the door into place. As Ridley had instructed, Yeager now took the nine inches of broomstick and slipped it between the handle and the door. This gave him just enough mechanical advantage to reach over with his left hand and whang the thing shut. So he whanged the door shut with Ridley's broomstick and was ready to fly.

At 26,000 feet the B-29 went into a shallow dive, then pulled up and released Yeager and the X-1 as if it were a bomb. Like a bomb it dropped and shot forward (at the speed of the mother ship) at the same time. Yeager had been launched straight into the sun. It seemed to be no more than six feet in front of him, filling up the sky and blinding him. But he managed to get his bearings and set off the four rocket chambers one after the other. He then experienced something that became known as the ultimate sensation in flying: "booming and zooming." The surge of the rockets was so tremendous, forced him back into his seat so violently, he could hardly move his hands forward the few inches necessary to reach the controls. The X-1 seemed to shoot straight up in an absolutely perpendicular trajectory, as if determined to snap the hold of gravity via the most direct route possible. In fact, he was only climbing at the 45-degree angle called for in the flight plan. At about .87 Mach the buffeting started.

On the ground the engineers could no longer see Yeager. They could only hear . . . that poker-hollow West Virginia drawl.

"Had a mild buffet there . . . jes the usual instability . . ."

Jes the usual instability?

Then the X-1 reached the speed of .96 Mach, and that incredible caint-hardlyin' aw-shuckin' drawl said:

"Say, Ridley . . . make a note here, will ya?" (*if you ain't got nothin' better to do*) ". . . elevator effectiveness regained."

Just as Yeager had predicted, as the X-1 approached Mach 1, the stability improved. Yeager had his eyes pinned on the machometer. The needle reached .96, fluctuated, and went off the scale.

And on the ground they heard . . . that voice:

"Say, Ridley . . . make another note, will ya?" (*if you ain't too bored yet*) ". . . there's somethin' wrong with this ol' machometer . . ." (faint chuckle) ". . . it's gone kinda screwy on me . . ."

And in that moment, on the ground, they heard a boom rock over the desert floor—just as the physicist Theodore von Kármán had predicted many years before.

Then they heard Ridley back in the B-29: "If it is, Chuck, we'll fix it. Personally I think you're seeing things."

Then they heard Yeager's poker-hollow drawl again:

"Well, I guess I am, Jack . . . And I'm still goin' upstairs like a bat."

The X-1 had gone through "the sonic wall" without so much as a bump. As the speed topped out at Mach 1.05, Yeager had the sensation of shooting straight through the top of the sky. The sky turned a deep purple and all at once the stars and the moon came out—and the sun shone at the same time. He had reached a layer of the upper atmosphere where the air was too thin to contain reflecting dust particles. He was simply looking out into space. As the X-1 nosed over at the top of the climb, Yeager now had seven minutes of . . . Pilot Heaven . . . ahead of him. He was going faster than any man in history, and it was almost silent up here, since he had exhausted his rocket fuel, and he was so high in such a vast space that there was no sensation of motion. He was master of the sky. His was a king's solitude, unique and inviolate, above the dome of the world. It would take him seven minutes to glide back down and land at Muroc. He spent the time doing victory rolls and wing-over-wing aerobatics while Rogers Lake and the High Sierras spun around below.

On the ground they had understood the code as soon as they heard Yeager's little exchange with Ridley. The project was secret, but the radio exchanges could be picked up by anyone within range. The business of the "screwy machometer" was Yeager's deadpan way of announcing that the X-1's instruments indicated Mach 1. As soon as he landed, they checked out the X-1's automatic recording instruments. Without any doubt the ship had gone supersonic. They immediately called the brass at Wright Field to break the tremendous news. Within two hours Wright Field called back and gave some firm orders. A top security lid was being put on the morning's events. That the press was not to be informed went without saying. But neither was anyone else, anyone at all, to be told. Word of the flight was not to go beyond the flight line. And even among the people directly involved—who were there and knew about it, anyway—there was to be no celebrating. Just what was on the minds of the brass at Wright is hard to say. Much of it, no doubt, was a simple holdover from wartime, when every breakthrough of possible strategic importance was kept under wraps. That was what you did—you shut up about them. Another possibility was that the chiefs at Wright had never quite known what to make of Muroc. There was some sort of weird ribald aerial tarpaper mad-monk squadron up on the roof of the desert out there . . .

In any case, by mid-afternoon Yeager's tremendous feat had become a piece of thunder with no reverberation. A strange and implausible stillness settled over the event. Well . . . there was not supposed to be any celebration, but come nightfall . . . Yeager and Ridley and some of the others ambled over to Pancho's. After all, it was the end of the day, and they were pilots. So they knocked back a few. And they had to let Pancho in on the secret, because Pancho had said she'd serve a free steak dinner to any pilot who could fly supersonic and walk in here to tell about it, and they had to see the look on *her* face. So Pancho served Yeager a big steak dinner and said they were a buncha miserable peckerwoods all the same, and the desert cooled off and the wind came up and the screen doors banged and they drank some more and bawled some songs over the cackling dry piano and the stars and the moon came out and Pancho screamed oaths no one had ever heard before and Yeager and Ridley roared and the old weatherbeaten bar boomed and the autographed pictures of a hundred dead pilots shook and clattered on the frame wires and the faces of the living fell apart in the reflections, and by and by they all left and stumbled and staggered and yelped and bayed for glory before the arthritic silhouettes of the Joshua trees. Shit!—there was no one to tell except for Pancho and the goddamned Joshua trees!

from West With the Night
by Beryl Markham

Before radar, wireless radios and sophisticated instruments, many pilots died attempting flights over water at night. No man or woman had ever flown the Atlantic from England to America when writer and adventurer Beryl Markham (1902–1986) made her 1936 attempt.

I have seldom dreamed a dream worth dreaming again, or at least none worth recording. Mine are not enigmatic dreams; they are peopled with characters who are plausible and who do plausible things, and I am the most plausible amongst them. All the characters in my dreams have quiet voices like the voice of the man who telephoned me at Elstree one morning in September of nineteen-thirty-six and told me that there was rain and strong head winds over the west of England and over the Irish Sea, and that there were variable winds and clear skies in mid-Atlantic and fog off the coast of New Foundland.

'If you are still determined to fly the Atlantic this late in the year,' the voice said, 'the Air Ministry suggests that the weather it is able to forecast for tonight, and for tomorrow morning, will be about the best you can expect.'

The voice had a few other things to say, but not many, and then it was gone, and I lay in bed half-suspecting that the telephone call and the man who made it were only parts of the mediocre dream I had been dreaming. I felt that if I closed my eyes the unreal quality of the message would be reestablished, and that, when I opened them again, this would be another ordinary day with its usual beginning and its usual routine.

But of course I could not close my eyes, nor my mind, nor my memory. I could lie there for a few moments—remembering how it had begun, and telling myself, with senseless repetition, that by tomorrow morning I should either have flown the Atlantic to America—or I should not have flown it. In either case this was the day I would try.

I could stare up at the ceiling of my bedroom in Aldenham House, which was a ceiling undistinguished as ceilings go, and feel less resolute than anxious, much less brave than foolhardy. I could say to myself, 'You needn't do it, of course,' knowing at the same time that nothing is so inexorable as a promise to your pride.

I could ask, 'Why risk it?' as I have been asked since, and I could answer, 'Each to his element.' By his nature a sailor must sail, by his nature a flyer must fly. I could compute that I had flown a quarter of a million miles; and I could foresee that, so long as I had a plane and the sky was there, I should go on flying more miles.

There was nothing extraordinary in this. I had learned a craft and had worked hard learning it. My hands had been taught to seek the controls of a plane. Usage had taught them. They were at ease clinging to a stick, as a cobbler's fingers are in repose grasping an awl. No human pursuit achieves dignity until it can be called work, and when you can experience a physical loneliness for the tools of your trade, you see that the other things—the experiments, the irrelevant vocations, the vanities you used to hold—were false to you.

Record flights had actually never interested me very much for myself. There were people who thought that such flights were done for admiration and publicity, and worse. But of all the records from Louis Blériot's first crossing of the English Channel in nineteen hundred and nine, through and beyond Kingsford Smith's flight from San Francisco to Sydney, Australia—none had been made by amateurs, nor by novices, nor by men or women less than hardened to failure, or less than masters of their trade. None of these was false. They were a company that simple respect and simple ambition made it worth more than an effort to follow.

The Carberrys (of Seramai) were in London and I could remember everything about their dinner party—even the menu. I could remember June Carberry and all her guests, and the man named McCarthy, who lived in Zanzibar, leaning across the table and saying, 'J.C., why don't you finance Beryl for a record flight?'

I could lie there staring lazily at the ceiling and recall J.C.'s dry answer: 'A number of pilots have flown the North Atlantic, west to east. Only Jim Mollison has done it alone the other way—from Ireland. Nobody has done it alone from England—man or woman. I'd be interested in that, but nothing else. If you want to try it, Burl, I'll back you. I think Edgar Percival could build a plane that would do it, provided you can fly it. Want to chance it?'

'Yes.'

I could remember saying that better than I could remember anything—except J.C.'s almost ghoulish grin, and his remark that sealed the agreement: 'It's a deal, Burl. I'll furnish the plane and you fly the Atlantic—but, gee, I wouldn't tackle it for a million. Think of all that black water! Think how cold it is!'

And I had thought of both.

I had thought of both for a while, and then there had been other things to think about. I had moved to Elstree, half-hour's flight from the Percival Aircraft Works at Gravesend, and almost daily for three months now I had flown down to the factory in a hired plane and watched the Vega Gull they were making for me. I had watched her birth and watched her growth. I had watched her wings take shape, and seen wood and fabric moulded to her ribs to form her long, sleek belly, and I had seen her engine cradled into her frame, and made fast.

The Gull had a turquoise-blue body and silver wings. Edgar Percival had made her with care, with skill, and with worry—the care of a veteran flyer, the skill of a master designer, and the worry of a friend.

Actually the plane was a standard sport model with a range of only six hundred and sixty miles. But she had a special undercarriage built to carry the weight of her extra oil and petrol tanks. The tanks were fixed into the wings, into the centre section, and into the cabin itself. In the cabin they formed a wall around my seat, and each tank had a petcock of its own. The petcocks were important.

'If you open one,' said Percival, 'without shutting the other first, you may get an airlock. You know the tanks in the cabin have no gauges, so it may be best to let one run completely dry before opening the next. Your motor might go dead in the interval—but she'll start again. She's a De Havilland Gipsy—and Gipsys never stop.'

I had talked to Tom*. We had spent hours going over the Atlantic chart, and I had realized that the tinker of Molo, now one of England's great pilots, had traded his dreams and had got in return a better thing. Tom had grown older too; he had jettisoned a deadweight of irrelevant hopes and wonders, and had left himself a realistic code that had no room for temporizing or easy sentiment.

'I'm glad you're going to do it, Beryl. It won't be simple. If you can get off the ground in the first place, with such an immense load of fuel, you'll be alone in that plane about a night and a day—mostly night. Doing it east to west, the wind's against you. In September, so is the weather. You won't have a radio. If you misjudge your course only a few degrees, you'll end up in Labrador or in the sea—so don't misjudge anything.'

Tom could still grin. He had grinned; he had said: 'Anyway, it ought to amuse you to think that your financial backer lives on a farm called "Place of Death" and your plane is being built at "Gravesend." If you were consistent, you'd christen the Gull "The Flying Tombstone."'

I hadn't been that consistent. I had watched the building of the plane and I had trained for the flight like an athlete. And now, as I lay in bed, fully awake, I could still hear the quiet voice of the man from the Air Ministry intoning, like the voice of a dispassionate court clerk: '. . .the weather for tonight and tomorrow . . . will be about the best you

*Tom Black, who taught Markham how to fly.

can expect.' I should have liked to discuss the flight once more with Tom before I took off, but he was on a special job up north. I got out of bed and bathed and put on my flying clothes and took some cold chicken packed in a cardboard box and flew over to the military field at Abingdon, where the Vega Gull waited for me under the care of the R.A.F. I remember that the weather was clear and still.

Jim Mollison lent me his watch. He said: 'This is not a gift. I wouldn't part with it for anything. It got me across the North Atlantic and the South Atlantic too. Don't lose it—and, for God's sake, don't get it wet. Salt water would ruin the works.'

Brian Lewis gave me a lifesaving jacket. Brian owned the plane I had been using between Elstree and Gravesend, and he had thought a long time about a farewell gift. What could be more practical than a pneumatic jacket that could be inflated through a rubber tube?

'You could float around in it for days.' said Brian. But I had to decide between the lifesaver and warm clothes. I couldn't have both, because of their bulk, and I hate the cold, so I left the jacket.

And Jock Cameron, Brian's mechanic, gave me a sprig of heather. If it had been a whole bush of heather, complete with roots growing in an earthen jar, I think I should have taken it, bulky or not. The blessing of Scotland, bestowed by a Scotsman, is not to be dismissed. Nor is the well-wishing of a ground mechanic to be taken lightly, for these men are the pilot's contact with reality.

It is too much that with all those pedestrian centuries behind us we should, in a few decades, have learned to fly; it is too heady a thought, too proud a boast. Only the dirt on a mechanic's hands, the straining vise, the splintered bolt of steel underfoot on the hangar floor—only these and such anxiety as the face of a Jock Cameron can hold for a pilot and his plane before a flight, serve to remind us that, not unlike the heather, we too are earthbound. We fly, but we have not 'conquered' the air. Nature presides in all her dignity, permitting us the study and the use of such of her forces as we may understand. It is when we presume to intimacy, having been granted only tolerance, that the harsh stick falls across our impudent knuckles and we rub the pain, staring upward, startled by our ignorance.

'Here is a sprig of heather,' said Jock, and I took it and pinned it into a pocket of my flying jacket.

There were press cars parked outside the field at Abingdon, and several press planes and photographers, but the R.A.F. kept everyone away from the grounds except technicians and a few of my friends.

The Carberrys had sailed for New York a month ago to wait for me there. Tom was still out of reach with no knowledge of my decision to leave, but that didn't matter so much, I thought. It didn't matter because Tom was unchanging—neither a fair-weather pilot nor a fair-weather friend. If for a month, or a year, or two years we sometimes had not seen each other, it still hadn't mattered. Nor did this. Tom would never say, 'You should have let me know.' He assumed that I had learned all that he had tried to teach me, and for my part, I thought of him, even then, as the merest student must think of his mentor. I could sit in a cabin overcrowded with petrol tanks and set my course for North America, but the knowledge of my hands on the controls would be Tom's knowledge. His words of caution and words of guidance, spoken so long ago, so many times, on bright mornings over the veldt or over a forest, or with a far mountain visible at the tip of our wing, would be spoken again, if I asked.

So it didn't matter, I thought. It was silly to think about.

You can live a lifetime and, at the end of it, know more about other people than you know about yourself. You learn to watch other people, but you never watch yourself because you strive against loneliness. If you read a book, or shuffle a deck of cards, or care for a dog, you are avoiding yourself. The abhorrence of loneliness is as natural as wanting to live at all. If it were otherwise, men would never have bothered to make an alphabet, nor to have fashioned words out of what were only animal sounds, nor to have crossed continents—each man to see what the other looked like.

Being alone in an aeroplane for even so short a time as a night and a day, irrevocably alone, with nothing to observe but your instruments and your own hands in semidarkness, nothing to contemplate but the size of your small courage, nothing to wonder about but the beliefs, the faces, and the hopes rooted in your mind—such an experience can be as startling as the first awareness of a stranger walking by your side at night. You are the stranger.

It is dark already and I am over the south of Ireland. There are the lights of Cork and the lights are wet; they are drenched in Irish rain, and I am above them and dry. I am above them and the plane roars in a sobbing world, but it imparts no sadness to me. I feel the security of solitude, the exhilaration of escape. So long as I can see the lights and imagine the people walking under them, I feel selfishly triumphant, as if I have eluded care and left even the small sorrow of rain in other hands.

It is a little over an hour now since I left Abingdon. England, Wales, and the Irish Sea are behind me like so much time used up. On a long flight distance and time are the same. But there had been a moment when Time stopped—and Distance too. It was the moment I lifted the blue-and-silver Gull from the aerodrome, the moment the photographers aimed their cameras, the moment I felt the craft refuse its burden and strain toward the earth in sullen rebellion, only to listen at last to the persuasion of stick and elevators, the dogmatic argument of blueprints that said she *had* to fly because the figures proved it.

So she had flown, and once airborne, once she had yielded to the sophistry of a draughtsman's board, she had said, 'There: I have lifted the weight. Now, where are we bound?'—and the question had frightened me.

'We are bound for a place thirty-six hundred miles from here—two thousand miles of it unbroken ocean. Most of the way it will be night. We are flying west with the night.'

So there behind me is Cork; and ahead of me is Berehaven Lighthouse. It is the last light, standing on the last land. I watch it, counting the frequency of its flashes—so many to the minute. Then I pass it and fly out to sea.

The fear is gone now—not overcome nor reasoned away. It is gone because something else has taken its place; the confidence and the trust, the inherent belief in the security of land underfoot—now this faith is transferred to my plane, because the land has vanished and there is no other tangible thing to fix faith upon. Flight is but momentary escape from the eternal custody of earth.

Rain continues to fall, and outside the cabin it is totally dark. My altimeter says that the Atlantic is two thousand feet below me, my Sperry Artificial Horizon says that I am flying level. I judge my drift at three degrees more than my weather chart suggests, and fly accordingly. I am flying blind. A beam to follow would help. So would a radio—but then, so would clear weather. The voice of the man at the Air Ministry had not promised storm.

I feel the wind rising and the rain falls hard. The smell of petrol in the cabin is so strong and the roar of the plane so loud that my senses are almost deadened. Gradually it becomes unthinkable that existence was ever otherwise.

At ten o'clock p.m. I am flying along the Great Circle Course for Harbour Grace, Newfoundland, into a forty-mile headwind at a speed of one hundred and thirty miles an hour. Because of the weather, I cannot be sure of how many more hours I have to fly, but I think it must be between sixteen and eighteen.

At ten-thirty I am still flying on the large cabin tank of petrol, hoping to use it up and put an end to the liquid swirl that has rocked the plane since my takeoff. The tank has no gauge, but written on its side is the assurance: 'This tank is good for four hours.'

There is nothing ambiguous about such a guaranty. I believe it, but at twenty-five minutes to eleven, my motor coughs and dies, and the Gull is powerless above the sea.

I realize that the heavy drone of the plane has been, until this moment, complete and comforting silence. It is the actual silence following the last splutter of the engine that stuns me.

I can't feel any fear; I can't feel anything. I can only observe with a kind of stupid disinterest that my hands are violently active and know that, while they move, I am being hypnotized by the needle of my altimeter.

I suppose that the denial of natural impulse is what is meant by 'keeping calm,' but impulse has reason in it. If it is night and you are sitting in an aeroplane with a stalled motor, and there are two thousand feet between you and the sea, nothing can be more reasonable than the impulse to pull back your stick in the hope of adding to that two thousand, if only by a little. The thought, the knowledge, the law that tells you that your hope lies not in this, but in a contrary act—the act of directing your impotent craft toward the water—seems a terrifying abandonment, not only of reason, but of sanity. Your mind and your heart reject it. It is your hands—your stranger's hands—that follow with unfeeling precision the letter of the law.

I sit there and watch my hands push forward on the stick and feel the Gull respond and begin its dive to the sea. Of course it is a simple thing; surely the cabin tank has run dry too soon. I need only to turn another petcock. . . .

But it is dark in the cabin. It is easy to see the luminous dial of the altimeter and to note that my height is now eleven hundred feet, but it is not easy to see a petcock that is somewhere near the floor of the plane. A hand gropes and reappears with an electric torch, and fingers, moving with agonizing composure, find the petcock and turn it; and I wait.

At three hundred feet the motor is still dead, and I am conscious that the needle of my altimeter seems to whirl like the spoke of a spindle winding up the remaining distance between the plane and the water. There is some lightning, but the quick flash only serves to emphasize the darkness. How high can waves reach—twenty feet, perhaps? Thirty?

It is impossible to avoid the thought that this is the end of my flight, but my reactions are not orthodox; the various incidents of my entire life do not run through my mind like a motion-picture film gone mad. I only feel that all this has happened before—and it has. It has all happened a hundred times in my mind, in my sleep, so that now I am not really caught in terror; I recognize a familiar scene, a familiar story with its climax dulled by too much telling.

I do not know how close to the waves I am when the motor explodes to life again. But the sound is almost meaningless. I see my hand easing back on the stick, and I feel the Gull climb up into the storm, and I see the altimeter whirl like a spindle again, paying out the distance between myself and the sea.

The storm is strong. It is comforting. It is like a friend shaking me and saying, 'Wake up! You were only dreaming.'

But soon I am thinking. By simple calculation I find that my motor had been silent for perhaps an instant more than thirty seconds.

I ought to thank God—and I do, though indirectly. I thank Geoffrey De Havilland who designed the indomitable Gipsy, and who, after all, must have been designed by God in the first place.

A lighted ship—the daybreak—some steep cliffs standing in the sea. The meaning of these will never change for pilots. If one day an ocean can be flown within an hour, if men can build a plane that so masters time, the sight of land will be no less welcome to the steersman of that fantastic craft. He will have cheated laws that the cunning of science has taught him how to cheat, and he will feel his guilt and be eager for the sanctuary of the soil.

I saw the ship and the daybreak, and then I saw the cliffs of New-foundland wound in ribbons of fog. I felt the elation I had so long imag-ined, and I felt the happy guilt of having circumvented the stern authority of the weather and the sea. But mine was a minor triumph; my swift Gull was not so swift as to have escaped unnoticed. The night and the storm had caught her and we had flown blind for nineteen hours.

I was tired now, and cold. Ice began to film the glass of the cabin windows and the fog played a magician's game with the land. But the land was there. I could not see it, but I had seen it. I could not afford to believe that it was any land but the land I wanted. I could not afford to believe that my navigation was at fault, because there was no time for doubt.

South to Cape Race, west to Sydney on Cape Breton Island. With my protractor, my map, and my compass, I set my new course, humming the ditty that Tom had taught me: 'Variation West—magnetic best. Variation East—magnetic least.' A silly rhyme, but it served to placate, for the moment, two warring poles—the magnetic and the true. I flew south and found the lighthouse of Cape Race protruding from the fog like a warning finger. I circled twice and went on over the Gulf of Saint Lawrence.

After a while there would be New Brunswick, and then Maine—and then New York. I could anticipate. I could almost say, 'Well, if you stay awake, you'll find it's only a matter of time now'—but there was no question of staying awake. I was tired and I had not moved an inch since that uncertain moment at Abingdon when the Gull had elected to rise with her load and fly, but I could not have closed my eyes. I could sit there in the cabin, walled in glass and petrol tanks, and be grateful for the sun and the light, and the fact that I could see the water under me. They were almost the last waves I had to pass. Four hundred miles of water, but then the land again—Cape Breton. I would stop at Sydney to refuel and go on. It was easy now. It would be like stopping at Kisumu and going on.

Success breeds confidence. But who has a right to confidence except the Gods? I had a following wind, my last tank of petrol was more than three-quarters full, and the world was as bright to me as if it were a new world, never touched. If I had been wiser, I might have known that such moments are, like innocence, short-lived. My engine began to shudder before I saw the land. It died, it spluttered, it started again and limped along. It coughed and spat black exhaust toward the sea.

There are words for everything. There was a word for this—airlock, I thought. This had to be an airlock because there was petrol enough. I thought I might clear it by turning on and turning off all the empty tanks, and so I did that. The handles of the petcocks were sharp little pins of metal, and when I had opened and closed them a dozen times, I saw that my hands were bleeding and that the blood was dropping on my maps and on my clothes, but the effort wasn't any good. I coasted along on a sick and halting engine. The oil pressure and the oil temperature gauges were normal, the magnetos working, and yet I lost altitude slowly while the realization of failure seeped into my heart. If I made the land, I should have been the first to fly the North Atlantic from England, but from my point of view, from a pilot's point of view, a forced landing was failure because New York was my goal. If only I could land and then take off, I would make it still . . . if only, if only. . . .

The engine cuts again, and then catches, and each time it spurts to life I climb as high as I can get, and then it splutters and stops and I glide once more toward the water, to rise again and descend again, like a hunting sea bird.

I find the land. Visibility is perfect now and I see land forty or fifty miles ahead. If I am on my course, that will be Cape Breton. Minute after minute goes by. The minutes almost materialize; they pass before my eyes like links in a long slow-moving chain, and each time the engine cuts, I see a broken link in the chain and catch my breath until it passes.

The land is under me. I snatch my map and stare at it to confirm my whereabouts. I am, even at my present crippled speed, only twelve minutes from Sydney Airport, where I can land for repairs and then go on.

The engine cuts once more and I begin to glide, but now I am not worried; she will start again, as she has done, and I will gain altitude and fly into Sydney.

But she doesn't start. This time she's dead as death; the Gull settles earthward and it isn't any earth I know. It is black earth stuck with boulders and I hang above it, on hope and on a motionless propeller. Only I cannot hang above it long. The earth hurries to meet me, I bank, turn, and side-slip to dodge the boulders, my wheels touch, and I feel them submerge. The nose of the plane is engulfed in mud, and I go forward striking my head on the glass of the cabin front, hearing it shatter, feeling blood pour over my face.

I stumble out of the plane and sink to my knees in muck and stand there foolishly staring, not at the lifeless land, but at my watch.

Twenty-one hours and twenty-five minutes.

Atlantic flight. Abingdon, England, to a nameless swamp—nonstop.

• • •

A Cape Breton Islander found me—a fisherman trudging over the bog saw the Gull with her tail in the air and her nose buried, and then he saw me floundering in the embracing soil of his native land. I had been wandering for an hour and the black mud had got up to my waist and the blood from the cut in my head had met the mud halfway.

From a distance, the fisherman directed me with his arms and with shouts toward the firm places in the bog, and for another hour I walked on them and came toward him like a citizen of Hades blinded by the sun, but it wasn't the sun; I hadn't slept for forty hours.

He took me to his hut on the edge of the coast and I found that built upon the rocks there was a little cubicle that housed an ancient telephone—put there in case of shipwrecks.

I telephoned to Sydney Airport to say that I was safe and to prevent a needless search being made. On the following morning I did step out of a plane at Floyd Bennett Field and there was a crowd of people still waiting there to greet me, but the plane I stepped from was not the Gull, and for days while I was in New York I kept thinking about that and wishing over and over again that it had been the Gull, until the wish lost its significance, and time moved on, overcoming many things it met on the way.

from The Information
by Martin Amis

We tell ourselves that flying is safer than driving, but it doesn't always feel that way. Such moments of doubt and their entertainment value are a jumping-off point for this passage from The Information, *a 1995 novel by Martin Amis (born 1949). Two writers on a book tour settle back in their seats for a short hop from Boston to Provincetown, and find themselves contemplating eternity.*

They rolled forward, soon to go. The seven passengers sat with their necks bent almost sideways, in postures of tortured compression. It wasn't just the low ceiling: it was also the embarrassing proximity of the tarmac, only a few feet beneath the soles of their shoes. Richard assumed that the engine was so loud that it was off the human scale altogether, and all you felt was vibration, in your every atom. More or less engulfed by his mail sack, he sat jammed into the rearmost row, next to Gwyn. They were both assessing the pilot—a figure of unusually enhanced interest: tall, fleshy, ginger-blond, a big man with a light step, he deployed a feminine delicacy in the arrangement of his peaked cap, his flightbox, his earphones. Turning sideways in his seat, comfortingly perfunctory, he had run through the safety instructions in a voice perhaps incapable of modulation anyway, and then attended to his controls—the sort of dashboard appropriate to a prewar spaceship or a glue-and-balsa nuclear sub, dials, graphs, metal switches coated in worn paint. Richard realized that the dash contained no plastic. Was that good, he wondered, and tried to lose himself in silent tribute to durable and horny-handed craftsman-ship and skills, now, alas, long vanished. The pilot wore a white shirt and lumpy cream trousers the texture of flock wallpaper. It was easy, somehow, to lose yourself in the expanse of his cream rump: firmly framed in the lower aperture of his seat, it filled its space solidly and proudly, soft-cornered, like a TV—like the shape of Richard's face.

So the little plane queued for take off. The little plane was a little plane, among all these big ones, and hoped it wasn't in the way. But it was. The passenger jets, dog-nosed (their noses black and damp in the dew or sweat of the coming storm), waited in line behind them like rigid pointers cocked for the hunt. Richard looked out through the propeller blades, which were moving invisibly fast, seeming to smudge the air or bruise it. Ahead of them, round the turn, were the tensed haunches of the important shuttles—to New York, to Washington—waiting to take Americans where they needed to go: around America. Over and above the compound anguish of the checked planes, all screaming at each other to get out of the way, you could hear the sky and the epic groan of the middle air. Darkness, night, was wheeling in from the north. But from the defiant south came a negligent and unanswerable demonstration of light, the elec-tromagnetic: god's whips, knouts and sjamboks of solder and copper.

No one spoke. Gwyn suddenly leaned forward and engaged the publicity boy. His inquiries were muffled by the headrest, and when the publicity boy replied he seemed to be talking or shouting to him-self, like a bum or a wacko, like American fever. *Come on, you seen what's behind us . . . They do this like nine times a day . . . No way is it a hurricane. It's a storm . . . You mean like a hurricane with a name?*

"Hurricanes used to be all girls," said Richard. He had spoken, really, to make the publicity boy seem saner. It made *him* seem saner too, though, and he continued ramblingly, "Now they alternate them. Girl, boy. Boy, girl. I think that's better, I don't know. Hurricane Demi. Hurricane Gwyn. Hurricane Gina. Hurricane Marius. Hurricane Anstice. Hurricane Scozzy."

"Hurricane who?"

"Nothing."

"Listen to this one," said Gwyn. "He's already flipped. Jesus. All this for a *party.*"

The pilot put his face into profile and monotonously informed them that it would be a whole lot cooler in here when they were off the ground. This was good news. Because the passengers were finding out what happened to the air on planes and what would happen to the air on jets unless they doctored and gimmicked it. How soon it was exhausted, and went blood-heat and pungent. How soon you were all breathing each other's yawn. On the jets you could wait at the can door for half an hour and step right in after some exploding nonagenarian had dragged himself out of there: that's how good these guys were. But on the little plane the air was already critically delicate. You wouldn't even want to worry it with speech . . . Now all the passengers were silent, giving themselves up to that strange modern activity, fancy-priced suffering, in which America leads the world; but when the plane rounded the last corner and found nothing ahead of it except sea and sky, and made its rattling gallop for the bruised yonder, and was up, away, exchanging one medium for a new and better one, and was immediately sent skidding sideways, windmilling its arms, then all eight of them moaned in harmony, answering the moan above their heads.

They steadied, and climbed. Over car park, over graveyard, over the harbor, over the bay. Soon the patchy whitecaps were no more than flecks of dandruff on the broad shoulder of the sea. Richard looked casually out of his porthole, to the south. And he couldn't believe it. The storm was there, like a gothic cathedral, with all its glaring gargoyles . . . Diurnal time was a figure for the human span: waking, innocent morning, full midday and the pomp of the afternoon, then loss of color, then weariness, then mortal weariness and the certainty of sleep, then nightmare, then dreamlessness. Outside, day was gone but it wouldn't go to bed. The day was dead and gone but wouldn't believe it and wouldn't accept it, the day and its sick comeback, trying to return and saying, *I'm still day. Don't you see me? Don't you like me* more? *I'm still day*, and not letting go, jerkily reanimated, hot-wired, and pulsing under the jump-leads. And the rain: the rain was wanting to lubricate this desperate tension between day and night, wanting to soothe and cleanse. But the rain was panicking and completely overdoing it and sounding like psychopathic applause.

"That red switch," said Gwyn. "What's he doing with that red switch?"

Next to the digital clock on the dashboard, which recorded their flighttime (nine minutes elapsed), there was a red switch and a flashing and beeping red light which did seem to be exercising the pilot in an unencouraging way. He kept twiddling it, as if hoping that the light would go off, or change color, or stop beeping. But his movements were perhaps more curious than agitated. The stiff cream carapace of his backside was still stalwartly ensconced in its chair.

"We're losing height. I think we're losing height."

"He'd tell us if something was up. Wouldn't he? Or wouldn't he?"

Without turning round the pilot said, "We're having a weight problem. Hopefully it won't be a . . . a problem. It'll keep us under this weather here." And now he did swivel round, eyeing each passenger in turn with reasonable suspicion, as if searching for a superfat stowaway.

"I'm not going to worry," said Gwyn, "until *he* starts to worry."

The pilot didn't seem worried. He had even started to whistle.

"That sounds wise," said Richard, and turned to his porthole. And the sea looked as close as the tarmac had looked ten minutes ago, and the plane suddenly seemed to be traveling not through the air but through the churned water. The dip, the climb, the crest, the fall. The wave, the wait, the wave, the wait, the wave, the wait, the wave.

"Oh man," said Gwyn.

"He's stopped fucking with that red switch."

"Has he? Good."

Above their heads the cabin lights dimmed and flickered and dimmed again.

• • •

It was when the patch of shit appeared on the pilot's cream rump that Richard knew for certain that all was not well. This patch of shit started life as an islet, a Martha's Vineyard that soon became a Cuba, then a Madagascar, then a dreadful Australia of brown. But that was five minutes ago, and no one gave a shit about it now. Not a single passenger, true, had interpreted the state of the pilot's pants as a favorable sign, but that was five minutes ago, that was history, and no one gave a shit about it now, not even the pilot, who was hollering into the microphone, hollering into a world of neighing metal and squawking rivets, hollering into the very language of the storm—its fricatives, its atrocious plosives. The gods had put aside their bullwhips and their elemental rodeo and were now at play with their bowling balls clattering down the gutters of space-time. Within were the mortals, starfished from white knuckle to white toe-joint, stretched like Christs, like Joans in her fire. Richard looked and now felt love for the publicity boy, his sleek, shaking, tear-washed face.

This would end. He reached for Gwyn's hand and said, loudly, in his ear, "Death is good."

"What?"

"Death is good." Here in America he had noticed how much less he cared, every time, whether the plane he was in stayed up. There was so much less, every time, to come down to. "Death is good."

"Oh *yeah?*"

Richard felt he had won. Because of his boys—because of Marius and Marco. Gwyn had a wife. And Richard had a wife. But who *was* your wife? She was just the one you ended up with who had your kids. And you were just the one she had them *with*. Childhood was the universal. *Everyone* had been there. He said,

"I'll survive."

"We'll survive. We'll survive."

No, not you, he thought. But he said, "The world liked what you wrote."

"Who fucking cares? No. Thanks. I'm sorry your . . . Gina loves you. She just . . ."

"What? She just what?"

Now came a thousand camera flashes through every porthole. The parting shots of the paparazzi of the storm. With rolling deliberation the sky gathered them into its slingshot, wound and stretched them back ("Death is good," he said again) and fired them out into silent night.

You could sense the presence of the peninsula, and see the lights of the airport. Some lights were fixed. Others moved.

"Avoidance apron," sobbed the pilot into his mike. "Avoidance apron . . ."

The passengers unwrapped their voices and sank back, harshly purring. Richard offered his handkerchief to the publicity boy, who accepted it.

"*Avoidance* apron. *Avoidance* apron!"

"What's he mean?" said Gwyn, jerking around in his seat. "What's the avoidance apron? Where you crash-land? Is the landing gear down? Is it gone?"

It didn't seem to matter and no one else seemed to care. They were getting nearer to their own thing, the ground, the earth. Not scored and seared by another thing, the fire, not covered and swallowed by another thing, the water, not plucked apart by another thing, the air.

Provincetown Airport was a baby airport, meant for baby planes, and it was shy about the fuss. With his case and his mail sack Richard had plonked himself down on a patch of grass—over on the civilian side of the airport's main bungalow. He patiently chain-smoked, and from a plastic bottle with a plastic tube patiently drank the brandy given to him by a sympathetic medic. On the airfield a scene of human and mechanical confusion was approaching its completion and dispersal point. There was a handsome fire engine, and two blue-cross station wagons on the lookout for custom (into one of which an elderly passenger had been levered, clutching his pacemaker) and a couple of cops creaking about . . . The pilot had left the plane last, attended by ground staff. He was wearing a shiny black mid-length skirt or pinafore. Two other passengers, slumped on chairs in the airport building, attempted to give him a cheer; but he shuffled on through, with marked modesty. Gwyn was in there now, with the publicity boy and a gesticulating young journalist from *The Cape Codder*.

He closed his eyes for a while. Someone took the cigarette from between his fingers and drew on it with audible hunger. He looked up: it occurred to him that they were both in a state that had a medical designation, because Gwyn resembled no one he had ever seen before. And maybe *he* didn't look that hot or that cool, sitting with his shoulders shaking on the frosted grass, and steam coming up all around him—animal vapors. But he laughed his tight laugh and said, not ramblingly anymore,

"I worked it out. You know the pilot? We thought he was shouting *avoidance* apron. But he wasn't. I heard one of the ladies here. He wanted a—*voidance* apron. She called it a shit-wrap." Richard laughed stealthily, under the cover of his shaking shoulders. He did think it was kind of great. You wouldn't want to radio ahead for a shit-wrap. That would offend the passengers. So you radioed ahead for a "voidance apron." And the passengers can remain unoffended as they prepare to crash-land or mass-eject onto the airport latrine. "A voidance apron," he said. "It's kind of great, I think . . ."

from Fate is the Hunter

by Ernest K. Gann

Ernest Kellogg Gann (1910-1991) flew DC-3s across the Alleghenies and C-54s across the oceans in the days when commercial flying was still an adventure for both passengers and pilots. This account of one memorable flight suggests just how much depended in those days upon a pilot's experience and judgement.

From spring until the beginning of winter there were remarkably few variations in the pattern of our flying. Occasionally I was assigned to captains other than Ross, but seldom for more than a single trip. These men were solid veterans of the line, even senior to Ross. They were Apitz, Dodson, Moore, and Cutrell, all of whom held regular bids on the Newark to Chicago route. The flights were mostly nonstop in DC-3's, thus tending toward dullness for a co-pilot familiar with the constant diversions of AM-21. I was treated with easy consideration and by direct inquiry picked up a few tidbits of knowledge, yet no deliberate effort was made to increase my paltry store of wisdom.

The reason was simple. I was not their regular co-pilot whom they might indulge as a son. I was Ross's boy. To interfere with his teachings would be crude and impolitic. I was expected to operate the landing gear and flaps on command, keep the log, the flight plan, and my mouth shut. All of this I endeavored to do efficiently, for it was certain that if I erred, Ross would hear about it.

In late November when the red and gold AM-21 faded and the first snow flurries dusted the northern stretches of the route, there came a general shuffling of crews and I was dispossessed of my now comfortable seat beside Ross.

The ever-watchful McCabe, believing that variety had in itself a special educational value, assigned me to a captain named Keim. This selection could not have provided greater contrast.

I had seen Keim a few times when the landings of our ships coincided along the route. According to custom, he had ignored my existence and reserved only a grudging salutation for Ross. Thus he was an unknown quantity and once again I went to Robbins for background. Though we were now friends, I received the same obtuse answers I had on Ross. I came away quite innocent of the startling differences to be found in two men who flew identical airplanes over the same route. My only salvation was in the fact that this time I knew my duties well.

Or so I believed.

Keim was of medium height and stocky. There were evidences of corpulence about his waistline emphasized by the manner in which he wore his belt—so low his pants seemed to remain in place without reason. His neck and shoulders were powerful, perfectly suited for the support of his rather massive head, which was topped with an array of curly red hair. It matched exactly a fine brush of mustache.

Keim's face was so constantly expressive and quick changing that it was difficult to leave its colorful collection of wrinkles and freckles to concentrate upon his eyes, which were the key to his complicated self. For here was a man at war with the world yet always loving it. He could be, in successive moments, a hilarious comedian and a sage. He could be outrageously dogmatic, stubborn, and raucous, until he chose to transform himself into a reasonable, very straight-thinking individual whose modesty often approached complete retreat.

His eyes were utterly fascinating and he had a trick of waggling the brows above them which contributed marvelously to their versatility of expression. Neither his eyes nor brows were ever entirely still, as if they were in continuous rebellion against the natural lethargy which normally held his body nearly immobile. Except for hunting, which Keim pursued avidly, he seemed to hate all forms of physical exertion. When he sat down he remained rooted in place, as fixed as a statue. When he stood up he floundered to the nearest supporting object, where he remained until absolute necessity compelled him to move again. Yet his eyes were always restless, darting mischievously and sometimes in high disapproval over all that passed before him.

Keim's wit flashed with electric speed and was most frequently voiced in a cutting snarl. It was always original, at times droll, occasionally whimsical, and often bawdy. When it pleased him to turn the same growl upon himself, the result was a sharp dagger of deprecation.

Keim was army trained, a fact which no longer worried me. He was more typically a line pilot than Ross and ever so much more inclined to observe regulations. He held an abiding faith in seniority and was enormously proud of his own length of service with the line. He thoroughly believed that seniority guaranteed security, a prejudice from which he could never be dissuaded. Numbers were his righteous sanctuary. It was terrible when they could not protect him against the incredible turn of fate which brought an end to his active flying career.

As a captain, Keim was the embodiment of caution and cunning. He had an inner sense about weather analysis, predicting its whims so truly that there seemed to be a secret pact between himself and the elements. He could stare at the swirling lines on a map designed to illustrate an air mass or a front and, muttering dark incantations to himself, come away with a detailed prognostication which invariably proved to be of astonishing accuracy. He never regarded bad weather as a potential physical challenge. Instead, he schemed and plotted, winning a mental victory before he ever left the ground.

In flight he was venturesome only to the minimum needs of the moment, and under no circumstances would he experiment or tempt his fortune. His creed, torn as always from the side of his mouth, was steadfast. "One thing I'm sure about. If my ass gets there, so will the passengers'."

Now, while the skies above AM-21 became sullen and heavier winds swept down from Canada laden with snow, other transformations occurred which were not so easy to comprehend.

Though we still flew many trips without enough passengers to pay for the fuel consumed, there were times when nearly every seat was taken. In a flurry of optimism the company ordered new airplanes, which meant hiring new co-pilots to replace those eventually promoted. I learned with pleasure that there were now more than thirty pilots with numbers higher than my embarrassing 267.

Almost overnight the airline business seemed to gain vastly in respectability. Agents even urged line pilots to buy insurance, and since we had hitherto been pointedly ignored, some were so carried away with the flattery they actually did so.

The entire atmosphere, from the mechanics working in the hangars to the exuberant poets charged with the advertisements, was infectious, and everywhere there seemed to be exhilaration and desire for doing. No one could explain the exact reasons for this new energy or pinpoint the exact time when the surge began. Some said it was sparked by the faltering, still phony war in Europe. Others credited the general safety record which had never been matched before. The enthusiasm and anticipation was not confined to one line; all of them fell in with the quickening rhythm of their teletypes and, like children long neglected, emerged cheering into the light.

Some substance was given to the rumors by the opening of La Guardia Field. All of the lines previously serving the New York area from Newark, except Eastern, moved at once into breathtaking grandeur. There were speeches loaded with touching phraseology about the dawn of a new age. There were people who said the entire project was a mad dream and someone should be investigated for stealing the City of New York's good money.

La Guardia Field became a symbol for the entire country, and other cities from Los Angeles to Washington and Boston were inspired at least to consider improvements on their own airports. A few of them haltingly turned their promises into action.

In truth, all the circumstances of American air transport were disgraceful. Except for the actual construction of good airplanes, we were so far behind the rest of the world that there was simply no comparison to be made. Imperial Airways had long been flying passengers in cocktail and full dinner service luxury. Their routes not only extended from England all over Europe but continued on all the way to India. Air France also sprawled over Europe and offered fairly reliable service across the Sahara to remotest Africa. Royal Dutch Airlines flew half around the world to the East Indies. Lufthansa was everywhere, and through shadow operations was firmly entrenched in South America. Even the confused Italians operated a regular service across the South Atlantic with Alor Littoria.

So air transport was accepted everywhere except in the United States. Unfortunately, our recent wave of enterprise and conviction stopped short at the hangar doors. We were still held in such distrust that many large firms forbade their executives to fly. And the price of the newly offered insurance for pilots was outrageous.

There was some reason for this rejection. Technically, we had barely emerged from strapping a parachute on our passengers and seating them on mail sacks. Flights across the continent were a slow ordeal, frequently hours late, and sometimes canceled altogether. Pilots were required to carry special form booklets which would enable them to put their passengers on a train.

Yet there were some tokens of progress. For example, we were suddenly authorized to carry our mail guns in our flight kits instead of strapping them, sheriff-wise, to our belts.

My first flight with Keim over AM-21 was not a success as far as I was concerned. He nursed a bitter hatred of the DC-2 heating system, to which, having at last learned its weird eccentricities, I had finally become attached. As if to ease his fury, Keim demanded the utmost from the boiler and kept the cockpit like a Finnish Sauna. Complaint of the temperature, voiced but once, met with the singular lack of enthusiasm I would soon learn to expect from Keim.

"Look. *I* happen to like it this way. You see that white stuff out there? It's called snow. I've shivered a million miles in these airplanes and I don't intend to do so any longer. If you feel yourself in a financial position to hire this airplane and employ me as pilot, then we might discuss the matter of heat. Until then I happen to be the captain, unless I've read our name platters on the door backward, and you're the co-pilot. So the temperature will stay the way I want it, which is the way it is now, period."

I glanced ruefully down at my still-new jodhpur boots in which my feet were slowly stewing. I had yet to learn that honest winter would soon come to AM-21 and all of Keim's heat plus my boots would do little to make cockpit life comfortable.

Keim also smoked cigars, which have an especially nauseating effect in an airplane. When he had made certain I disliked them his enjoyment of every puff increased immensely. In gasping self-defense I left the cockpit frequently and went back to the cabin. My absence did not disturb him in the slightest since he rarely relinquished the controls all the way to Cleveland. He did not even suggest giving me a landing or a take-off, a denial of confidence sorely felt after my months with Ross. He even did his own reporting on the radio, cupping the microphone tightly in his hand and growling our altitude and position from the side of his mouth as if daring the ground to answer. His every action marked my presence in the cockpit as nonessential.

Keim did not employ the rod in the manner of Ross. Since I could now handle the physical chores well enough, although not always to his entire satisfaction, it is doubtful that he would have troubled himself to punish me in any event. On the return flight he gave me a take-off at Buffalo which he observed without comment.

On our next flight he moved the quota up to two and added a landing, which, thanks to a soft bed of snow at Syracuse, proved to be what was known as a "greaser." Ordinarily such landings provoke some obligatory comment from the other pilot—"Are we down?" or, sarcastically, "Of course you do that every time."

Not from Keim. He chose to remain silent, but as the one eye I could see swam around to fix upon me, the attendant eyebrow climbed, and then descended slowly. There was no other evidence that he had even seen the landing, but such signs from him were enough to give me hope of his approval.

I could not know that while Ross concentrated upon perfecting my actual flying technique, Keim was equally determined to do something about my thinking. To him my flying brain was still woefully immature in flight planning, almost devoid of caution in maneuver, and altogether lacking in weather wisdom. He proceeded, in embittered patience, to set these matters right. After three trips his occasional grunts of approval held for me the thrill of a trumpet flourish.

Now winter came to AM-21 in all seriousness, and the land below was dead beneath a white shroud. Only the sky remained active, interchanging moods of bluster and stealthy cold silence.

The sun was timid and rarely visible from the ground. When we climbed through the nearly permanent cloud deck and emerged to fly on top, the sun came as a complete surprise, for its existence was nearly forgotten. Wrapped in his overcoat, Keim would alternately frown menacingly over his shoulder at the heater and then sit in resigned misery, blinking owlishly at the sun. Unlike other captains, he never left the cockpit. The very thought of appearing before what few passengers we carried seemed to terrify him.

My growing confidence irritated him beyond measure. When I ventured an opinion, which in the joy of baiting I sometimes deliberately made as wild as possible, his reaction inevitably began with an angry semaphoring of eyebrows. Then his voice would rise into a high-pitched complaining whine, tragic in forbearance, mightily abused. His eyes, darting from the instruments to the sky and finally fixing balefully upon me, spoke of a man asked to endure a crushing burden.

"Of course! Why *not* go down and have a look at Syracuse? Why should we pass it over? They're *only* reporting a ceiling of three hundred feet and half a mile visibility with blowing snow. Why not, indeed? What are we fooling around up here in the sun for? Obviously I have been completely wasting my time trying to learn a few things about this route the last five years! I should have consulted you much sooner! *Indeed!* I've never met a co-pilot who knew so very much. I should inform the payroll department they've made a serious mistake. *You* are the one who should be paid for doing the thinking around here! Obviously my stupidity can never be overcome by what very *little* experience *I've* had. Go ahead! *You* take her down! *You* have a look at Syracuse! Kill us all! Who wants to live forever?"

Such moments with Keim were exquisite and well worth retreat with wounds.

While I absorbed aerial wisdom from Keim, my contemporaries serving other men of equal experience matured in kind. McGuire was learning, and Watkins, and Mood, and Petersen, and Gay, and Carter, and Owen. We now appreciated the niceties of a low approach well done. A failing engine was not an exciting lark but a serious problem to be solved. Fuel, especially in winter, was like an always diminishing bank account and should be expended judiciously. Ice was a phenomenon to be avoided like the plague, and we anticipated the customary uselessness of radios when flying through snow.

It became important to think as well as fly. All of our captains were required by law to choose an alternate airport which they could certainly make should the place of destination prove impossible. We saw that this thinking went much further, and understood that good line pilots held an alternate in their minds for every eventuality. If this did not work out, then they would do that. Expecting the worst, they skipped one emotion when trouble appeared, and thus moved without pausing past disappointment to decision and action.

All of this and much more came to us in time, which was measured and carefully recorded in our logbooks. So many hours and minutes of nighttime, so many of day, and so many of flight on instruments. Together with the dates and the names of those captains we served, it was all set down.

One fundamental of our training had, for most of us, still to be experienced. We had been bewildered, amazed, humbled, and excited. We had not yet been thoroughly frightened or forced to look disaster directly in the face and stare it down. This omission in my own curriculum was corrected on a certain February night.

My escort to fear was a captain named Hughen.

The locale was new to me: AM-23, which designates the air space between Nashville, Tennessee, and New York.

Only the plane was familiar to me. Because the last available DC-3 had been grounded for maintenance, an elderly DC-2 had been substituted to fulfill our schedule. It was airworthy but far from beautiful. It bore a haggard look and its scars were like hard-won decorations. Oil and exhaust flame had left permanent stains along the engine cowlings which no amount of burnishing could ever remove. There were hail dents about its nose, and deeper depressions on both sides of the fuselage where the propellers had cast off countless chunks of ice. A glance at the logbook proved it had flown over ten thousand hours. Someday soon it would be sold off to a more modest line in Africa or China or Central America where it might continue a grubby career for years.

We walk toward the ship in the moonlight. The night is cold and penetrating, without the crispness of northern air. The sky is clear except over the city of Nashville itself, where a thin matting of stratus cloud reflects the surface light. There is no wind and the click of our heels echoes sharply across the concrete ramp. It is just possible to see the vapor of our breaths in the moonlight.

Hughen is a large and dignified man who speaks in short, quick word groups, as if all that he had to say was assembled, chained neatly together, and then released only when ready. He flew the mail in open-cockpit planes and has been with the line so long I must consider that time as forever. The architecture of his face is solid and heavy, contrasting strangely with the infantile smoothness of his skin. He bears one unmistakable talisman of the true early bird—a barely perceptible wisp of mustache which at one time was as much a part of self-respecting pilots as their helmet and goggles. He is quite bald except for a few strands of black hair comprising another wisp just forward of his cranium. These remnants of a pompadour are carefully combed straight back.

Hughen has been considerate and friendly, but the gap between his experience and mine is of such vast dimensions that our relationship naturally remains that of master and apprentice.

We are bound for New York on what should be a four-hour flight. The weather has been forecast as favorable except for a mild warm front some hundred miles to the east. There is no reason to believe it will present any difficulty. There will be eight passengers. They are already waiting patiently behind the wire gate, shuffling about in comfortable ignorance of their immediate future, watching the moon and murmuring the shyly polite little clichés so necessary to strangers embarking on a common journey. Their fates must soon be joined with our own, which is a pity, for on this night they too will know the rancid taste of fear.

Hughen is not happy about the substitution of a DC-2.

"I thought I was through flying these damn things."

But he straps himself into his seat with a sigh of resignation and methodically checks off every control and instrument in the cockpit, calling forth each item from his memory. The ritual performed to his satisfaction, we start the engines and taxi away. In a very few minutes we are climbing toward the moon.

Hughen is a meticulous man and, knowing little of my experience, has worked out the flight plan himself. He has chosen Columbus, Ohio, as our alternate, a convenient place, where the weather is forecast to remain excellent. It now lies far over the night horizon to the northeast. We have sufficient fuel aboard to reach New York and if we should find it closed we have enough to turn about and proceed easily to Columbus. We carry an additional forty-five minutes of fuel to cover any conceivable delay after arrival there. This is the law, and we have complied with it although there is absolutely no reason to believe this reserve fuel will ever be needed.

By the time we have reached our cruising altitude the lights of Nashville are lost beneath the tail. There are times, particularly during day flights, when pilots are much given to conversation in the cockpit, though the noise of the engines and slip stream causes them to raise their voices unnaturally. At night the reverse is true, there seeming to be a muffling of all outward sounds by the darkness until the cockpit becomes a cozy place well suited to meditation. If the night is fair and strewn with stars, or phosphorescent with a moon, then pilots have been known to turn down every light in the cockpit and sit in absolute silence, savoring their uniquely remote peace as long as they can.

On such nights contact with the earth is lost more completely than at any other time. Radio calls from the ground stations are considered an intrusion and answered resentfully. Few pilots are immune to this nocturnal spell. It has a mystical quality which lays a pleasing coverlet over the usual technical thought patterns necessary in a cockpit, and once again the airplane becomes an argosy afloat in space instead of a mere machine.

On such nights, with the horizon lost, it is possible to look down upon certain stars, an illusion which causes the altimeter to become meaningless. The hands pointing to seven and zero could indicate seven thousand feet or seventy thousand or seven hundred miles, for the eerie spectacle from the cockpit is presumably the same.

I have been staring at the moon.

Now, reluctantly, I turn up the lights, place the logbook on my knees, and prepare to mark down our moment of passage over Knoxville. I will radio this information back to Nashville. Based on our ground speed, an easy calculation when a computer is used, I will also report the wind we have experienced and a new estimate of our arrival over Roanoke, which lies to the north.

Hughen has so far done all of the flying and is apparently lost in contemplation of his instruments. He has not spoken since our take-off. I wait, expecting to see the lights of Knoxville before he nods his head to confirm that we are actually over the range station. And the waiting is easy, for there is still the moon.

I lift myself in the seat, inspecting the darkness below. There are no lights of any kind. Instead, the earth is obscured by a veil of cloud which I take to be ground fog. Its presence is unimportant since we have no intention of landing at Knoxville. I toy with my pencil and watch the luminous clock on the instrument panel. The sweep second hand quivers through the smallest units of time, which are now without particular value. The hand appears to move slowly, as it must do to those rich in leisure and safety. Time speeds only when we would halt it.

We are now four minutes late over Knoxville, yet Hughen has made no sign. Thinking I may have missed his signal, I flip a switch at my side and so cut myself in on the range. No, we are still approaching Knoxville. The invisible wind outside must be much stronger than forecast. Twisting the dial on my computer, I find it must be over forty miles an hour. I can solve the equation exactly when I know our exact time over the station.

Now there is a division in the sky ahead which appears to be shaped like a wedge. It divides our forward view into layers. First there is the blackness far below, which has become confused with globules of minor cloud, then the wedge protruding from what proves to be a solid mass. Finally there is an uppermost plateau of vapor, which is almost exactly at our altitude. It is thin, gossamer-like, and relatively brilliant beneath the moon.

Hardly more than a minute passes before we are sliding swiftly along just above the surface of the plateau. The sensation is delightful, for the only way the true speed of an airplane may be visually appreciated is to fly it close to a relatively stationary surface. In barnstorming days we frequently sought this same exhilaration by skimming over the fields and trees, even following the contours of hills as closely as we dared. It was, at least, a stimulating prelude to disaster, which was all too frequently the end result. Such gay foolishness in an airliner is of course unthinkable, but the same sensation can be achieved by finding a flat-topped deck of cloud and flying along its surface until the bottom arc of the propellers slice into it. This is a harmless diversion and when, as now, a moon illuminates a great mattress of vapor, the effect is intoxicating.

I glance at Hughen and find him smiling. What else, when this is fulfillment, the ghostlike, swift, and sensual tonic of true flight? These moments are the sinew of our devotion, the physical excitation to be found in our way of life.

Hughen nods at the tiny glowing light on the instrument panel. We are over Knoxville.

I write down the time on the flight plan form, place a pencil dot on the marking side of my computer, and discover we have been bucking a fifty-mile-an-hour wind. This is thirty more than forecast and I cannot believe my figures. I repeat the calculation and get the identical answer. I reach across the cockpit and hold the computer so Hughen can see it.

He frowns and takes a moment to smooth the wisps of his hair.

"You sure?"

"Yes. I'm sure."

"We'll get a better check between here and Roanoke. Maybe our climb threw your figures off."

"I allowed for the climb."

"Even so."

Hughen turns north for Roanoke as I radio our findings back to Nashville. The moon slides around until it is over my right shoulder. But I have lost interest in the moon. Nashville is sending me a series of weather reports for various cities, and these must be recorded in a special shorthand which most nearly resembles the hieroglyphics of the Egyptians. When the transmission is finished I find that all is the same as on our departure except for Nashville itself, which is now reporting an overcast condition with lower broken clouds.

This is an abrupt change and had not been predicted.

There is also a southerly wind. At Nashville a wind from the south is not good.

"Did you hear the Nashville weather?"

Hughen nods his head. "No matter. As long as New York holds up."

He reaches forward and turns the fuel valve to the right auxiliary tank. Then for a moment he thoughtfully works the wobble pump at the side of his seat to guarantee free flow of the precious liquid. After several strokes, when it is obvious the fuel system is functioning properly, he stops pumping and again retires within himself. I cannot account for his strange preoccupation and believe it must be a personal habit rather than due to any demands of our flight.

I spend some five or ten minutes at my paper work. There are baggage and mail forms, fuel, loading, and logbook to be looked after, in addition to the flight plan. When these are all completed I hand the open logbook to Hughen with a pencil placed in the jaws so he can easily sign his name. I hold the controls while he scribbles with a flourish. And after his name he marks down his seniority number. If my number were 64 I would sign my name with a flourish too.

Enviously, I close the logbook and place it on the floor. Yes, it would be wonderful if my number were 64. When you are young how can you hasten age? What is there to do with youth when you are youth and therefore impatient with waiting? Yet I can only wait and find such comfort as I can in the moon.

It has vanished. There is not even a glow in the sky. Instead we are wrapped in vapor which swoops around the snout of the DC-2 and whips against the windshield. Then we must be in the front which the meteorologists had located almost exactly. They explained that it would lie nearly stagnant in a long trough extending from the Blue Ridge Mountains as far north as Baltimore. Its promised length does not displease me. Certainly Hughen will not wish to fly the full two hours necessary to emerge from this long band of weather. Certainly, when his eyes tire, he will relinquish the controls and if I cannot do anything about my number I can at least add to my instrument time.

There is a new roughness to the air and I become vaguely uneasy. Hughen is absorbed in his instruments and I soon become aware that he is paying particular heed to the outside temperature gauge. It stands at thirty degrees.

I remember from my days in Lester's school that this temperature is supposedly ideal for icing conditions. Yet so far there is no evidence of ice and I am even a little disappointed because the most I have ever seen is a delicate tracery across the windshield. Meteorologists are frank in confessing their inability to forecast the existence of ice in a cloud mass. They seem positive about one thing only. Any cloud holding a temperature between twenty and thirty degrees harbors the potential of ice. It might be there. Or it might not.

The air is still not rough enough to require the passenger seat belt sign. There are jolts, but they are few and far between. I lean back in my seat, thinking about Hughen. How I envy his flying experience! And his fortune, what of that? He was lucky enough to fly when there was romance and stirring adventure—and constant hazard. He came through unscathed to this solidity. His face and body are now those of a comfortable man as secure in his position as the proprietor of a long-established store. He has a wife, two children, money in the bank, and a home. He is a sensible man and serene—certainly not of the swash-buckling type who must sometimes destroy themselves in a search for self-justification. Then why is he still here? Why is he still sitting in a worn leather seat, surrounded by a hundred things of such harsh mechanical nature they can offer him little comfort? Why is he not at home, this solid man, sprawled in a leather armchair? His home will be dark now. It is long past the family bedtime. Yet the head of the house is aloft with the moon.

Our first warning is an insistent hissing in our earphones. It builds rapidly until it becomes an abrasive squealing, the nasty and continuous scratching of fingernails along a slate. The screeching becomes a diaphonic howl and the range signal of Knoxville is buried in it.

Hughen, pained at the sound and consequent lack of guidance, presses his lips tightly together.

"See if you can tune in Knoxville on the D.F."

The direction finder is a completely separate radio installation and is controlled by a tuning dial and a small crank for turning the receiving loop. By cranking the loop a bearing may be taken on any convenient station and thus a navigational line of position established. Because of its construction the loop can often bring in signals when the regular antenna fails its purpose.

I lean forward to crank the loop so that its position is best for receiving the Knoxville range. Nothing. Only the hideous sound of those fingernails.

I turn the volume far down and crank the loop back and forth, a few degrees at a time. Listening intently, both of us press the headphones hard against our ears. Nothing.

"Try Roanoke."

I retune the receiver and rock the crank slowly back and forth. Again, nothing penetrates the screeching.

"Try Charleston."

I am ashamed. The route is new to me and I do not know the call sign of Charleston by heart. I could find it in the book which is in my flight kit, but it is quicker to admit my ignorance and ask Hughen, who must surely know.

"The identification is C.H."

I tune the receiver quickly and crank again. Nothing. Nothing . . . nothing.

"Give Columbus a shot."

I know the frequency of Columbus since it is sometimes used on AM-21. It is far away, but there is always hope in the freakishness of radio.

Yet again . . . nothing. There is no break or recognizable signal to be plucked from the strident discord. We are swallowed in a crazy region of utterly useless sound.

I have been so preoccupied with tuning, listening, and cranking that I have given little heed to the windshield. Now it has become opaque. Our world ends in a gray panel approximately eighteen inches from our faces.

"Start the de-icers."

I flip the switch above my head which will activate the rubber boots, then turn on the landing lights to observe their operation.

Looking back at the wing, I watch the intermittent pulsations of the boots and find their movements strangely fascinating. So this is true ice. It looks more like pie crust. The rubber boots, ponderously swelling and collapsing like elongated hearts, break the pie crust off in great flakes. The rhythm of the operation is a slow one, allowing the ice to form in a thin layer before it is torn apart, spat back at the night, and sucked away.

There is also ice forming on the rim of the engine cowling and the propeller hub. It does not seem to be more than half an inch thick.

Turning back, I find Hughen adjusting the carburetor heat levers. He must reach around to my side of the control pedestal to get to these controls, and I am astonished to see that his bald head glistens with perspiration.

"Too hot in here for you?"

"No."

Hughen is concerned although I can see no reason for being so. This is as nothing to a thunderstorm.

I wonder if Hughen might be one of those pilots secretly afraid of airplanes. There are a very few such men, anxiously nursing their dread until the day when they can retire. Experience has worn them out instead of hardening them. They exist in a half-frightened daze, like punch-drunk fighters, and everyone is sorry for them.

Suddenly someone is throwing rocks at me. There is an erratic banging upon the fuselage just behind my seat. I instinctively twist and dodge, then realize the hammering is also behind Hughen.

"Shoot some alcohol on the props!"

Of course. The propeller blades, like the wings, are accumulating ice, which is retained only until centrifugal force whirls it off. Chunks the size of baseballs are being hurled against the resounding aluminum. And since one blade retains more than another, the delicate balance of the three-hundred-and-eighty-pound propellers is disturbed. An uneven vibration seizes the entire ship. It passes beneath my feet from one side of the cockpit to the other, surging to a maximum, falling off, and then returning again. I do not like this vibration. There is something wicked about it.

I turn a valve marked "props" and labor strenuously at a hand pump which is just behind me. At once the cockpit becomes pungent with the smell of alcohol. My pumping will send the liquid to the propeller blades and supposedly free them of ice.

In less than a minute I am also sweating. Things are beginning to happen very fast. They are not good things.

The vibration is increasing in spite of my pumping. The racket of banging ice is becoming a fusillade. The air is still not unduly rough, but unless the instruments and the seat of my pants are lying, the ship is beginning to porpoise in an unbelievable manner. Hughen is having a very rough time with the controls. Now the sweat is dripping from his cheekbones and he is breathing heavily.

"Try Knoxville again! On the loop!"

He is afraid. I am certain he is afraid. His voice is controlled, but there is the constriction of fear beneath his control. The ordered words come like pistol shots.

I stop pumping, tune the D.F.'s radio to Knoxville frequency, and reach for the loop crank. In doing so, my attention is caught by the air speed. One hundred and twenty miles an hour! Only a few minutes before we were cruising at one hundred seventy. Yet Hughen has not touched the power. A queasy sensation passes through my stomach. The blood rushes to my head until my cheeks feel aflame. My hands are suddenly hot and throbbing. I catch myself working my lips. These I know to be the beginning signals of fear. I cannot seem to stop it.

Because my lips insist on making these silly formations, I cannot say anything about the air speed. One hundred and twenty. We must not lose any more. With a load of ice this ship will cease to fly at one hundred, possibly even sooner.

What the hell is wrong with those fancy de-icer boots? They are not performing the task for which they are intended. Come! Function!

I glance furtively out the window at my side. The blinking red-light indicator shows the de-icers are in operation, but outside there is visible proof that they are lying down on the job. The leading edge of the wing is now one long, unbroken bar of ice. And it is clear ice, rumpled as if there were rocks beneath.

Yes, the boots are working. But they are expanding and contracting *beneath* the sheath of ice and consequently useless! The ice has accumulated too fast for them.

"Get Knoxville!"

I try. I try with all that is in me to hear Knoxville. I strain my senses, allowing the squeaking to sear my brain as I listen for the treasure of a signal. I must hear it, for now a new threat is evident. I am dismayed to see that the altimeters read a mere five thousand feet. We have lost two thousand. We are foundering like a ship. The rate of climb shows we are sinking at a steady two hundred feet per minute, which at least makes for very simple arithmetic. At such a rate we will descend to sea level in twenty-five minutes, whether we like it or not.

Hughen moves the propeller controls to full low pitch. Now I realize that he has every reason to be afraid. We cannot possibly descend to sea level or anywhere near it unless we are ready for surrender. The Blue Ridge Mountains are buried in the night below. We are already below the level of the highest peaks.

"We're getting out of this!"

Hughen pounds his feet on the rudder pedals. They are immovable. The rudder, far back on the tail of the ship, is frozen. There is, of course, absolutely nothing we can do about it. Yet by constant movement Hughen has kept the ailerons free, so a turn is still possible. He must execute the turn very slowly, taking great care not to bank more than a few degrees at a time, for at this speed and with the efficiency of the wings so damaged, a turn can be the introduction to a spin from which, under the circumstances, there can be no possible recovery.

I watch Hughen start into a slow left turn. At once the air speed slips to an agonizing one hundred and five. The ship has abandoned the easier porpoising and is bucking viciously. I cannot believe that an airplane is capable of such idiotic action. There is absolutely no explanation for it.

Hughen is a man tiptoeing along a very tenuous wire. The wire is swaying crazily in the wind, he is being bombarded with rocks, and if he loses balance for one second, we are done for. How can this all have happened so suddenly? Fifteen minutes ago all was as it should be.

"Call Nashville. Get emergency clearance at five thousand. Tell them we are returning on account of heavy ice. Accumulation fast . . . clear ice."

"Do you want me to call first or try to get Knoxville range?"

"Call first. Tell them to clear that altitude."

I repeat the message into my microphone, trying to control the tendency of my voice to become a quavering falsetto. It is I who should be in a leather armchair before a fire. I cannot bear to look at the instruments as Hughen is obliged to do. Their readings are bringing me very close to panic. Where is that rambunctious youth intrigued with the essence of danger? What is happening so very quickly to the young man who thought the present world suffered from oversecurity and produced only mice-hearted men? Captain Hughen, this is all an anachronism. We belong to the modern world and should therefore be secure. Please arrange a remedy for this grievous mistake at once.

One hundred miles per hour. Altitude four thousand eight hundred feet. Still sinking. Maybe if I refuse to look the readings will go away.

There is no reassuring reply from Nashville. I can only assume they received our message and will clear all other planes from our altitude.

A sudden, terrible shudder seizes the entire airplane. At once Hughen shoves the throttles wide open and the nose down.

The shuddering ceases. Hughen wipes the sweat from his eyes.

"She almost got away from me!"

The incipient stall has stolen an additional three hundred feet from our altitude. We must not risk a repetition, and yet the engines cannot remain at full power forever. But Hughen leaves the throttles where they are.

I crank the loop desperately although the hope of hearing anything is dissolved in noise. I abandon the frequency of Knoxville and again experiment with Columbus, which is so much farther away. Then quite clearly I hear a new whine, distorted yet unmistakably genuine. It is interrupted by the code letters C.O. Columbus!

I crank through a null and note the bearing. At once I tune to Charleston and find it also readable.

"I have Charleston and Columbus! Fix in a minute!"

I don't know why it seems so terribly important to know where we are. What *is* important is our altitude, a factor we can do nothing about. If it continues to diminish, our position is of little consequence. Both Hughen and myself would be indifferent as to which of the Blue Ridge Mountains we actually hit.

I manage to take two good bearings when Hughen at last completes his turn. I plot them at once on the chart drawn from my flight kit.

"Here is a fix. Only second-class bearings, but they make sense."

Hughen glances at the two intersecting lines I have drawn on the chart. They show us to be approximately fifty miles to the north of Knoxville—directly over a long hump in the mountains. There is a peak somewhere in this area. Its summit is marked as 4,150 feet. We are now at 4,500 feet and still sinking.

Even as we study the chart we are approaching or leaving the vicinity of the peak. Which it is, we cannot know until I plot another fix. There is no way to make an airplane wait.

"Take another shot in two minutes."

In two minutes the effort might be entirely superfluous.

We have merely nodded to fear. Now we must shake its filthy hand.

Both engines suddenly begin cutting out—first one and then the other. For one awful moment they both subside together. And there is a silence which is not really a silence but a chilling diminuendo of all sound.

This is the way you die.

At three minutes past two in the morning.

And as suddenly the engines regain themselves. We can feel the surge forward, but we have lost five hundred precious feet! We are below that peak, wherever it may be.

Something must be done about the engines. Nothing else is of any importance whatsoever.

Hughen has yanked on full rich mixture to the carburetors. He switches back to the main fuel tank and works the wobble pump. All the while he struggles to keep the ship in a semblance of straight and level flight.

Again the engines grow feeble. They are stricken with a mysterious disease. We might argue with our flying senses, but we cannot argue with a manifold pressure gauge. Both instruments show a slow and steady loss of power. This cannot be due to carburetor ice. We are certain of that because other instruments tell us the heaters are working.

We lose another two hundred feet. Hughen anxiously jockeys the throttles. He checks the magnetos. Perfect. He seems more perplexed than frightened and I cannot think of a way to help him.

We are much too low. We can only be flying in a valley, but it is impossible to determine which valley since there are several shown on the chart. Nor can we know when this convenient valley will come to an abrupt end. Hughen begins a slow circle. Flying so, we will at least use up less territory.

"Maybe I'd better go back and start heaving things overboard."

We must, absolutely *must*, have altitude.

"Wait. I may need you."

Hughen has switched on the landing lights again and yanked open his side window so he can see the left engine clearly. After a moment he hauls the window shut. Then to my horror he cuts off the fuel mixture to his engine. Starved of fuel, it backfires angrily. At once Hughen pulls the fuel lever to full rich again. The response is like a cheer. His engine is putting out full power once more. He repeats the action with the right engine controls. Again, after a moment's startled regurgitation, a welcome return of power.

We are able to climb at fifty feet a minute!

"Air scoops . . . icing over. Watch them. Soon as the power falls off, cut the mixture until they backfire. Then slam them on again."

I must lean forward to see past the accumulation of ice along the fringes of my side window. It is swelling rapidly and is easily three inches thick in places. Beyond it, in the ghostly light, I can see the engine, now grizzle-bearded in ice.

The carburetor air scoop is an oval-shaped metal mouth on top of the engine. Through it must pass the air, which is as important to any combustion engine as fuel. Without air the engine dies as surely as a drowning human being. Normally, the mouth is approximately four inches wide. Now the reason for our loss of power becomes all too obvious. Even as I watch, the ice accumulates around the lips of the mouth. It builds upon itself, decreasing the size of the opening like a closing iris until it is merely a black hole hardly more than the size of a dollar. The same thing is happening on Hughen's side. Our engines are simply suffocating. Something must remove the ice before it closes their mouths entirely.

Hughen has had the nerve and courage to find a way. By backfiring the engines a tongue of flame spurts from the air scoops. It is not the flame but the force of air from the bowels of the engine which knocks away the closing ice. Two hefty belches seem to do the job nicely. Then there is a wait of three or four minutes until the danger point is reached again. It is a terrible abuse of the engines, but not so bad as asking them to fly through a mountain. Gradually, Hughen is able to nurse the ship to 4,300 feet. But even at full power, that is all. He holds the course reasonably steady on southwest, the direction from which we have come.

Between backfirings I am heavily engaged with the loop antenna. With luck, our position will again become important.

I am able to plot a series of bearing fixes. They show without doubt that retreat might be our salvation. We are crawling across the chart like a wounded insect. But it is very important that we are indeed creating a series of marks rather than a single X, which would, with due finality, designate the very end of all movement. Lower terrain is ahead and presumably better weather. We have actually been in the ice less than thirty minutes, not a very long time to so incapacitate an airplane. And yet the half hour has had the smell of eternity.

Then, quite unexpectedly, we stumble out of the cloud and sail beneath the moon. I refrain from yelling and pounding on the leather crash pad before me only with difficulty.

Hughen, as befits his age and experience, maintains his dignity. His relief is confined to a great sigh, the sound of a shipwrecked sailor throwing himself at last upon a beach.

The propellers fling their final collection of rocks at us, and the vibration which has shaken the ship for so long gradually melts away. We are skating above the plateau again, although its presence is only dimly visible through our side windows. Our forward windshields are solid with ice; hence the moon itself is invisible. But it is quite enough to sense its light.

"Shoot some alcohol on the windshield."

I turn the valve to the proper marking and pump. It is a fruitless procedure. The liquid spews out of small pipes along the glass and creeps between the crenelations of ice. I can see it. I can also see that it is completely ineffective except to fill the cockpit with fumes. It is a stupid arrangement. What could the engineers have been thinking? Somehow the glass itself should be heated.

"I'm getting drunk."

"Forget the alcohol, then. Rig the elephant's pecker."

Hughen refers to a large flexible duct which draws hot air from the main heater. It is hung on a wire and may be adjusted like a fire hose so that its spray of warmth can be directed on any desired portion of the windshield. In very light ice it can, with patience, melt a hole barely two inches in diameter, providing just enough forward visibility for an emergency landing. With this kind of ice it proves as ineffective as the alcohol.

Hughen cannot set up the hose by himself. He is a very busy man. Though we are flying in clear, smooth air, and thus no longer accumulating ice, the load we already have still renders the ship nearly unmanageable.

It is twenty minutes past two. We know that we have no sound reason to smile at each other, but a smile now seems very necessary—a congratulatory salute directed more to an invisible patron rather than to each other. It is a feeble smile, wanting much in confidence. For we are by no means acquitted; both judge and jury are still out. Still, Hughen is relieved enough to think of our passengers.

"Go back. Explain we are returning to Nashville. Keep moving and it won't take you long."

I leave my seat without enthusiasm. For some reason I am stiff all through my body, as if I had been soundly whipped in a fight. I button my coat and clamp on my cap. Assuming what I hope is an easy manner, I move back past the baggage compartment and open the door to the cabin. Given the choice, I would have closed it at once.

For it is difficult to reconcile myself to this wholly sane and luxuriously comfortable atmosphere. Here are eight people who had been just on the border line of relinquishing their roles as human beings. A very few minutes before, they almost became mixed elements of viscera, bone, and blood, squashed into shapeless blobs which would quiver through the last of life and then be still. Had Hughen lost a mere five miles per hour air speed for even thirty seconds, this could easily have happened. Yet he did not lose those five miles, and as a result the passengers are quite alive. Do they owe anything to Hughen? Not according to the earthy theories of Captain Keim. But I think they do. They owe him for being superbly skillful at his job. They owe him for being enough in love with his work to be where he is instead of at home in his armchair, or better yet—at this hour—in bed.

Their poise astounds me. They could not, of course, see the instruments or appreciate their frightful information, but even here in the cabin there must have been enough commotion for alarm. Two of the passengers are asleep or pretend to be. The others are obviously miserable, yet somehow able to feign reasonable calm. I can only admire them. Helpless and trusting, they had the nerve to sit quite sedately and await their fate.

"I'm sorry. We are returning to Nashville."

The man who sits alone mutters an oath and without further interest returns to his copy of *Time*. I cannot help wondering what he would look like with that magazine as an integral part of his guts.

"I am sorry to tell you we are returning to Nashville."

"Why?"

Why indeed? Because it is the closest place. Because we know the weather is good there. Because the captain knows the field at Nashville, having studied its nature for years, and also it will be much easier for you, lady . . . and because. . . .

"We are returning to Nashville."

"What about the motors? I saw flame. Is something wrong? I felt a little sick."

And "No," speaks the officially appointed liar, "nothing is wrong."

Nothing at all. If I speak the truth it will accomplish nothing. Can I now explain to this man and his wife the cruel and unalterable principles of aerodynamics? Can I say to him while his extraordinarily dull-eyed wife listens without comprehension that this airplane is a scientific masterpiece, intended to remain air-borne at a certain speed carrying a certain weight . . . and yet, because of our newly acquired weight, none of which is pay load, the very basic design of this flying machine has been sadly altered . . . so that all of the previously reliable figures may now be thrown out the window? Can I say that under normal conditions we are supposed to consume ninety gallons of fuel per hour, but for the past hour we have been exploiting our reserve through circumstance, and so consuming twice that amount? And can I say there is nothing we can do about regaining it? Can I say that we have been very lucky?

"We had some backfiring on the engine which is on your side. It's cleared up now. But we think it's better to return to Nashville."

The stewardess is new enough to be frightened. She is huddled on her small seat next to the door although there are many of the regular seats available. She is fussing with her commissary report, as if its completion were a last will and testament.

. . . the coffee was cold when placed aboard . . . the rolls were smashed and there was only half enough butter. . . .

She has her problems.

"What's wrong?"

"Nothing. We're going back to Nashville. You can see the same movie again."

"What shall I tell my passengers?"

"I've told them. Serve some coffee if it will perk them up."

"I don't know what's the matter with those Nashville people. The coffee is always cold out of there. I'm going to report them."

"Do."

"How will my passengers get out of Nashville? Two of them have connecting flights."

"I don't know."

"I don't like that banging against the fuselage. I wish I was back in Los Angeles taking a sun bath. Are you scared?"

"Always."

How a man can parade in front of a woman! How insignificant his fears, how humble his courage. Could this young woman have seen the poltroon within me only a little while ago, the present stuffy stalwart would have collapsed before her eyes. Yet because she is a woman who might see me again, I walk back up the aisle with a confident swagger.

Inside, I am aerodynamically ill. Because Lester, in his school, had taught me to understand aerodynamics. And I do not wish to look like Lester.

After the hypocrisy of the cabin, the cockpit is almost a relief.

"Want to fly awhile?"

I want very much to fly this airplane now that we are in the clear. I want to see what it is like to fly an airplane that is not really flying but merely lingering in the air. After all, Hughen is present to catch me if I fall off the tightrope.

He has reduced the power slightly, but we are still using much above the requirement for normal cruising. Even so, it is barely enough to maintain a faltering one hundred and twenty miles per hour. He waves for me to take over the controls. I flounder uncertainly for a moment, shocked at the heavy, drunken feel of the ship. After a little time I manage fairly well.

The standard radio is tuned to the Nashville beam. It is loud and clear and thus sweet music to our ears. I could almost relax were it not for Hughen. Out of the corner of my eye I can see him fidgeting in his seat. He wipes his face with his handkerchief, opens his collar, then smooths the wisps of hair again and again. His head is in constant motion as his attention alternates repeatedly between the instruments and the window at his side. His fingers drum a nervous, inaudible rhythm on his knees. For a time he tinkers halfheartedly with the heating duct. It has not made the slightest mark upon the windshield ice. Forward, we are as blind as if the oblique sections of glass were marble slabs. We are sitting in a crypt.

It will not be an easy landing at Nashville; therefore Hughen certainly has cause to drum his fingers. But as long as the side windows can be opened, it can be done. In thirty minutes at the most we should be on the ground.

Nashville is calling us on the radio. Hughen quickly takes up his microphone and acknowledges our attention.

"Nashville special weather . . . ceiling estimated four hundred over-cast . . . visibility one mile . . . light freezing rain. . . . "

Now then! What is this? We are returning to an airport which little more than an hour before was bathed in moonlight! We are returning because we could hardly have been considered as really on our way. And there was no hint in the forecast that the city of Nashville and all of its environs should do anything but continue to sleep peacefully beneath the moon. It has no right to sour on us. There *must* be some mistake. The operator must be reading a report from some other station.

Luck has a miserly reservoir. It seems that unless you are willing to accept impurities, you can draw out just so much at one time. There has been cause to believe that we may have consumed our ration for one night, and it is even more certain that we are in no shape to make an instrument approach through freezing rain. Yet outside my window, past the wedding-cake display of ice, there is not a shred of cloud between what has become our private plateau and the moon. This makes it much easier to believe the next report from Nashville will be more cheerful.

Twenty minutes pass. Our course is now west, straight for Nashville. Our propeller ice is entirely gone and the air continues smooth. But we have not lost a millimeter of our wing ice. We cannot will it, or wish it, or melt it, or blow it, away. Where are the engineers again? The wings should somehow be heated. And our rudder is still frozen solid.

We pass through the cone of silence over Nashville station. Hughen takes the controls and starts a gentle left bank. As we circle, the moon appears in my side window. It gives luminosity to the ice decorations around the frame, then slides out of sight. Our traffic clearance has instructed us to hold over the station as another ship is in the process of landing. So we wait and the moon wanders twice across the area of my window. The cloud deck is not far below. Somewhere in it the approaching ship should be plowing through the murk, and when it has found the runway, it will be our turn. We would appreciate it if the other ship would hurry. We have had quite enough of this limited scenery.

Nashville is calling us. Our clearance?

"Message. Nashville special weather. Pilot reports ceiling estimated three hundred feet . . . visibility one half mile. Eastern Airlines missed second attempt approach and is proceeding to alternate. Pilot reports moderate icing in approach. Do you wish further clearance or will you hold? Signed Garrow."

This ambiguous message is actually studded with suggestions. It must be interpreted beyond the mere figures, weighed for its nuances, and applied to our own touchy situation. Translated, it means that for the moment the weather at Nashville is below our company standards, but this may change. Therefore if Hughen thinks he can afford to linger in the vicinity awhile, he might descend for a "look." If he then finds the weather legal, he may land. If not, he is in trouble and he'd better have fuel enough to go elsewhere. It is up to him, and the dispatcher on the ground, who is not influenced by either ice or moon, will abide by his decision. Yet there is a further hint in the wording itself. "Pilot reports ceiling. . . ." This is far more trustworthy than a report from a ground observer. Also it was not just any pilot but an Eastern Airlines pilot who decided to pass up the field. This is more than a delicate admonition and one which the dispatcher knows will be understood and appreciated by Hughen. He must now weigh a separate factor which affects the whole business of airline flying. And, after evaluation, fit it in with the more tangible elements.

He must give at least some consideration to the fact that airline pilots are separated into tribes in spite of their common occupation. Gossip has provided legend, which in turn leads to unavoidable generalization. Thus United pilots are considered colorless and sticklers for regulations. American pilots are thought to be a mixed lot, prone to independent complaint and rebellion. TWA pilots, highly regarded individually, are pitied for the chameleon management of their company. Pan American pilots, admired and envied for their long-range flying, are thought to be shy and backward in foul-weather work. The tribes are each healthy and strong in their way, but their characteristics, conditioned by their aerial territories, are as different as the Sioux, the Navahos, and the Cherokees. All of this is recognized as debatable. Yet the legends had to start somehow.

Now it is important for Hughen to remember that Eastern Airlines pilots are singularly determined and clever. They are not given to timidity, and if the pilot now beneath us has refused to continue his approach, then the conditions must be very unpleasant indeed.

Hughen, newly concerned with our fuel reserve, takes less than a minute to join all the factors together and reach a decision.

"We are proceeding to our alternate. Request clearance direct to Columbus instead of via airways."

We will save a few miles by flying a direct course, but it means I shall be very busy with cross bearings. Before the clearance is received, Hughen has already swung off toward the northeast.

In five minutes it will be three o'clock in the morning. It is over four hundred miles to Columbus—at our present speed, some three and a half hours' flying.

On Hughen's demand I check the amount of our fuel.

"We're fat. Four hundred and twenty gallons remaining."

Hughen is not so easily persuaded that all is now well. He holds his computer before him and regards it dubiously. His lower lip slides up to brush along the wisp of mustache; then he shakes his head.

"We're using a hundred and thirty gallons an hour. I doubt if we'll be able to reduce power very much. So we can't make Columbus even in still air and keep any reserve. Get the Cincinnati, Louisville, and St. Louis weather. Ask for the winds aloft."

I call, staring at the ice. If it would go away, then we might fly like an airplane. If. . . .

My request is answered directly from New York, evidence that those on the ground are beginning to take a special interest in the proceedings. The reports are not encouraging.

Louisville . . . closed. St. Louis . . . closed. Cincinnati appears on the border line with a five-hundred-foot ceiling, rain, and a mile of visibility. We are homeless beneath the moon. Columbus, our original alternate, which is now beyond our hopes, is the only haven reporting favorable weather. Hughen is biting his mustache again.

The voice from New York drones a report on the winds aloft. I copy the series of figures which presume to reflect the movements of the upper air levels in our vicinity. They are the offerings of an inexact science and not to be trusted implicitly. But they do serve as an omen for good or evil.

I hand the paper to Hughen. Even when things are not going well in a cockpit, there are certain social amenities to be observed, and a man who finds malicious satisfaction in spreading gloom is a wretched airmate. I would rather have kept the winds aloft a secret from Hughen, thus permitting him to concentrate on what was now inevitable.

New York has said that the winds will blow from the north at this altitude and their force will be thirty miles an hour. They will subtract from our speed a like amount and leave us plowing upstream at a time when we need every blessing. It not only means that we *must* land at Cincinnati but Hughen must make his instrument approach unerringly. There will not be fuel for a second pass at the field. We must now consider minutes rather than hours.

Hughen is starting to sweat again. He smooths the pitiful hairs as he reads the figures. For some reason they seem even less in number. At this moment Hughen is the loneliest man in the world.

"Give me a fix every five minutes."

The next hour was checkered with quick change from hope to disappointment, from certainty to doubt, and at last resolved itself into an atmosphere of angry determination. If fate was bound to defeat us, then it should have chosen fewer and more subtle harassments. We might have been tricked into becoming wastrels of time and, feeling entitled to some relaxation, have thrown away as much as five minutes. But we were overly beset and the consequence was a team perfectly agreed that if we were compelled to leave the moon and go down into the blackness forever, it would not be the result of our neglect or surrender.

Our combat against the series of misfortunes was without any sign of confusion. Nor could anyone say, when all was done, that we should have fought in another way. The pandemonium of noise was gone, the radio was so clear we could turn the volume far down, and once more the night enclosed our cockpit. There was then a relative hush, which would have been truly restful had it not been so contaminated with forebodings.

Hughen devoted himself entirely to keeping immediate life in our airplane and yet reserving the last drop of its vitality. He set the propellers in full high pitch and reduced the power until we mushed through the air. He leaned the mixture of fuel so that the proportion of air was increased vastly beyond normal. All of this placed a tremendous faith in our engines, but it cut down our fuel consumption until it was a wonder they ran at all. He was gambling because he had to, but the cards he held were good and he was a skillful player.

Above all, Hughen flew—although the term is inadequate to describe his handling of the airplane. The fact was that he urged it along, his tense body seeming actually to lift the DC-2 every time it appeared on the point of aerodynamic exhaustion. This crisis threatened again and again because as we burned fuel and therefore became lighter in the air, Hughen would correspondingly reduce the power. And so the uneasy relation of weight to minimum speed for flight was set up once more. Throughout this interminable struggle he spoke once.

"If this were anything but a DC-2 we just wouldn't be in the air."

And I remembered McCabe felt the same way about a DC-2 and how on a spring morning he had said I might one day learn to love the machine in spite of its cantankerous nature. The only inaccuracy in McCabe's prediction was that my passionate love affair began at night.

I had more time for thought than Hughen because my work came in bunches. So between radio fixes I not only had moments to fall in love with a haggard and middle-aged collection of aluminum but I had also time to wonder at its presence. The schedule called for us to be flying a DC-3, which would undeniably have had a much worse time carrying this same load of ice. And since our past margin had been nil, it followed that what Hughen had said must be true.

Then why? What combination of events, over which we could not possibly have had the slightest control, caused the last-minute substitution of an airplane that would carry more ice than the type we were supposed to fly? Who . . . what did this? What was luck? Were we, for some reason, more deserving of its mystic attention than others who encountered a series of circumstances—which culminated in their destruction? If we were favored, then I wanted to know why, and so perhaps manage to continue the relationship.

I did not have a great deal of time to twist my way through such imponderables. But I had enough.

A final fix showed us to be twenty miles out of Cincinnati. Just before we flew through the cone of silence, we were called on the radio.

"Cincinnati weather now measures three thousand feet . . . visibility better than three miles . . . wind calm. . . ."

Our rejoicing was short-lived. It expired when I checked the fuel still aboard. Fifty gallons.

The dawn was barely apparent when we slithered out beneath the overcast. Through Hughen's side window I caught a glimpse of the airport dozing in the soft twilight. The man deserved respite for he had been nearly five hours at the controls. But he had two problems still remaining. He had to line up with a runway though he was quite blind forward, and he had to be right the first time. He could not skid the ship and so align it exactly during the last moments of descent. The rudder, in spite of our combined kicks at the pedals, remained frozen. Thus he would be obliged to approach the runway at the end of a banking circle, keeping it in sight as long as he could and then at the last moment straightening out and holding a fixed line of flight. I thought to help him during this maneuver by peering from my side window and calling course corrections. None were necessary. Hughen nailed the runway down somehow and held his descent as if sliding down a banister. He said later that he was not overly worried about the runway. He had a far more serious problem.

Even Hughen had never flown an airplane so laden with ice. By experimentation he now knew its demands and behavior when cruising. But what would happen when those aerodynamic conditions were abruptly changed? Leaving level flight, our angle of attack would be quite different, although presumably this change would be to our benefit. It seemed that a wing so grotesquely malformed with ice would regain some of its efficiency when its attitude was tipped in descent. It seemed. We did not know.

Then when the landing gear and flaps were lowered and contributed their enormous drag, what happened? Normal approach speed was one hundred and five miles an hour. Touchdown to the runway should be at least eighty. In the usual situations there was always warning of an incipient stall and thus time to increase speed and recover. This was something we knew.

But now? How much warning would there be from our distorted wings? Or would there be any at all? How much steeper should the descent be, how much extra air speed maintained to compensate for our infirmity? There was nothing in any regulation about the matter because no one knew.

There was an ancillary complication. Like all airports, Cincinnati had its geographical limits. The southerly side was bordered by a high dike. The runways were black, wet, and slippery from the rain. If the landing was too fast toward the south we might consume the entire width of the airport and slide into the dike. The westerly runway terminated before the passenger terminal, which could also effectively stop an airplane. When an irresistible force. . . .

It was like fitting the head to the hat, and Hughen's choice was a beggarman's. It was perhaps best that once we were out of the cloud, he had less than a minute to dwell upon the alternatives. Our fuel meters yelled starvation.

There is a runway. I snap the landing gear down, then the flaps. Our speed slacks off alarmingly. Hughen slams on full power and the engines gulp the last of our fuel.

Hughen banks slightly, daring not to chance more than a few

degrees. His face is pale; his eyes dart from instrument to instrument. He allows our speed to increase with the descent. One hundred and thirty miles an hour. I try to convince myself that this speed is not outrageous for the restricted bowling alley ahead. Yet Hughen, sensing the ship through the controls, must believe he needs this speed.

"We're past the wires!"

Hughen flies the ship right down to the ground. Not until the wheels hit does he cut the power. We hit hard and stay earth-bound. There is no life left in our wings for bouncing.

Good morning to the city of Cincinnati.

These were the truths of that morning:

We skated along the rain-soaked runway for nearly one thousand yards and came to a halt directly before the concrete terminal. We were spared the vision of its swift approach because of our opaque windshield.

In all of our fuel tanks there was a total of thirty gallons remaining. Because of the tank design most of this would have been unavailable to our engines; therefore a second attempt to land would almost certainly have failed before completion.

It took the mechanics two hours of hard labor to knock the ice from our wings, engine cowlings, and empennage. In most places it had reached a thickness of four inches.

Nashville was not declared open for flights until past noon. Louisville and St. Louis cleared somewhat later. We were not interested in Columbus since we could never have reached it no matter how great our determination.

We ate a strangely silent breakfast in the airport café. There was really nothing to say and even the click of our coffee cups seemed intrusive upon our thoughts. We did not see the stewardess or the passengers until much later in the morning. They were taken to a hotel for breakfast and for this we were unaccountably grateful. It seemed very important not to see them. It seemed very important not to see anyone and to lean back against the backs of our chairs, blow smoke at the ceiling, and only look at our thoughts.

We could have rested in Cincinnati for the day. And the temptation to do this was powerful, for, having lost both desperation and fear, we were now very weary. We sat for a long time, joined not in conversation but in great sighs.

It happened that there were no local crews available and possibly this influenced Hughen's decision to proceed, although it was doubtful that he felt any pressing call to duty. He simply wanted to reach his home, he said, and lie down, and think things over. I understood his desire and hoped that after he had slept he would spend some time in an armchair drinking beer. On my own, I was still wondering about the substitution of the DC-2 and the remarkable clearing of the Cincinnati weather. And I wondered about the valley into which we descended blindly without hitting anything. And I thought that something must be done about ice on airplanes because next time there might not be a valley.

So we flew on to New York through weather which was not good but merely routine. In my logbook I wrote down the time of our flight from Nashville to New York.

It was eight hours and fifty minutes.

Beside these figures I placed a short notation. "Ice."

from Flight of Passage
by Rinker Buck

In 1966, the young Buck brothers Rinker (born 1950) and Kern (born 1948) set out to cross America in an old 85-horsepower Piper Cub; they would be the youngest fliers to make the trip. Their ultimate test came at Guadalupe Pass, in the Guadalupe Mountains of West Texas.

For five hundred miles east of the Continental Divide, the high plains of Texas and New Mexico sweep up as a long, imperceptible incline, rising steeply at the end as the stately massif of the Rockies comes into view. From our dawn takeoff at Albany to our afternoon arrival at Carlsbad, New Mexico, where we launched for the Guadalupe Pass, we climbed more than 2,000 feet in land elevation, to almost 4,000 feet above sea level. We flew west through Sweetwater, Lamesa, and Seminole, the fabled "southern route" of the early airmail flyers, but a pilot must fly that stretch at least once to understand what the land is doing to him. Usually we were looking only five or ten miles ahead, not enough to sense the corrections for height we should have been making. All morning, the ground seemed to be stealthily rising up and trying to swallow the plane. Every hour or so we realized our land error and climbed to avoid obstructions and terrain.

The country, too, changed. After Midland, Texas, the beige and red prairie, with its occasional clumps of green draws, rapidly gave way to sandy desert littered with boulders and rocks, the earth all dirty yellow and black, with spectacular mesas and ravines forming the serrated foothills of the Rockies. There were bizarre, disc-shaped cirrus clouds that day, screening the sunlight into weak shadows. The featureless terrain obliterated into featureless sky, erasing the horizon. Deprived of clear ground reference, Kern occasionally experienced problems with vertigo, or spatial disorientation, and was forced to fly by peering constantly at his turn-and-bank indicator and altimeter. I had my hands full navigating by the compass and my time-elapsed calculations. We were flying through an extra-planetary abyss. Even the towns we passed along the way, many of which we never actually saw, had a far-off ring. Big Spring, Odessa, Pecos.

Farther along the clouds broke up and the sun scalded down. Oil fields, the first that we saw, popped out of the empty landscape. Dozens of black and orange derricks methodically pumped away, and the dirt tracks leading up to them radiated off into the desert like the spokes of a sundial. But the oil installations must have been unattended most of the time because there was virtually no sign of human activity below.

Adding to our feelings of flying into a lunar cosmos, it was to be a day of mishaps and freak events. The big mountain pass ahead, which we knew we would brave by midafternoon, seemed to be pushing us back, warning us off by a series of aberrant mechanical and natural frights.

As we turned in for our first refueling stop of the morning, at Avenger Field in Sweetwater, the tail suddenly rattled and shook as violently as a truck hitting a pothole. The airframe resounded with a bang! The sticks sagged, heavy and hard, the nose dropped, and I had to grab the controls myself to help my brother pull the plane away from the ground. He lunged with both hands for his stick and yelled back.

"I've got the stick! You work the throttle and rudders! Just get me down Rink, work me down."

It was a pretty decent spot of flying we did that morning, but we couldn't appreciate it right away. We didn't know what had happened to the plane. All the possibilities ran through my mind. Had we collided with another plane? Maybe we'd lost our elevator struts and the tail was about to vibrate off. Or a bird-strike—we'd seen low-flying vultures all morning. They were awfully big birds, and if one of them was hung up on our rudder, the plane might act like this.

It only took us a half-minute or so to reach the ground, but that's a long time when your heart is pounding like a pile driver. Kern was holding up the plane all right, but with little jerks and bumps, because two hands cannot be as coordinated as one. All the way down he kept yelling for me to work the throttle and rudders better for him, which wasn't an easy thing. A single mind flying alone gracefully choreographs the body—stick hand, throttle hand, the feet on the rudders—into a coordinated landing approach. Two minds doing it together, especially two frightened minds, are an uncoordinated jumble.

"Power, Rink!"

"Not that much! C'mon!"

"Trim. Give me some nose up."

"Wind drift! Jesus, could you watch that? Left rudder, Rink."

But gradually I got into my brother's head and got the hang of that strange descent. We mushed into a soft cushion of air over the runway. To help stall the plane, I furiously cranked in all the nose-up trim I could get, scraping some skin off my knuckles against the metal flange on the carburetor-heat knob as I flew the handle around. I didn't notice the blood on my pants until we stepped out of the plane.

At the gas pumps, which were deserted at seven in the morning, we couldn't find anything wrong with the plane. There were no dents or breaks in the fabric, everything was in place, and when we took off the inspection plates on the tail and peered inside, everything seemed to be in order. But the stick was completely dead on us and we could never fly the plane as it was. It was a mystery. My brother sat on the wheel of the Cub with his chin in his hands, miserable with himself. Our plans for reaching the mountains that day seemed dashed.

The airport mechanic arrived in his pickup a few minutes later. He was a tanned, gentle fellow in a greasy ball-cap, and he smiled knowingly when we explained what happened. He reached into his pocket for a key and unlocked the fuel pumps.

"You may as well gas up now," he said. "Let me get a couple of thangs from the hangar. You'll be outta here in ten minutes."

When the mechanic returned he was carrying a flashlight, needle-nose pliers, and a shiny galvanized-steel spring, slightly larger than the ones used on screen doors, fresh out of its box. He reached inside the tail inspection plate up to his elbow, grappled and winced, and came back out with two broken pieces of a rusty spring.

"It's what I figured," he said. "Busted elevator spring."

"Goddamn it," Kern said, angry at himself. "It's the one part I didn't fix."

"Ah, go easy on yourself young fella," the mechanic said. "Nobody replaces an elevator spring. You fix 'em when they break. You're just lucky that I got a new one that fits."

"What would break a spring in flight like that?" my brother asked.

"Well, where you flyin' from?" the mechanic said.

"New Jersey."

"Nu Jursa! Whoa here. Are you them boys on the radio?"

"We don't have a radio in this Cub."

"No! The AM band boys. You're all over it. Evrabaddy's lookin' for you boys. They're saying you're the youngest aviators ever to fly coast to coast."

We were astonished. It was the first indication we had that there was press interest in our flight, and it had never occurred to us that we might be the youngest aviators to fly the continent. It seemed bizarre to us, too. Here we were out in this lonely, remote stretch of Texas, which felt like the end of the world, and we were enjoying the isolation and the complete freedom from everything we knew. Meanwhile, newscasters were talking about our flight on the radio. Both of us instinctively suspected that my father was behind it. He was probably trying to build as much interest as he could, so there'd be a big splash once we got to California. Neither of us minded very much. We just hadn't expected my father to pull a fast one like that on us in the middle of the country, and we hadn't expected newscasters to be interested either. What did everybody see in this trip?

"Anyways, that's what did it to you," the mechanic said. "You been flying in a lot of turbulence?"

"Yeah, lots," my brother said. "Straight, almost, for three days."

"Well, it's too much for an old spring like that," the mechanic said. "She just gave out in the stress, that's all."

The new spring that the mechanic had wasn't designed for a Piper Cub. It was for a Piper Pawnee cropduster. But by crimping back the ends of the spring and making adjustments on the armature of the elevator, the mechanic adapted it for the Cub. As he set the new spring in place, the mechanic explained that the controls would be lighter now.

"The thang'll be kinda loosey-goosey on you now, know what I mean?" the mechanic said. "But it'll be better. Real responsive-like."

The airport owner and his wife arrived and opened up the pilots' shack. We went in and bought some crackers and soda. The mechanic came in for his morning coffee, and we all sat outside on the porch and talked.

The air was pungent with the dry, woody smell of the high plains early in the morning. There was a thick coating of dew on the macadam ramp and the gas pumps, and glistening on the sagebrush beyond—surprising, I thought, for this dry terrain. The biggest jackrabbits I had ever seen were bounding across the ramp, running circles around each other.

The woman walked out to the pumps to empty the waste barrels. Returning, she called to her husband.

"Dear," she said. "Look at that pretty little Cub on the ramp. It's perfect. Perfect! I've never seen a plane so beautifully restored."

Kern beamed, took off his cowboy hat, and ran his hand through his sweaty, flaxen hair. I was laughing my ass off for him that morning. Kern saw me doing it, looked over and smiled, and started laughing at himself too. He looked ridiculous in that big ten-gallon hat he'd bought for himself. But he was happy and self-confident out here in the far reaches of Texas. I could see him changing and growing, it seemed, with every leg we completed, and he was a lot more fun to be with when he was relaxed on the ground like this. I couldn't get over how much I enjoyed being with him now.

"Ah, lookey here," the airport owner said. "Are you them boys from Nu Jursa? It's on the radio. Everybody's trying to find you two."

"Yeah. That's us," Kern said, but he felt a little sheepish about it. "Look. I'm just doing this to build time for my commercial license. We didn't do this for publicity."

"Oh it's okay!" the fellow said. "This'll be good for aviation, you know? They'll be a pack of people waiting for you once you get over the mountains this afternoon."

The airport owner was a licensed pilot who flew the Rockies all the time, mostly in big Cessnas and twin-engine planes. He went over the maps with Kern and me and showed us how to fly the Guadalupe Pass. From west Texas, it was better to cross northwest into New Mexico and launch for Guadalupe Peak from the north. Then we could head almost due south for the twin Guadalupe Peaks, flying a parallel course with the mountain range until we reached the pass. That way, the Guadalupe Range would protect us from the prevailing wind from the west until we were up above 9,000 feet. Facing the pass straight on for fifty miles would just expose us to heavy winds and leeward turbulence.

The owner at Sweetwater didn't discourage us from taking on the pass, but he didn't make it sound easy either. There were a couple of planes on the strip with 85-horse engines, a Luscombe and a Cessna 140, that had been through the pass, so it could be done. The big thing to watch, he said, was altitude loss. We should turn and face the pass about three or four miles out. If, during the first mile toward the pass, we could hold our altitude and course against the wind and the turbulence, we'd probably be okay. But if we started losing height and couldn't regain it, we should turn back right away.

He said one other thing that cheered us.

"It'll actually get better for you *inside* the pass. It's like the eye of a storm in there, a lot calmer. So, the last mile going in, when it's hell, just know it'll actually be better inside."

As we turned to go, Kern pulled out his wallet. We owed them for a new elevator spring, labor, a tank of gas, crackers and soda. The three of them just stared at us and smiled. They wouldn't take our money.

Kern tried to insist, but it was no use.

The owner removed his tattered ball-cap and ran his hand through his hair.

"Boys," he said, "Just go. Evrabaddy's real excited for you two. Fly hard, and you'll make the mountains by noon."

We refueled again at Wink, Texas, a tiny desert hamlet just south of the New Mexico border. The gas jockey there was a gaunt, unshaven ranchhand type with holes in his boots, filthy jeans, and a hideously sweat-stained straw hat. While I supervised the fueling, Kern walked across the ramp to stretch his legs.

"Ah, listen here fella," the gas jockey called out. "Check out the hangar."

Kern doubled back for the hangar, figuring that there must be some kind of nice airplane in there, a restored biplane or something, that the gas jockey wanted him to see.

As he filled the wing tank, the gas jockey kept looking over his shoulder toward my brother and the hangar, and he spilled gas on the fabric.

"Hey," I said. "You're spilling gas. Watch that wing."

"Frig the wing. Watch your brother."

"I said, watch that wing! You're spilling gas."

"And *I* said, watch your brother."

A sound like a hundred snare drums and cymbals going off all at once resounded from the hangar, echoing off the corrugated tin walls.

Kern came running out of that hangar almost airborne. His cowboy hat blew off, and his big brown eyes were as wide open with terror as the Gettysburg dead.

Crashing into the Cub's wing strut, Kern leaned on it for support. He was panting and heaving, trying to catch his breath. Meanwhile, the hangar in front of us was rattling and heaving with a deafening roar, like it was about to come loose from its foundation.

"Jesus Christ, Rinker. Jesus. Lord."

The gas jockey fell off the wing, laughing hard, a mad dervish of gas hose, 80-octane fuel and clattering ladder. Haw, haw, haw, haw! He hadn't laughed this hard in months, since he sent the last jackass in penny loafers into the same hangar.

"Snakes," my brother expelled. "Snakes. Hundreds of them, thousands. *Rattler snakes.*"

It was true. Still bending over with laughter, the gas jockey led us over to the hangar and we crept up to the shadowy interior by the door. He threw the door wide, and the roar of rattlers went off again, so loud I held my ears. There were thousands of rattlers in there, in wire cages stacked all along the walls, with a large, open pit near the far end crawling with a hundred or more snakes all twisted around and slithering over each other. Smaller, wooden cages, stacked in the middle of the floor, held a huge colony of breeding rats—rattler food. A few of the snakes from the open pit began slithering over for the door as soon as they saw the light poking in, and Kern and I jumped back.

My father had told us a story once from his Texas days, about a young air cadet returning late at night from a drunk in town. Against all standing orders he took a shortcut through the prairie and walked across a runway. From the barracks they heard his screams, and everyone scrambled into Jeeps and drove out there. The airman was already dead, scarred by more than a dozen rattler bites. To me, it was just more barnstorming blarney, typical of my father's need to concoct stranger, more macabre tales as his standard fare of tailspins and midair collisions wore thin over the years. Turns out, though, the one about the rattlers was true.

"Oh yeah, haven't you heard about this?" the gas jockey asked. "Don't you ever, ever cross a runway at night in Texas. Them rat'lers will get you before you ever see them."

Rattlers are heat-seeking reptiles. From the frequent deaths of their mates, most of them knew to keep off heavily trafficked roads at night. But small airport runways are generally deserted, and after sunset, when the desert cools quickly, the rattlers crawl by the hundreds onto the warm macadam strips. At Wink, and a number of other airports around, the owners had developed a lucrative second income, harvesting the snakes at night with ten-foot snake poles and selling them live by the pound to meat-packing plants in Dallas and San Antonio. In some parts of Texas, fresh snake meat was still considered a delicacy. But most of it was packed like tuna into cans and shipped to Asia. Once a month, a big semi rolled into Wink and hauled off the rattlers.

The chucklehead gas jockey had a fine time describing to everyone in the pilots' shack how he had scared the balls off another out-of-town pilot. But he had a fraction of decency left. One of the people inside told him that he'd heard about us on the radio, so he too wouldn't let us pay for our fuel either. We were on the freebie roll again, and everyone seemed to be behind our flight now, cheering us toward the mountains. As a makeup gift, the gas jockey gave us several tins of rattler meat.

"Coast to coast, huh?" the gas jockey said. "Well, good luck. Evrabaddy's rootin' for ya."

The heat was up, our height above sea level was now almost 3,000 feet, and it took us forever to get off the runway at Wink. The Cub dismally wallowed in the climb. We were just one hop away from launching for the pass, and we didn't want any extra weight. As soon as we were out of sight, mushing up over the gray-beige desert, we threw the tins of rattler meat out the window.

Now that we had reached the hard desert, we knew that we were supposed to follow one cardinal rule: remain over highways in case the engine acted up. But from Wink we would have to fly all the way back to Pecos to pick up a road. We looked at the map and decided to take a shortcut, flying northwest until we picked up the Pecos River, which we could follow up toward Loving and then into Carlsbad, New

Mexico. The midday heat had churned up some low cumulus clouds, which clung to the foothills of the Rockies in the distance, so we would have a decent horizon. We struck out over open desert for Carlsbad.

Kern let me fly, and I was enjoying it, skimming the bottom of the clouds in a Texas sky and ruddering over now and then to look for the Pecos River.

Whabang, Whabang, Whabang, bang, bang, bang, bang, bang, bang! Shit.

What was happening? Violent, irregular vibrations were shaking the plane.

The stick and rudder pedals trembled. The engine cowling up front leapt so violently on its mounts I was afraid that it was going to cut loose and cartwheel into the windshield. The airframe and fabric shook. We were finished, done for, fifty miles from the nearest airport over uninhabited desert, without so much as a dirt road underneath us. It was exactly the situation we had vowed to avoid. Instinctively I throttled back and slowed the plane.

Kern took the controls right away.

"Don't panic Rinker! We've still got an airplane here. Navigate. I want to know our exact position."

He inched the throttle forward and set up a slow flight at about sixty-five miles per hour, and we limped across the desert like that, saving every inch of height for as long as we could, with the front of the Cub banging violently and the floorboards trembling and vibrating underneath us.

We couldn't figure out what was wrong. The rpm on the tachometer was smooth and consistent, the oil pressure and temperature normal. The engine was responding well to the throttle. It was a partial engine failure of some kind, we guessed. Four-cylinder Continentals were famous for their endurance, even with a cylinder out. We knew of pilots who had kept damaged engines running for half an hour or more. But it didn't seem likely that we could make Carlsbad. The plane was shaking even more violently than before, and everything from the altimeter to the windows was rattling. And now the turbulence had picked up too, and it was very difficult to fly it properly in the slowed, vibrating plane. As the nose porpoised up and down, we were very uncomfortable, so drenched with sweat that our shirts were wet, and our hearts pounded along with the plane. While I looked for spots below where we might land, Kern struggled to keep the Cub straight and level and to maintain our altitude. He was extremely disciplined and levelheaded about that—he didn't want to lose an inch of altitude until we had decided what to do.

But it was a nauseating sensation, wallowing along in a wounded plane like that, and it was hard to resist the urge to just ditch the plane. It would be a relief, going down in the desert, and I began to sweat and tremble from that horrible claustrophobia known to pilots and their passengers in a panic. At any cost, I wanted out of that plane.

"Kern! We can put her down. If we ditch sideways and wipe out the wheels, we'll be fine."

"No! No Rink. I'm not ditching 71-Hotel. I've got an airplane here. I think we can make Carlsbad."

It was a hellish hour, getting to Carlsbad. But after about twenty minutes, by making minute adjustments to the throttle and trim, Kern found a kind of queasy, nose-up attitude that reduced the vibrations and the trembling of the controls. We were still being kited all over the place by turbulence but we could stand being in the plane.

But our trip was doomed. I knew that my brother was thinking the same thing. Every second that we ran the engine was only damaging it more. Even if we made it to an airport, we probably couldn't afford the repairs or, more likely, the new engine we'd need. We'd have to leave the plane in New Mexico and take a Greyhound bus home. The indignity of that seemed pathetic. Everybody knew about our trip by now, and it was going to end just east of the Rockies with engine failure. And what fools we'd been. Without a radio, we couldn't call in our position as we went down.

And the waterbag. The fucking waterbag. I looked down to the hard-tack desert below us. I wasn't the least bit worried about walking out—

we both could make the fifty or sixty miles to Loving, even in our penny loafers. But we probably wouldn't last until evening without water. Suddenly it seemed incredibly imbecilic for us *not* to have a waterbag, and incredibly wise for my father to have suggested one. We had boxed ourselves into exactly the situation he warned against. Barnstorming blarney had provided for this contingency, but we hadn't listened.

Whabang, Whabang, Whabang! Sticks and floorboard and baggage compartment thundering, we struggled over the desert.

Making agonizingly slow progress over the scorched and rocky wasteland below, we finally picked up the Pecos River and followed it north into Loving. But it was work, nasty, hot work, all the way. When the big strip at Carlsbad came into view, my brother pushed back his cowboy hat, rested his throttle hand on the instrument panel, and handed me back his Ray-Bans to wipe free of sweat.

"Rink! We're going to make it. We're fucked, but we've made it to an airport."

Waffling onto the runway at Carlsbad, we shut down the engine and coasted into a pile of tumbleweed on the side of the runway. I threw open the door and jumped out to inspect the engine.

As soon as I could see the plane from the outside I started to laugh.

"Kern! It's fine!"

"What?"

"It's just the cowling gasket! It blew off in flight. It's nothing! Just some ripped fabric."

The rubber and asbestos gasket that ran along the underside of the engine cowling and two of its three metal fittings were hanging down to the ground. Those fittings were another casualty of all the turbulence we'd flown the Cub through. In flight, one of the fittings had sprung loose, fell out into the slipstream and sucked the rest of the gasket out. Only one fitting held, and the rest of the assembly dangled out underneath the plane like a kite tail. The banging and vibrations were caused by the heavy metal fittings striking the landing gear and the underside of the plane as we flew along at over sixty miles per hour. The cowling was jumping up and down from the kite-tail effect of the heavy gasket and fittings billowing in the slipstream. This in turn set up secondary vibrations along the rest of the airframe that shook the plane.

The damage was relatively minor—a badly scraped landing gear, and a long, neat tear in the fabric underneath the plane—which we could probably fix ourselves. I was overjoyed that the plane wasn't damaged any more than that. But our assault on the mountains was delayed by at least a day.

But the airport breed, a crop-dusting man, in fact, saved us again. There was a large fleet of Piper Pawnee cropdusters from Seminole, Texas, working out of Carlsbad that week. They were spraying irrigated farms up around Artesia and Roswell. Every night the duster crew staged their planes back at Carlsbad for maintenance and repairs. A four-passenger Cessna-180, stuffed up past the windows with oil, parts, and tools, served as the operation's traveling shop.

When we pulled onto the Carlsbad ramp, dragging the broken gasket along the taxiway underneath us, the crew chief for the crop-dusting operation, a licensed mechanic, was lounging under the wing of the Cessna. He got up and strolled over for a look.

"Lost your gasket, huh?"

"Yeah," my brother said, trying to hide his disappointment.

"Hey," the duster chief said, "Are you them boys flying to California?"

"Well, we're supposed to be," Kern said.

"Jeez, it's a big deal now," the man said. "You're all over the radio. There's a bunch of reporters waitin' for you in El Paso. They called here lookin' for ya."

"I guess they'll have to wait until tomorrow," Kern said. "We've got to get this plane fixed."

"Tomorra? Whad'ya mean, tomorra?" the duster chief said. "It's just a gasket—window dressing, noise abatement, extra weight. On my Pawnees here, I rip 'em off as soon as they come from the factory."

This cheered us some, because a Pawnee was just a reconfigured and enlarged Cub, with a big engine thrown on front and the wings mounted on the bottom instead of the top. Probably this fellow knew what he was talking about.

To prove the point, the duster chief squatted beneath the cowling, pried off the remaining fitting with a screwdriver, and ceremoniously threw the dismembered gasket across the ramp.

"There," he said. "Now you've got a real airplane."

He looked underneath the Cub, walked over to his shop-plane, and came back with linen fabric tape, coffee cans of dope, and a blowtorch.

"Lookey-here," the duster chief said. "My planes are all up and I don't have a thang to do until tonight. If you boys are still game, I can have this Cub airborne in an hour."

"Really?" Kern exclaimed. "That would be great."

"It's nothing. Go get yourselves some pop."

The duster chief gave the underside of 71-Hotel what he called a "hot patch." His Pawnees were hitting sage brush and hopper trucks all the time, ripping tears in the fabric, and the operation lost too much money if they kept a plane out of the air all day just to patch some fabric and let the dope dry. So he "hot-patched" fabric all the time.

Slapping a length of linen tape over the tear in the fabric and painting on some dope, he gingerly flamed it dry and hard with the blowtorch. Two coats of nitrate, torch it, two coats of butyrate, torch it. He even produced a spray can of official Piper white paint and touched up the patch and the scrapes on the landing gear. When he was done, we couldn't even tell that the plane had been damaged.

"Okeydokey," the duster chief said. "That patch ain't never comin' off. My Pawnees? The hot patches are the strongest part."

That duster chief liked Kern. I could tell from the way the corners of his mouth trembled when he smiled that he got a big charge out of my brother. He couldn't resist a boy this earnest, all sunburn and freckles, the penny loafers and the man's cowboy hat on a boy's head, sticking out like a burro's ears.

"Son," the duster chief said, "Anything else bothering you?"

Kern took off his cowboy hat.

"Well, the engine, sir. We've just really pushed it hard across the desert—all those vibrations and everything. We're going to fly the mountains this afternoon. What do you think?"

"Stand by," the duster chief said. "I'm giving this Cub an annual inspection, right now. Go inside in the shade and relax. I said an hour and I meant it."

Kern was fiddling with the cowboy hat in his hands.

"Ah, well see. I don't think we have enough money for an annual."

"Ah, frig your money son. This is nothing for me. I can do an annual faster than a skunk can piss scent."

We knew a good mechanic when we saw one. If there was anything wrong with the Continental, we were confident that the duster chief would find it.

The duster chief brought his toolbox over from the Cessna and threw open our engine cowling. He pulled all the rocker arm covers, the plugs, and the filters, checking carefully for metal filings and other tell-tale signs of trouble. He ran compression checks on the cylinders, and went over the magneto ignitions, the wiring, the manifolds, and the carburetor. He didn't like the way the Continental was idling up at these high altitudes, so he propped the engine himself and adjusted the mixture and timing.

We used that time to plan our flight across the pass. It was a Tuesday afternoon, and there weren't any local pilots or geezers around Carlsbad that afternoon. They would have told us that there was one major fault in our plans. We were planning on launching toward a 9,000-foot mountain at the height of density altitude conditions. It was two in the afternoon, when the heat, turbulence, and headwinds were at their worst. We should have waited until evening, or better, the next morning, when a lower sun and cooling temperatures might have given us another 500 or 600 feet of service ceiling. But we didn't think of this ourselves and we were determined to fly as soon as the mechanic was done. It was the worst time of day to do it, a foolhardy moment to attempt our ascent.

Our route of flight was obvious. We could see that we'd pick up the bottom of the Rockies as soon as we took off from Carlsbad. A southwest-running spine of peaks lay just a few miles from the field, and it climbed steeply up toward Guadalupe Peak. As the airport owner back in Sweetwater had told us, the ridge line of the peaks would protect us from the worst winds during our long climb. On the map, the terrain-colorings changed as dramatically as we would have to fly, from the soft beiges and grays of the 4,000-foot desert floor to the ugly smudge of orange and black peaks that rapidly swept up to 9,000 feet. But we would need more than that to safely cross the Pass— 10,000, 11,000, even 12,000 feet, whatever we could coax out of 71-Hotel. We knew that we faced a difficult hour of flying, but we weren't raising any objections against ourselves. We'd flown too hard all day to turn away from the mountains now.

The duster chief called us out to the Cub. Everything was fine, he said. The compression on the cylinders was strong and he'd only found one plug that was fouled with oil, ordinary enough on an old Continental engine, and he'd cleaned that and regapped the spark. As we took off and climbed, he said, we'd be surprised by the extra noise. Without the cowl gasket, the engine would roar. But it was only noise and we'd get used to it after fifteen or twenty minutes. In fact, the engine would run a little cooler and better without the cowl gasket, because more air could get through now.

Kern went for his wallet.

"Look, maybe I should just try and pay you what I can afford. I want to be fair about this."

"Put that away son," the duster chief said. "What you owe me is that mountain. Get across. This trip of yours is gettin' kinda famous. There's people waitin' in El Paso."

It was a wonderful feeling I had for people, the afternoon we launched for the pass. All day, all week in fact, strangers were buying us meals, giving us free tanks of gas, fixing up our plane, and cheering us on west. I was afraid of that peak ahead, and I admit it. But I wanted that mountain now—not for myself, not even for Kern and me together. Everybody had been good to us and expected us to get across, so now we had to pay them back and do this thing.

There's one last memory I have of Carlsbad, New Mexico.

Under the baking sun, with the desert wind pasting my hair to my perspiring forehead, I stood underneath the tail of 71-Hotel and held it level to the ground on my shoulders. Kern was up in front of the wing on a ladder, fueling the tank himself. He wanted the plane level so that he could squeeze in every last ounce of fuel. It was only sixty miles to the pass. But we'd be climbing at full throttle all the way.

Guadalupe.

Looking south from the Carlsbad ramp, I could see the purple-black rim of mountains towering up toward the peak. I wasn't going to like it up there one bit, I knew, but then Kern yelled from the cockpit and it was time to go.

"Contact!"

Kern. Somehow he always got us through. My only choice now was to grit my teeth and fly, so I threw the prop, ran around to the back, and strapped myself in.

The runway elevation at Carlsbad was 3,293 feet above sea level. We could see right away what the high altitude conditions and the scorching heat did to 71-Hotel's performance. Wallowing down the sticky macadam, we ate up nearly a third of the runway before we labored into the air. This was not a good omen for our assault on Guadalupe.

The sun at its zenith burned through our glareshield and the engine roared louder than ever through the opening created by the missing gasket. Kern gingerly climbed us up to a safe height above the desert plateau. At 1,000 feet, once he could see that the engine was running smoothly, he hauled back on the stick and hung the plane on its prop. We would need a very high "angle of attack" to climb in this thin, hot air. Uncomfortably nose-high, throbbing with the vibrations of the straining Continental, we would not see over the nose again for more than an hour.

The black wall of the Rockies rose on our right, climbing higher and

higher as the range slewed southwest. It presented a tantalizing, maddening barrier. Each time the altimeter bobbled up another few hundred feet, up past 4,000, 6,000, then 8,000 feet, we looked directly out
the side and found ourselves nearly level with a conical summit, or a
jagged, naked pinnacle of rock. Over the mountain, there was a slice of
clear air and we could see to the west. But the sensation of space
opening up and the joy of seeing over to the other side was always
short-lived. There was always more wall rising ahead of us to the right,
black-gray and sandy, with spectacular rockslides and grotesque outcrops and false ridges that made my mind race. The Rockies were a
quandary, both beautiful and cruel. How could mountains be so end-
lessly enticing to the eye, yet so impassable?

As we climbed we were rifled by the westerlies, which lifted up the
right wing and resounded over the fabric like a drum roll. The wind
slammed against the far side of the mountain, rocketed straight up and
over the peaks and then roiled up thousands of feet more in a magnif-
icent, invisible volcano, depositing down on us its leeward turbulence.
We were ascending into a furious eddy of air that stretched all the way
down the range. The pounding from the west was so continuous that
my brother flew with the right aileron pushed up to keep the wing
down, keeping the plane straight with the opposite rudder, so that we
climbed in a queasy-feeling slip. The high angle of climb we were
forced to maintain against the steadily thinning air was disorienting.
Now I was attacked by the worst kind of vertigo, one of my own mental creation. From his position up front, my brother could still see the
peaks out of a portion of his windshield. But my view was almost completely blocked by the pitched-up nose and the downed wing, and I
hated the agonizing feeling of a mountain that I couldn't see rising to
my side. I was sitting at the bottom of an obtuse triangle that had been
turned awkwardly on its side. At the apex, up over my brother's head,
there was only clear sky, burned white by the sun. Over my right knee,
I looked straight down to the rocks.

But once in a while the wind pounded us hard enough to lift the
wing again, and then I could steal a quick glance left into the tepid

slipstream. We were inching along the little blacktop highway that paralleled the east face of the mountains, down through Carlsbad Caverns, Whites City, and Pine Springs. With the steep climb, the engine developing only two-thirds of its power in the thin air, and the wind pushing us back from the range, our progress was excruciating. At best we made only fifty miles per hour over the ground. And we were alone, completely alone. Everything below us was lifeless—hardbed desert on one side, colorless rock on the other. There wasn't even a passing car that I could judge our progress by. We were punishing ourselves and our plane fruitlessly, it seemed. Our fuel would be exhausted by the climb, leaving nothing for the pass.

Kern didn't seem to notice. As we clawed up in that queer climb, I looked forward to him, perched high above me, almost over my head. His cowboy hat, nonchalantly pushed back on his head, bumped up against the cockpit struts whenever we hit turbulence. With his left hand he held the throttle all the way forward in a lock-grip, and with his right hand he kept up the nose with the stick firmly in his lap. I begged him with my racing heart and trembling limbs to feel my agony and discomfort. Then he might level the wings and lower the nose. We could turn back now, before we were inside the mountains and it was too late. My brother did look back several times, quickly, so that he didn't lose control of the plane, flashing that determined half-smile of his. But I didn't want to show him how I felt so I smiled gamely and gave him two thumbs up.

It wasn't simply bravado, or reluctance to betray my cowardice to my brother. The sun and the throbbing plane, the mountains rising unseen over my right shoulder, surrounded me in a kind of hallucinogenic chamber, carrying me beyond myself. This was fear becoming spiritual. I wanted that mountain badly, and the pulsating cockpit and the sun were lulling me into a senseless, anesthetized state that blurred out fright.

During that climb, I thought a lot about Saint-Ex and Ernest Gann again. Nothing in particular in their writings came back to me, and in any case I was too dulled by the throbbing, engine and airframe to recall their books clearly. I just thought of Saint-Ex and Gann, the men.

They were always scaring the hell out of themselves in airplanes, then coming back down and transforming the experience into metaphysical poetry. They were very candid about their fears in the air. Saint-Ex was even candid about his own death, which he expected at any time. In his last book, *Flight to Arras*, written while he was a fighter pilot during World War II, Saint-Ex analyzed his chances of surviving the war and concluded that they were nil. He prepared himself and his reading public for his inevitable demise by creating the impression that he was indifferent to his fate—no one should even search for him once he was downed. The only purpose in his life had been the existential search for meaning in the air. Dead, there was no point to Saint-Ex anymore. This was prescient enough. Returning from a mission over North Africa in 1943, Saint-Ex was jumped from behind by German fighters, who filled his P-38 full of holes before he could lose them. He fell to a watery, unknown grave somewhere in the Mediterranean, and no trace of him or his plane was ever found. Saint-Ex appeared to have willed the ultimate existential act. He had vanished, and the only part of him that was left was his writings. Would he know fear during his last moments? He didn't know. He only knew that he felt resigned to death, thinking about it on the ground.

These were the kind of dreamy, melancholy thoughts I had, inching up to the peak. The effects of the heat, the throbbing of the plane, and the lack of oxygen brought a lot of this on, I suppose, but the worst part was not being able to see out the side. Once we cleared 9,500 feet though, and I could see a clear patch of air for a while, I felt better. The important thing, I told myself, was keeping my head and making myself available if Kern needed any help.

It was chilly up at 10,000 feet. Neither of us had ever flown a plane that high. Judging the distance from an intersection on the road below, I guessed that we were now approaching Pine Springs and the cut through the mountains. Without asking my brother I reached forward on both sides and pulled shut the windows. It was a shock, closing off that slipstream. The absence of wind blowing over my face only made my vertigo worse, and my arms and legs trembled involuntarily.

At 10,500 feet my brother leveled the wings and the Guadalupe Pass came into view. The pass was an immense V, opening up between the twin Guadalupe peaks, more than a mile across at the top. At the summits, black, vertically crenellated sides guarded the opening, but lower down the slopes rounded out and softened to a soothing beige. Rockslides and windblown sand collected in the crevices and overflowed to the valley floor. The ferocious headwinds ripping through the cut blew up a hazy inferno of vapor and dust. We could already feel the first ripples from the wind tunnel ahead—sharp, choppy buffets and powerful, elongated downdrafts.

We were still three miles from the pass, flying a parallel course with the mountains, so that the peaks themselves appeared to us at right angles. Even though our altimeter read above 10,000 feet, which should have put us well above the summits, they still looked higher than we were. At the time I thought that our sideways angle distorted the view, but we later realized that the density altitude conditions contributed to a large altimeter error, by as much as 1,000 feet. In fact, we were still below the peaks. In any case it was an academic question. Though we remained in a climb and we were penetrating an ascending column of air, the Cub was nearly maxed out before we reached the mountains. We would gain only another 900 feet.

When we were directly opposite the big space of hazy air in the middle of the V, my brother hove over 90 degrees, to directly face the pass and the headwind. The wings immediately answered to the force of wind and pushed the nose up even higher. Momentarily leaving the throttle unattended, my brother yanked hard on his seat belt.

"Rink! Pull your harness tight!"

"It's tight!"

"Well pull it harder. Here we go!"

Perhaps we waited three seconds for the first belt of turbulence to hit us. Perhaps it was thirty seconds. But time soon meant nothing. Once it hit, all time ceased.

Whong!

It happened very quickly and violently. One second we were level and facing the pass, squinting down out the sides to see the clear patch of V ahead of us, the next second we were down so hard on the left wing that the tip was pointed straight onto the desert, 90 degrees over. Sky, desert, and mountain wall gyrated around as in a centrifuge. From the force of the blast, our shoulders banged up against the throttle casement and our feet momentarily went weightless off the rudder pedals.

It was a physically arduous thing, getting out of it. My brother lunged forward with the stick to arrest a stall, pushed hard over on the ailerons and rudder, and waited for something to happen. There was no determined half-smile now. He was scrambling up there, fighting G-forces with his arms and legs, to get the plane upright again. But we were now so high, over 11,000 feet on the altimeter, and the force of the blast was so strong, that the controls simply wouldn't answer. In that high, thin air, there literally weren't enough molecules passing over the controls to receive our commands. Our Cub just wasn't meant to be that high. Unbelievably, the wing tucked under even farther, and we hung there motionless and weightless for a few seconds more, suspended on one side and almost inverted, before the plane slowly righted itself.

Damn. We'd lost 300 feet. Kern felt the stick for flying speed and hauled back again on the nose to regain the lost altitude. We had just enough time to catch our breath before the next blast hit.

We were just a fisherman's cork bobber, severed from the line, careening over white water and rocks. The next two miles to the pass were like that, our wings rocking violently over, against which our flimsy controls seemed almost powerless. But by skittering and jockeying the stick sideways in a kind of mad wiggle and dance, my brother kept us tracking straight toward the middle of the pass.

This area just outside the pass was the notorious back quadrant, where the wind racing through the cut had already boiled over itself many times, churning up a wake turbulence on itself. The wind and the air disturbances here are generally worse than within the pass itself. As we got closer to the mountain wall, about a mile off, we began to probe a calmer patch of air. Now the wings were slamming over only 20 or 30 degrees.

I still didn't see how we'd make it. The peaks looming on either side, just ahead, were still above us. The winds and the downdrafts kept beating us back. Passing 11,500 feet, Kern dipped the nose a bit to penetrate the headwind and make some forward progress. Then he hauled back again to regain the altitude. But as soon as he lifted the nose we got beaten back once more. We were just crawling to the pass, motionless in the headwind, like crabs scrambling up a beach in the intervals of waves, then spinning backward again in the receding surf.

Now the steep sides of the V were clearly visible just ahead of us, a fractured and veined massif of rock sloping up to meet us. In the turbulence, we were often pitched sideways, nose down. The aperture of the pass was quite narrow down below and didn't fill the windshield, so that it didn't seem possible that we could fit through. From these strange, uncontrolled attitudes, immense boulders and broken-toothed pillars of rock came into view, as if they were spinning up sideways to meet us. Individual rocks boldly stood out from the mass—I felt that I could see every pit mark and sandy abrasion. From a distance the pass had a harsh beauty. Closer in, it was ugly and gritty.

Hypoxia, or aeroembolism as the old pilots called it, is oxygen starvation. We had now been flying at 10,000 feet or above for over half an hour, the period of time it normally takes for pilots to feel the effects of oxygen denial. We had been concerned enough about hypoxia while crossing the mountains to discuss it several times before the trip, but it is typical of hypoxia that pilots forget all that they have learned once they are suffering from it. Hypoxia can work oppositely on different pilots. Some pilots become euphoric, swell with a sense of well-being and want to climb their plane even higher. Others turn morose and lethargic and are flooded with panic. As a flying team we were suffering both effects. I was definitely of the darker persuasion. Frightened and claustrophobic in the glassed-in interior of the plane, desperate to see again over the nose, I was boiling and shivering all over at once. Kern up front seemed content, and his smile had returned. He was happy to finally be in the mountains and a calmer patch of air.

Kern never seemed to lose his flying sense either. Fishtailing with the rudders, dipping the nose a bit and then goosing back with the stick, he worked to squeeze out of the plane and the wind every last foot of air.

Now it didn't matter how either of us felt. We were inside the pass, and the edge of the mountain range on either side of us had disappeared. Ahead we could only see burned white sky, ugly walls of sand, and black veined rock. North and south had ceased to exist; there was just an east-west hole in the rock. We couldn't turn back now, because the walls looming up on either side of us were too close, denying us a turning radius. And if we'd given up the wind on our nose, we would immediately have plunged to the rocks.

That final entry into the pass was a hallucinogenic blur for me. There was so much heat and noise in the cockpit, the glareshield above my head looked too hot to touch, and now the walls on either side of the pass tumbled up, quite close. There were moments when I looked out and the twin peaks were more or less level with us, and other moments when we were in a downdraft and they disappeared above the top of the wing. I felt exhausted, wanting to cry, but not wanting to, overwhelmed by a desire to escape into sleep.

I'd read about this, too, in war books, and Robert L. Scott in *God Is My Co-pilot* had written about it. In the middle of the worst combat mission he'd ever flown, or struggling to hoist an overloaded DC-3 over the Himalayas, suddenly he would be overwhelmed by the urge just to give up and fall off to sleep.

Yet with panic arrived a great inner calm and resignation. My father and my brother had been too cavalier about this. It wasn't safe taking on the Rocky Mountains in an 85-horse Cub. So what? Cratering into the walls would be immensely pleasurable right now. I wouldn't fight it, and the experience would be interesting, extrasensory, even. In a hurry, it would end this misery of light-headed, claustrophobic flight.

I was startled awake from this torpid fatalism by my brother calling back.

"Rinker! Take the controls."

"What?"

"Take the stick! It's your airplane! My arms have given out. I can't hold it up anymore."

My heart must have doubled its output just then, because I was instantly awake. Kern needed me to fly, and I was overjoyed to be able to do so, as if I had been thrown a life-rope. Gaining control of the plane, I knew, would revive me.

I grabbed the stick in my lap, wiggling it and the rudders a bit to show him that I had the plane. He immediately stretched out his arms and cracked his knuckles, then began massaging his muscles. Clutching the struts over his head, he leaned forward over the instrument panel and peered out to the walls of the pass.

"I'm going to keep a real careful eye on these peaks," Kern yelled back. "You fly."

I was shocked by what I found. I caressed the controls forward and back to feel the play of air over the wings. There was almost nothing there. In that high air, we were flying just a few miles an hour above the stall. The great wind on our nose was the only thing holding us up.

We flew that way through the rest of the pass. It could have been six minutes, or twelve, or twenty. It doesn't matter. Time had disappeared. I fought the turbulence and the downdrafts and kept the wings level, and didn't give up an inch of height. I was fixated on altitude, an anti-dote for my hypoxia, or maybe a symptom of it. When my brother handed me the plane, the altimeter read 11,600 feet, and I was deter-mined not to lose a foot.

"Eleven-six."

That was my mantra. Eleven-six. I wasn't going to give an inch back to this mountain.

"Eleven-six," I kept repeating to myself, drunk on those numbers.

I constantly peered forward to the altimeter on the instrument panel up front, whacking my brother on his shoulder when he let it get in the way. The little hand on the dial couldn't move off that 6, and when it did, I wiggled and fish-tailed and nudged the stick to move the nose into better wind, to get us back up.

"Eleven-six. Eleven-six. Eleven-six."

My other fixation was my throttle hand. There was only one place for the throttle to be—all the way forward. I braced my arm in a lock-grip against it and never once relaxed the pressure.

It was an odd, wondrous experience, flying like that. Kern had handed the plane over to me, so matter of factly. Now we were so nose-high that he was perched almost directly on top of me, as if I were following him up a ladder. I didn't worry at all about our position against the peaks because I could see him peering attentively from side to side. He was alert, in control, and I was gratified every time he showed the slightest movement, because it showed that he wasn't keeling over from hypoxia, which would have left me all alone with the plane. He gave me hand signals from the instrument panel, or reached back and squeezed my legs, steering me left or right as we crawled past the outcrops inside the pass. He was the eyes, and I was the flying arms and legs. With him riding above me like that, and the throbbing, pulsating plane and the winds, I was an Atlas holding the whole works up, hoisting us over the pass.

I was very confident too, and all dangerous, indolent thoughts of cratering into the sides left me. We could easily make the rest of the pass, flying this way. There was still a lot of flying to do, and turbulence to fight, but I was euphoric about our progress so far and the rest of the challenge, now that there was some adrenaline flowing from me to the plane.

I was still deprived of vision and couldn't see much. All I was doing, really, was staring straight up over Kern's head to polarized sky, and fixating on the altimeter and Eleven-six. I coordinated the stick entirely by seat-of-the-pants feel and the altimeter and airspeed indicator. I couldn't see the sides of the pass anymore because the angle of the wings was too high, blocking my view out the side. But I trusted Kern up front to correctly judge our distance from the walls. With transcendent happiness and belief, I just hung on and flew Eleven-and-six.

Eleven-and-six. Eleven-and-six. I held it for as long as I thought I could stand it, but still we weren't through the pass yet and I held it some more. My arms were starting to hurt but I didn't want to give up the plane until I absolutely had to. The far-side turbulence was supposed to be awfully bad too, and I wanted Kern fresh and rested for that. That cheered me some too, because I realized I was suffering the effects of hypoxia but I still had enough left to think.

Buffet-jolt, buffet-jolt, wham-wham-wham. This was very different turbulence now, unique, very choppy and quick, with violent sideways movement that shook the stick. Good. I never welcomed a spot of bad air so much, because this meant that we were beginning to hit the rotor turbulence on the far side.

I could do this for another minute, I thought. Summoning that last ounce of strength beyond all strength, I flexed my muscles against the throttle and the stick and counted to sixty.

"Kern! Are we through?"

"Just about! Just about."

"All right! Listen, take back the plane."

"It's my airplane!"

My body cracked with relief. My throttle arm was as hard as cast iron and there were spasms and coils in my shoulders and hips, from the mental and physical tension of holding up the plane. But there wasn't any room in that tiny cockpit to stretch myself out, so I just sat there like a scarecrow in the wind, bobbing and jerking on a stick.

We had enough presence of mind to remain high for another ten minutes. If we tried to descend through the hellgate of air on the windward side, the violent downdrafts would suction us back into the mountain. So we just hung up there as long as we could stand it, bong, bong, bong, bong in that awful air, Eleven-six, Eleven-six, hating with every bone in our bodies the God who made mountains. But I was mentally at rest, now that I knew we were past the peaks and that my brother had the plane. I closed my eyes and leaned my head on the window railing, exhausted and physically drained but satisfied with myself. I waited for the calm air to return and the sound of the engine idling as my brother let us down.

Finally, gulping in air as we fell, we dove for oxygen and the desert floor on the far side. It was a visual relief to finally be able to see out through the windshield and the side windows, and I realized that I must have dozed off for a few minutes as Kern held us up through the rotors. We were clear of the mountains now.

In the desert just beyond the pass there were shallow salt flats filled with water, a blue meringue shining under the sun, stretching north and south. Tiny white caps and gently swirling pools lapped up against sand, an exotic, bizarre marine display after so much time staring at desert and hard rock. The air above the liquid flats was cool, and it cleared our heads. Over desolate mesquite country, we steered due west for El Paso, seventy miles away.

We were immensely contented now, enjoying the kind of deep, peaceful sense of well-being that is nourished by delivery from danger and fatigue. The big barrier, the only real obstacle that stood between us and the Pacific, had been crossed. Since November, and more intensely since May, I had worried about the Rockies. I didn't see how we could possibly cross them in a Piper Cub. Now we'd finally done it, even if I couldn't account for the aerodynamics of it. We were done and through, and there was no further need to figure it carefully and subject our crossing to logical analysis. It wasn't logical at all, in fact it was downright irrational, what we'd just accomplished. I would never know how close we came to killing ourselves getting through that pass, because my side vision wasn't adequate enough to judge that. Maybe we flew the mountains perfectly, maybe not so well. But none of that really mattered now because we were whole, on the far side. The gateway to California had been breached. I was overjoyed that it was behind us.

The country was changing again. The blacks and hard yellows of the high desert were giving way to the tessellated ochers and painted sands of the low desert on the western side of the Rockies. The country was falling toward the ocean again. The flying was easy and Kern shook the stick when we came up on a ranch, and I took the plane and dropped down to buzz the cows.

El Paso rose out of the desert like an emerald. Glittering roofs, green lawns and yucca trees were framed by the graceful, sweeping oxbow of the purple Rio Grande. It was the first habitation of any size we'd seen since Pittsburgh.

Our fuel cork was riding on EMPTY again, but we felt inured to worry now. We had the windows open and all the way across the mesquite I kept glancing back over the tail to the fading wall of the Rockies and the two peaks guarding the pass, until they disappeared into the blue meringue of water on the salt flats.

Guadalupe. Before that day I always thought of Exupéry and Ernest Gann, and the early airmail pilots who flew the pass, as distant, heroic figures, brave men who conquered peaks. They seemed very aloof to me and I could never emulate them. Now I felt closer to them all, and I had learned something else. It wasn't bravery. Bravery isn't what it's cracked up to be. They were just stubborn, that's all, and afterward they were very tired.

from Carrying the Fire:
An Astronaut's Journeys
by Michael Collins

Space flight was still a new and uncertain enter-prise in 1966, when Michael Collins (born 1930) and John Young roared off Pad 19 atop a Titan rocket. Collins' description of his space walk between their Gemini craft and an Agena satellite three days into the mission shows just how sketchy things often got up there.

As dawn arrives, I am precisely on schedule and ready to go. It never occurs to me that the ground might not agree. "Gemini 10 . . . you have a GO for the rest of the stationkeeping." John sounds a bit nonplussed. "Roger. How about the EVA? You want it?" "That's what we mean exactly." "Glad you said that, because Mike's going outside right now." And so I am. My first job is to get back behind the cockpit next to Thruster 16, where the nitrogen valve is and where a micrometeorite detection plate has been exposed for the past two days. I remove the plate with no difficulty, making sure that John doesn't fire 16 while my hand is practically crammed down its nozzle. "Watch that thruster there, babe. All right, don't translate down. I'm by it." "O.K.," John replies, but not O.K. for long, as it's not more than a few seconds before he blurts, "Well, babe, if I don't translate soon, we're going to run into that buzzard." I have no idea where the Agena is, as I am facing the side of the Gemini with my feet lazily swinging back and forth as I try to make my way along a handrail with the micrometeorite plate in one hand. I guess I'm far enough away from 16 now. Or am I? "Wait! O.K., go ahead." I now manage to reach the cockpit, hand the plate in to John through the open hatch, and then start back to connect my gun to its nitrogen supply. Again I warn John, "Don't translate down," and again I get the same answer, "O.K., we're going to hit this thing if we can't translate down pretty soon." I get out of the way. "Go ahead, translate down now. You're pretty clear." John gets a new idea. "Hey! Can we back out a little?" I don't care about those thrusters, I'm not near them. "Yes, go ahead, you want to go down?" "No, I want to back out." "O.K., back out. O.K. Don't go down until I tell you."

My problem is that there are two handrails, one raised manually by me, and the other, which is supposed to pop up automatically. I have raised the former prior to retrieving the micrometeorite plate, but the latter has only popped up at one end, the end farthest away from the cockpit, and the near end is still almost flush with the skin of the Gemini. My plan calls for winding my nitrogen line under the handrail and then connecting it to the nitrogen valve, but clearly there is not enough room to get the bulky nitrogen connector under the flattened rail, despite a couple of good healthy tugs. Finally, I decide to make the connection without the loop under the rail. I remove the cover plate from the nitrogen valve, get positioned as best I can, using the two handrails to torque my body into place directly above the valve; and then, holding a rail in my right hand and the connector in my left, I ram the connector down onto its mate. Missed! The sleeve on the connector has sprung forward and must be recocked (a two-handed operation). In the meantime, the reaction to my shove has caused my body to lurch over to one side, and my legs bang up against the side of the spacecraft. John feels the commotion and so does the Gemini's control system, which resents the unwanted swaying motion I am creating and fires thrusters to restore itself to an even keel. "Boy, Mike, those thrusters are really firing." What can I say? "O.K." John continues, "Take it easy back there, right?" I'm trying, as I am now poised for another stab at the nitrogen connector. When my body is in the right position once again, I quietly release both hands and—floating free for a second—reach down and recock the connector, find the handrail again, and give the connection another shove. Made it! "O.K. I'm hooked into the nitrogen." "O.K.," says John.

Now we have to contend with the floating loop in the nitrogen line, which is the result of my having hooked it up without first detouring it around under the handrail. If the slack is not taken up, it will assuredly drift over on top of good old Thruster 16 and get severed just when I need it. The solution lies in the cockpit. "I'm coming back into the cockpit area for just a second here." John is apparently drifting away from the Agena, because he replies, "O.K, I have to translate up. O.K.?" "All right. Just a second. O.K., go ahead. Translate up, that's all right. See that loose nitrogen line? You're going to have to snub that down some place. Can you do that?" "Where is it?" I dangle it down inside the open right hatch. "See it?" "Yes." "Got it?" "Yes." I don't know what he's going to do with it, sit on it if necessary, but he's in a better position to cope with it than I. Perhaps we can trade jobs for a moment. "Good boy. O.K., I'll watch the Agena while you take care of the nitrogen line. O.K.?" As I hang on to the open right hatch, I look up and slightly to my right at the Agena, which must be twenty feet away. I can't see the earth, only black starless sky behind the Agena, so I guess the earth must be somewhere behind me. I realize with a start that I have not been conscious of the earth one instant since I opened the hatch; I really don't care where it is; all I care about is assembling the claptrap I require to get over to that Agena and retrieve that micrometeorite package. The position of the earth is immaterial. So is our speed, which is nearly eighteen thousand miles per hour; but so what? What counts is our speed relative to the Agena, not relative to the earth. "O.K., I've got it secured." John has solved the nitrogen line problem and is now maneuvering us closer to the Agena. "What I'm trying to do is put you right next to it." Great! Peering out through his tiny window over on the left side, John edges us slowly forward and upward toward the end of the Agena, the end with the micrometeorite equipment on it. But now he comes to his limit. "If I get in closer to it,

I won't be able to see you or it." I can see it just fine, not having to peer out through John's paltry window, and I can tell we are in good position. "O.K., I can almost leap right now, but I'd rather not if you can get a little bit closer. I'll give you directions, John . . . John?" It takes John two seconds to decide. "O.K." I take John forward from fifteen feet . . . ten feet . . . six feet—he's blind now, as the Agena is almost directly over my head. "O.K., better stop right there, John." "O.K." I want him to back out a bit now, but he will be doing it without me. "Translate aft. O.K., you're in a good position. I'm going to leap for her, John." In a soft, fatherly voice he lets me go. "Take it easy, babe." "O.K."

Gently, gently, I push away from Gemini, hopefully balancing the pressure of my right hand on the open hatch with that of my left hand on the spacecraft itself. As I float out of the cockpit, upward and slightly forward, I note with relief that I am not snagged on anything but am traveling in a straight line with no tendency to pitch or yaw as I go. It's not more than three or four seconds before I collide with my target, the docking adapter on the end of the Agena. A cone-shaped affair with a smooth edge, it is a lousy spot to land, because there are no ready handholds, but this is the end where the micrometeorite package is located and, after all, that is what I have come so far to retrieve. I grab the slippery lip of the docking cone with both hands and start working my way around it counterclockwise. It takes about 90 degrees of handwalking in stiff pressurized gloves to reach the package. As I move I dislodge part of the docking apparatus, an electric discharge ring which springs loose, dangling from one attaching point. It looks like a thin scythe with a wicked hook, two feet in diameter. I don't know what will happen if I become ensnarled in it; I suspect it is fragile and will pull loose easily from the Agena, but on the other hand, it *is* made out of metal of some sort . . . Best I stay clear of it. By this time, I have reached the package, and now I must stop. But, I'm falling off! I have built up too much momentum, and now the inertia in my torso and legs keeps me moving; first my right hand, and then my left, feels the Agena slither away, despite my desperate clutch. As I slowly cartwheel away from the Agena, I see absolutely nothing but black sky for several seconds, and then the Gemini hoves into view. John has apparently watched all this in silence, but now he croaks, "Where are you, Mike?" "I'm up above. You don't want to sweat it. Only don't go any closer if you can help it. O.K.?" "Yes."

Where I am slowly comes into view and perspective. I am up above the Gemini about fifteen or twenty feet, in front of it and looking down at John's window and my own open hatch. I must be just out of John's view. The Agena is below me to my left, and slightly behind me. A loop of my umbilical is stretched out menacingly toward the fouled front end of the Agena, which is why I don't want John to get any closer, but that is a very ephemeral worry, because I am moving so as to take the slack out of the umbilical, moving up and to my right on the end of my cord. My motion is taking me away from the Agena, but it is tagential relative to the Gemini, which is not pleasant, because the laws of physics tell me that as I get closer to it (as my radius decreases), my velocity will increase and I may splat up against it at a nasty rate of speed. This conservation of angular momentum is what causes twirling ice skaters to spin faster as they pull their arms in closer to their bodies. This isn't what I had in mind. Fortunately, I have my gun, my maneuvering unit, stuck on my hip. It can nullify, or at least reduce, my tangential velocity so that I can safely make it back to the Gemini. I reach for it. It's gone! I grope until I find the hose leading to it, and discover the gun isn't really gone, it's just trailing out behind me. I reel in the hose, open the arms of the gun, and start hosing. I am squirting nitrogen out through two tiny nozzles pointed in a direction I have selected to (1) reduce my tangential velocity, (2) increase my radial velocity toward the Gemini, and (3) keep me pointed toward the Gemini. By the time I begin this procedure, I have swung up higher above the Gemini and off to its right, so that it is now low down to my left and I am moving off toward the rear of it. The gun is not capable of changing this path entirely, but it does modify it enough so that I come sailing around in a slow arc and straighten out as I fly behind the Gemini, a location I have never intended to explore. "I'm back behind the cockpit, John, so don't fire any thrusters." "O.K., we have to go down, if we want to stay with it." "Don't go down right now. *John, do not go down."* If he does, it will not only fire thrusters near me, but, worse yet, it will cause my target to sink below me just at the moment I am having difficulty getting down to it. "O.K.," he says. Now things are getting better: I am approaching the cockpit from the rear, and I have only that one thruster next to the nitrogen valve to worry about. "O.K., John, do not fire that one bad thruster, O.K.?" "Which one bad one?" It's no time for numbers games! "You know, the one that squirts up." "Oh, 16."

My approach to the Gemini isn't exactly graceful, and it's still a bit too swift for my liking, but as I reach the open hatch, I snag it with one arm and it slows me practically to a stop. It is now a simple matter to get the umbilical cord pulled in, and to stuff it and myself back inside the open hatch. Time for another try. "O.K., John. Want to give it a new try over there?" "Yes." "O.K., let's try it one more time." "O.K" This time I decide to use my gun to translate over to the Agena, so John doesn't have to fly so close to it that he loses an important part of his visual field. If he stays fifteen feet or so away, he should be able to see most of it and all of me. When John gets us into position, below the Agena, I depart the cockpit by squirting my gun up, pointing it right at the end of the Agena. Up I glide, miraculously it seems, pulling myself up by my bootstraps. As my left bootstrap reaches the top of the instrument panel, my foot snags on something briefly and causes me to start a gentle face-down pitching motion. Just as a diver wants to hit the water headfirst, not flat on his back, so do I wish not to splat into the Agena back first, so I have some quick adjustments to make with the gun. I hold it in the proper position to create an upward pitch, and after a few seconds of squirting in this direction, I have restored my desired orientation. I now discover to my horror, however, that I am gently rising up and that my path is no longer taking me to the end of the Agena but just above it. Fortunately, I have just enough time to make one last frantic correction, and as I cruise by, I am able to reach my left arm down and snag the Agena, just barely. As my body swings around, in response to this new torque, I am able to plunge my right hand down into the recess between the docking adapter and the main body of the

Agena, and find some wires to cling to. I'm not going to slip off this time! After all this, I have lost my bearings, and I don't know which way to move to find the meteorite package. Of course, since the end of the Agena is circular, I will wind up at the right spot eventually, but I don't want to discover the Indies by sailing west, especially if that means getting entangled more easily in that dangling metal loop. John is worried too. "See that you don't get tangled up in that fouled thing." I see what he means. "Yes. I see it coming." I continue, hand over hand, past the menacing obstacle. John is still worried. "Don't get tangled up in that thing. It's going on behind you now."

I can't stop now, and I can't see my trailing umbilical anyway. "If it starts to look bad, let me know. I'm going to press on up here." Finally, I make it around to the meteorite package, which is protected by a fairing and held in place on rails. The fairing can be removed by depressing two buttons and then yanking. It is attached to the micrometeorite package itself, a square metal plate some six inches on a side, by two wires ending in pins imbedded in holes in the package. I am supposed to remove the fairing, dump it, and then pull the micrometeorite experiment itself off and hang on to it for dear life. At this stage of the game I wouldn't be at all surprised if the whole thing were welded in place on the side of the Agena. Therefore, what a pleasant surprise when the two buttons stay depressed and the fairing jerks loose with only a moderate pull, bringing with it the package dangling by the two wires! For some reason the precarious nature of my hold on the package never enters my dull skull, and I am delighted that I have the whole thing in one hand with no fuss or bother.

John is still worried about my getting fouled with the Agena, which is starting to move now. I have yanked, pulled, and twisted the end of it on two occasions, and its response has by now become obvious to John. I can't see its motion, but I can feel that when I push against it, it seems less than rock-steady. John registers his alarm. "Come back . . . get out of all that garbage . . . just come on back, babe." I have my package, which has been on this Agena for three months, and although I am supposed to replace the old micrometeorite experiment with a new one, it doesn't seem a wise move. The Agena is tumbling slowly, John is worried, and the loose, hook-shaped wire is uncomfortably close. I am ready to return to Gemini and so inform John. "Don't worry. Don't worry. Here I come. Just go easy." "You want me to turn around to meet you?" John asks. He is offering to maneuver the Gemini around until it faces me directly, an unnecessary frill. "No, don't do a thing." This time, with no tangential velocity to worry about, I am coming home the easy way, hand over hand on my umbilical, but *slowly*, to avoid going fast enough to splat up against the side of it when I get there. I just don't want John firing thrusters in my face. "Don't fire any thrusters if you can help it. I'm getting back that way," meaning I have swung around toward the rear of the Gemini. John is obviously concentrating on *my* position, for suddenly he asks, "You don't see the Agena anywhere, do you?" "No. Yes. I see it. O.K." I find it up above us, and behind the Gemini for the first time, which is why John can't see it. We are well clear of it.

I am now back at the open right hatch, and I make a very sad discovery. I have lost my camera, the 70mm still camera which I had stuck into a slot on the side of my chest pack. I have no one to blame but myself, for this unconventional rig is of my own design. A couple of months ago I asked for a special bracket to be made, so that the camera could be attached by wedging a metal finger on the bracket into a keyhole-shaped slot on the chest pack. The system really worked well during training, and I had gotten quite adept at one-handed operation of the camera film advance and shutter mechanisms, even in my unwieldy suit. As a safety measure, I had a lanyard connecting the camera to a ring on the chest pack. Throughout the past half hour I have found that my zero-G wrestling match with the Agena caused the camera continually to work free of the keyhole slot and to dangle aimlessly on the end of its tether, banging and twisting from side to side. This has happened half a dozen times, and each time I have grabbed it, taken a quick picture, and stuffed it back into its slot. In addition, I have taken quite a few other exposures along the way, so that this roll of film must have at least a dozen of the most spectacular pictures ever taken in the space program—wide-angle pictures of Gemini, earth, and Agena—and now it is gone! I can't see the camera anywhere, but the lanyard dangles forlornly from my chest pack, making aimless little pirouettes to draw my attention to it. Each time the camera came loose and banged around, the screw must have backed off a little bit, until finally—*pfft!* Adios, beautiful pictures.

The next task in this EVA is to evaluate the gun properly, and I have mapped out a series of maneuvers which I will do out on the end of my tether, in front of our Gemini, where John can see me. The precision with which I can perform these maneuvers, as measured by John's movie camera and my impression, will allow engineers to evaluate the potential of the gun as a maneuvering device. But first, a couple of other things have to be done. I report my camera loss to John and he sounds sad, but he still has his mind on the Agena. "We're not going to hit the thing, are we?" "No. We're clear. I'm watching it. We're good and clear." Adios, 8 Agena. We've finished our three-month love affair with you, and now you are once again a derelict free to drift, a menace to be avoided. The next thing I must do is talk to the ground, before they chew us out again. All the talking John and I have been doing has been on intercom and the ground has heard none of it. The way it works, if I just talk, John hears me, but the only way the ground can hear is if my microphone button is held down, and it is back in the cockpit where only John can reach it. Thus, I need his help to talk to the ground, and so far both of us have been too busy to fool with it. But now, with the Agena gone, I had better make my report before the ground has a baby.

"How about pushing my mike button. Can you do that?" "Yes. Go ahead." "O.K., Houston, this is Gemini 10. Everything outside is about like we predicted, only it takes more time. The body positioning is indeed a problem, although the nitrogen line got connected without too much of a problem. I—when I translated over to the Agena, I found that the lack of handholds is a big impediment. I would—I could hang on, but I couldn't get around to the other side, which is what I wanted to do. Finally, I did get around to the other side and I did get both the S-10 package and the nose fairing off. John now has them. However, there is a piece of shroud hanging—or part of the nose of the Agena that came loose, and I was afraid I was going to get snarled up in that. So did John, and he told me to come on back. So the new S-10, which I was going to put on the Agena, I didn't, and I just now threw it away. Also, I lost my EVA Hasselblad inadvertently, I'm sorry to say. I'm getting ready now to do some gun evaluations. O.K., John, you can let go." The ground has other ideas. "We don't want you to use any more fuel. No more fuel, over." This means that John won't be able to maneuver the Gemini, to hold it steady while I practice my little routine out on the end of my string. John grumbles, "Well, then he'd better get back in." The ground agrees. "O.K. Get back in." John now serves me formal notice. "Come on back in the house then." I don't wanna, I don't wanna, but there's no basis upon which I can argue the point and I know it. The main thing was to get the micrometeorite S-10 package off the Agena, and besides—if we're out of gas, we're out of gas.

John has to remind me to disconnect the nitrogen line, and then I let the ground know what we're up to. "O.K., Houston, Gemini 10. I've disconnected the nitrogen line and I'm standing up in the hatch here. John's not firing the thrusters any more. We're just going to take a little rest here and make sure we both know what we're doing before we press on with the ingress." "Roger. This is Hawaii. Take your time and get all squared away and they'll pick you up over the States shortly." Houston, Hawaii—what difference does it make what piece of real estate we are over? It's all "the ground" in my mind, and besides, they make it sound as if the hatch won't shut properly unless we're over the States. They don't have the remotest idea of my problem, which is that this umbilical cord is wound around me at least a couple of times and I don't seem to be able to get far enough down to . . . Just don't think about it. John sees my predicament and is able to reach over far enough with his stiff pressurized right arm to unloop one coil. Now I have to back out, and John guides my feet and yanks a bit, and I am nearly free, with only one persistent loop around me. The rest of the fifty feet seems somehow to be all down in the cockpit, a nearly opaque mass of white coils that obscures the instrument panel and John and everything else below the level of the hatch frame. Good grief, a full house already, with most of me still outside. I wedge my body down through the coils, forcing my legs deep into the footwell, jackknifing my knees until my torso swings down and inward in that old familiar motion I have practiced a hundred times in the zero-G airplane. I grab the hatch above me and swing it gingerly toward the closed position. Its first contact will be either the hatch frame or my helmet. If the latter, I will have to repeat this ghastly process all over again. Click! Success! Now I have only to unstow the hatch handle, and crank and crank, until—*voilà*—it is actually sealed shut! Somewhere along the line the ground wants to know if John can give them a propellant quantity reading. "Get serious," he growls.

Neither one of us can see much besides links of umbilical cord as we fumble for the valve which will fill our cabin up with oxygen, allowing us to depressurize our suits and get on with the monumental task of restoring some semblance of order to our tiny home. I manage, in my thrashing around, to turn off the radio by accident, which at least gives us a few moments of blissful silence. When we finally reestablish contact, John tries to be funny. "He's down in the seat because there is about thirty feet of hose wrapped around him. We may have difficulty getting him out." I try to be funny. "This place makes the snake house at the zoo look like a Sunday-school picnic." Pretty thin humor, but we are trying to tell them just how glad we are to be back inside again, with the spacecraft pressure up at a comfortable five pounds per square inch.

We have one more EVA to go, the final one being simply a quick hatch opening to dump all unnecessary equipment. We prepare a tremendous duffel bag, into which we manage to cram the finally tamed umbilical, the chest pack, empty food bags, and everything else we don't absolutely need. This time I wedge myself way, way down in the footwell before dumping cabin pressure, so that the hatch will swing open and closed a good six inches above my helmet. All goes according to plan; I pitch out the bag, and finally the cabin pressure is up again, and we have (hopefully) trusted the little old ladies of Worcester and their glue pots for the last time. The next time my hatch opens, the only thing I want to worry about is blue Atlantic seawater gushing in. The cockpit has taken on a new aura of spaciousness, especially over on John's side, as for the first time he is able to stretch his legs full-length without bumping into equipment lashed to the floorboards. Somewhere along the line we have lost an experiment package we wanted to keep and our flight-plan book. Finally, we find the flight plan, flat on the floor under John's feet (where he couldn't see it until after the equipment dump), but the experiment apparently really is gone, presumably having floated out the right hatch somewhere along the line.

We have a couple of things to do before this day is over, but not too many, please, as the propellant quantity gauge tells us we have but 7 percent remaining. First, and most important, we want to get our orbit down from 250 miles, and we use up most of the 7 percent in a burn which reduces our perigee to 180 miles. The lower the better, in case we have difficulty with our retrofire burn tomorrow morning. The retrofire energy comes from four separate solid propellant rocket engines, but in case one doesn't fire, or we have difficulty controlling the direction of the thrust, we want to be as low as possible. A perigee of 180 isn't the greatest, but it beats 250. Once we are safely in our new orbit, we make up for some lost experiment time and race through an involved sequence designed to determine whether the positively charged ions whizzing past our craft can be used to determine the direction we are pointing, a very simple scheme compared to the complex and heavy gyroscopes we now employ for this task. It seems to work well, and the needles connected to our ion sensors move in close agreement with the information coming from the gyroscopes.

Once this is behind us, we are on our own for the first time in the fifty-three hours since we left Cape Kennedy, with a ten-hour sleep period ahead of us, with no Agena to keep us rigidly upright, with no navigation or rendezvous or other complicated tasks to consume our every minute. We have only one constraint, and that is, we must not use fuel, as our gauge is nearly on zero, but that is no hardship as we drift carelessly over the world. We congratulate ourselves and receive compliments from our friends on the ground. "We'd like to let you know that we're pretty doggone happy down here . . . it was a great job today. It was fabulous." John agrees. "I tell you it was a tremendous thrill. It was really incredible. I didn't believe part of it myself." I think he's talking about my climbing on the Agena, which God knows *was* unreal. Who would believe it? "Hope those pictures come out" is all I can say.

Meanwhile, we have turned off our attitude-control system, to save gas, and are doing some very un-airplane-like things. In a fighter it is possible to do loops and rolls, even spins, but one never goes sideways or backward—at least not without violent consequence. But we are tumbling now—slowly, smoothly, aimlessly—and as we go, the square snout of our spacecraft traces graceful arcs in the sky, sometimes in front of our direction of travel, sometimes to one side or the other, sometimes behind. It is a three-dimensional roller-coaster ride in slow motion, with no noise, no banging around, no hollow feeling in the pit of the stomach. If this is what the old Edwards test pilots meant about an astronaut just being along for the ride, being a canned man, then I am for it. It is suppertime now and I have missed lunch in the hurly-burly of EVA preparations; I am famished, and have finally gotten a chance to fill up a plastic tube of dehydrated cream of chicken soup with cold water (the only kind we have). After kneading it for a couple of minutes, I snip off the end of the feeding tube with my surgical scissors (which are powerful enough to cut through the fifty-foot umbilical in case of an emergency, like being unable to disconnect from the nitrogen valve. I know, I have tried it). Anyway, I finally get my first swig of soup and it is the best thing I have ever tasted, better than a martini at Sardi's, better than the pressed duck at the Tour d'Argent. And the view out of the window is absolutely breathtaking!

I will try to explain it. First, some arithmetic. At two hundred miles above a sphere whose radius is four thousand, we are just skimming along one twentieth of a radius above the surface. The atmosphere itself is ridiculously thin, thinner than the rind on an orange, and we are just barely above it. The curvature of the earth is apparent, sure, but it is not a dominant impression, not any more than running your eye over a curved dinner plate causes you to think about its concavity rather than the design on it. Nor is the speed impressive. It's certainly not the blinding speed of the Indianapolis 500. The rate at which something appears in the window, crosses it, and vanishes is not much faster than in a commercial airliner. That is because our much faster orbital velocity is balanced by our higher altitude, so that angular changes (the most important visual cues of speed) are still within the realm of the commonplace. These, then, are the similarities, to which one must add color, for, although the sky is absolute, unrelieved black instead of blue, the colors below look about the same as they would if seen from an airplane. Let a six-year-old child have a peek and he would be back at his coloring book within a minute. Then what is so impressive, what makes it different? It is the eye of the adult, which balances what he sees with a lifetime of crawling the surface of the planet. Supertourist is up, and what a feeling of power! Those aren't counties going by, those are countries or continents; not lakes, but oceans! Blanche, we can still make Yellowstone today, if we drive six more hours. Forget all that, baby! In six hours we will have circled this globe four times! Look at that, we just passed Hawaii and here comes the California coast, visible from Alaska to Mexico, and my cream of chicken soup not yet finished. San Diego to Miami in nine minutes flat; if you missed it, don't worry, it will be back in ninety minutes. Another difference is that we are above it, and it is uniformly bright. No misty days, no towering thunderheads; all that is below, and super-bright in the unfiltered sunlight, which spreads a cheeriness over the whole scene below. No doom, no gloom, only optimism. This is a better world than the one down there. Fantastic!

Up until now we have charted our progress by the clock, not the scenery. The fuel cells must be purged at 51:36; never mind that it's over the delightful island of Ceylon. Now, as we munch on pressed bacon cubes and suck thin grapefruit juice out of plastic bags, we pay attention to the chunks of real estate which grandly parade past our windows as the Gemini slowly cartwheels. The Indian Ocean flashes incredible colors of emerald jade and opal in the shallow water surrounding the Maldive Islands; then on to the Burma coast and nondescript green jungle, followed by mountains, coastline, and Hanoi. We can see fires burning off to the southeast, and we scramble for our one remaining still camera to record them. Now the sun glints in unusual fashion off the ocean near Formosa. There are intersecting surface ripples just south of the island, patterns which are clearly visible and which, I think, must be useful to fishermen who need to know about these currents. The island itself is verdant—glistening green the color and shape of a shiny, well-fertilized gardenia-leaf. Then back over the Pacific again in a race for Hawaii and the California coast. I could stay up here forever! Er, amend that, I don't want to stay up here past 70:10, which is retrofire time, and it is now 56:14 and time to get some sleep. Up the girls go on the windows, blotting out the bright shiny world, and leaving John and me with our thoughts in the darkened cabin.

As I drift off to sleep, I can't help but compare this night with the previous two. Let's face it, the first night was miserable, with the twin embarrassments of the Module VI fiasco and the excessive rendezvous fuel, plus my painful knee and my generally keyed-up state, resulting from this strange and apparently hostile environment. The second night was different, better certainly, but still full of unknowns, and my extra tiredness had created gloom, not giddiness. Tonight is something else again. We have carried off that second (and more difficult) rendezvous, and I have actually spacewalked from one satellite to another and retrieved a package from it! I can't get it out of my mind. Too bad it got cut short, too bad I didn't have a chance to savor the experience, to let the view soak in a bit. Funny there was no sensation of motion, or of falling, especially considering that I get a bad feeling in the pit of my stomach when I peer over the edge of the roof of a tall building. I really wasn't very conscious of the earth at all, only the Agena and the spacecraft—one at a time, depending on what had to be done next.

Work, work, work! A guy should be told to go out on the end of his string and simply gaze around—what guru gets to meditate for a whole earth's worth? I think nirvana must be at an altitude of 250 miles, not down below in the teeming streets of Calcutta or up above in the monotonous black void. I am in the cosmic arena, the place to gain a celestial perspective; it remains only to slow down long enough to capture it; even a teacupful will do, will last a lifetime below. "I found truth in orbit." Wrong, I haven't. "I found God outside my spacecraft." Wrong, I didn't even have time to look for Him. Would that I could, like Mercury of the winged heel, convey some swift message of value, a message of splendor and beauty, of hope and praise, a message which accurately mirrors what I have seen today. John Magee would have known how to do it. Behind my head, stowed away in a small bag with some flags, rings, and other trivia, is a small file card on which my wife, Pat, has typed his poem "High Flight."

> *Oh, I have slipped the surly bonds of earth*
> *And danced the skies on laughter-silvered wings;*
> *Sunward I've climbed, and joined the tumbling mirth*
> *Of sunsplit clouds—and done a hundred things*
> *You have not dreamed of—wheeled and soared and swung*
> *High in the sunlit silence. Hov'ring there,*
> *I've chased the shouting wind along, and flung*
> *My eager craft through footless halls of air.*
> *Up, up the long, delirious, burning blue*
> *I've topped the windswept heights with easy grace*
> *Where never lark, or even eagle flew*
> *And, while with silent, lifting mind I've trod*
> *The high untrespassed sanctity of space,*
> *Put out my hand, and touched the face of God.*

from Father Goose
by William Lishman

Canadian sculptor William Lishman (born 1939) wanted to fly like a bird. His wish carried him through a series of disasters and near-disasters with ultra-light aircraft (imagine hang gliders with go-cart engines).

T he hard part was to lift the entire aircraft up and get it balanced on the small of your back while keeping dead to the wind. That was no mean feat, considering that the craft weighed more than a hundred pounds and had nearly a thirty-foot wingspan. If the nose got too high and the wind was a little brisk, it tried to throw you over backward. Similarly, if the nose got too low, it added immensely to the weight.

Once in position, feet apart and bracing yourself against the backrest, it was imperative to hold it at the perfect angle of attack. Then, quickly moving your left hand and letting that side sag a little, you hit full throttle. The engine revs to a scream, the propeller turning a few thousand rpm six inches from your butt. In a moment the thrust is too much to hold back. It is either go forward or fall flat on your face. One step, two, three—with each step the load gets lighter, your strides become easier. Within a hundred feet the wings are flying free under your armpits. Another few feet and you feel yourself lifted. The wings are beginning to take you away faster and lighter, faster and lighter. Your legs move with ease as the weight is lifted from them. You are running faster than you would have ever thought possible, great long wonderful strides, feet just brushing the ground and at last totally free of the ground. Your legs, not believing it, are still flailing open air. You are free, truly airborne. The field drops away beneath you and a great vista opens up. I have never experienced such a contrast in extremes— at one moment fear-weakened, overburdened, and awkward, clamped down by gravity and entangled in a banshee-screaming, cumbersome contraption, then within seconds becoming lighter, lighter, freer, and freer. Even the noise seems to drop away with the gravity in the most graceful manner.

That is, if everything goes right.

Many times things went quite wrong. There was the time—my sixth powered flight—at about a hundred feet when the right wing stalled and dropped away. Pointed straight down, I spit the kill switch. Miraculously the Riser pulled out and I was skimming the ground downwind at thirty miles an hour with a ten-mile-an-hour wind. A downwind landing then would be a disaster, for the full weight of the aircraft would be on me while I would be attempting to run on foot at twenty-something miles an hour. I attempted to bring it around to the wind. The right wingtip caught the ground and did two marvelous big slewing cartwheels into a jumble of tangled aluminum.

It was almost a year before my next attempt, and then came the time when the tip of my heel connected with the tip of the propeller on the final paces of takeoff. I had devised a safety guard to prevent such occurrences, but in the long final strides of takeoff the heel of my shoe rotated around the guard just enough to clip the tip of the prop. The prop exploded and took out most of the right lower wing. I spit the switch and rolled into a ball of bent aluminum and fabric. I survived with only minor bruises.

In the years that followed I built and rebuilt, tried different engines, carved prop after prop, and bought and made reduction drives. In short, I lived the romance and evolution of this new form of aviation and my Easy Riser became a refined little plane with a three-cylinder, electric-start radial engine, an elevator, one-stick control, and steerable tricycle gear. With meager funds I built a hangar and put in a minimal six-hundred-foot airstrip. It was the only way to enjoy flying that little craft, for its wing loading was so minimal—less than two pounds per square foot (a modern airliner is ten to twenty times that)—that any turbulence was keenly felt. And I only wanted to fly when it was enjoyable. So the aircraft stood ready. When the weather was right, I could be airborne in short order.

The best scenario was to rise at daybreak and take a cruise before the regular day began and then close the day watching the sunset from my own private mobile mountaintop. The Riser cruised nicely at thirty miles an hour. It looks flimsy as a butterfly, yet it is extremely strong. Being a biplane, it has the strength of a box and also the drag, which prevented me from flying at speeds beyond its limit. For several years I cruised the local countryside, observing the changes in seasons and occasionally watching flights of birds from my birdlike vantage. Many mornings before breakfast or on clear evenings before sunset I would wander off through the air currents like a lone hawk, turning lazy circles a few hundred feet in the air, absorbing the countryside, living in that sea of air above the ever-changing terrain. In early spring when the grass has just turned green and the hardwood forests are transparent without their leaves, it's possible to see how the land was formed. I discovered many mansions tucked away in wooded lots and saw the personality of each farmer written in the patterns of his fields. On occasion I would come on a flight of gulls or would see a blue heron and fly behind them at a distance. Several times I was able to catch a thermal with a hawk and spiral up a few hundred feet, for they have no fear of the aircraft. I always felt that they just considered my craft another bird. Many times I was within feet of them. And always the lure of flying with the birds was there. Even though I knew I wasn't really making much headway, the dream wouldn't go away.

True flying with the birds began for me on one of those autumn dawns when pools of mist lie in the hollows, the air does not move, and the long shadows of the fencerows are drawn across the stubble fields by the rising sun. The farm woodlots of southern Ontario were beginning to show splotches of golds and reds among their summer greens. I had flown east from my airstrip at Purple Hill in the Easy Riser—absorbed in the clear crisp beauty of the day. To the north, Lake Scugog sat mirroring wisps of vapor, the rising ghosts of yesterday's warmth. After about twenty minutes a long, lazy semicircle pointed me homeward at about five hundred feet. As I approached the Swain farm I noticed a stubble field almost black with birds. Throttling back, I started dropping down for a closer look. The birds sensed my approach and rose as one, like a blanket of ducks, thousands of ducks, and in a moment I was in their midst. I powered up to climb out of the flock, but they were climbing too, our airspeed matched. They made no attempt to dive away from me; by default, they had accepted me into their number, save the two that were directly in front that kept glancing nervously back, maybe worried that this might be some new predator that would devour them in midair. When it became obvious to them that I was not a threat, they just winged on. The air was full of ducks—in front, below, above, behind, some in ragged chevrons, some in amorphous clusters, wings flashing in the early light. The thrill was indescribable. Caught in their mass spirit I winged along, just another bird in this autumnal squadron headed for the marshes to the northwest, my attention focused on a duck off to my left holding perfect formation about four feet off my wingtip, just as if I had always been his wing mate—and for a moment I felt I had.

I drank in this wonder, the experience one of those that transcends time. Below and to the south, through a myriad of ducks, I glimpsed my house and airstrip slipping by, as if they were a child's model seen on the bottom of some great river of ducks.

As we went on, there was a flow within the flights, a movement of groups smoothly shifting their positions as if under the baton of some unseen conductor. Then the open fields gave way to the dark green of the forest and there, with this great massing of wings, I was in a time before man had surrounded the planet, filled with a primeval feel dating from eons, ages, before freeways and television.

I became aware that we were descending. I too had tuned in to the flight conductor.

The reality of my mechanical bird wings interceded, and the fear of my engine quitting over the woods brought me out of this marvelous trance. Reluctantly I pushed the throttle forward and climbed up, through, and out of the mass of wings. They flowed aside, letting me through. I winged over to the left, and full of what at that instant I didn't have a word for, can only describe as glee, I swept around to head home, watching the sparkling of wings receding lower and lower into the dark scrub of marsh that had not yet received the sun.

In a few moments I was rolling down my bumpy airstrip, shaken back to ground reality, feeling that I had for a moment experienced something of great significance. I could not get this joyful feeling to leave. I kept my flying machine, the Easy Riser, at the ready, craving to spend more time with these creatures in their element, and experience the world from their vantage again.

It was not to happen that year. Once, returning from a sunset flight, I did spy a flock of about thirty Canada geese, higher and a little off to the south from me. I swung around and made an attempt to join up. It was not their wish. Even with my machine at full throttle they gradually outclimbed me into the twilight. The snows came. I put the Riser away in my makeshift hangar (capital cost, twelve dollars) and busied myself with the major sculpture commission I was working on for Expo '86. Then, later that winter, disaster struck, neither the first nor the last in my long affair with ultralight aircraft and geese. The hangar collapsed under a huge snow load and completely crushed the Riser, putting that part of my life back to square one.

So where should I go from there? Get another aircraft, obviously! I immediately started thinking about getting a Lazair, a second-generation ultralight designed by Dale Kramer and the late Peter Corley when they were little more than teenagers. For a few years it was the darling of the ultralight crowd, the aircraft to have. In its original form it had two six-horse-power converted chain-saw engines and one stick that controlled everything. The Lazair had long, gracefully tapered wings with a little upsweep at the tips, and an inverted-V tail. It was and still is a beauty in the air, both visually and to fly. It also afforded wonderful visibility. I must admit I lusted after one for years. On the demise of the Riser, I found a good used Lazair for sale. I paid half down to clinch the deal, and one fine day in April 1986 1 went to take delivery of it a few miles from my airstrip. The man who was selling it to me flew it over to a huge sod field a few miles from our home, a good level area for me to take my maiden flight. Like most ultralights of the time, it was not a two-seater. The usual procedure was for the instructor to stay on the ground, giving lots of advice and watching the student learn.

The day was perfect, without a wisp of wind. I thought flying it would be a piece of cake. After all, I had had several hundred hours in the Riser by then and assumed I would not have a major problem converting to the Lazair.

Wrong assumption! This was a Mark II Lazair with rudder pedals, an overhead stick, twin nine-horse engines, and narrow landing gear. The Easy Riser was single pusher-prop, with single conventional stick and wide and easily steerable nose gear.

Terry, my instructor, instilled great confidence in me. He flew the craft up the field at about three feet of altitude as steady as a rock—yellow prop spinners, yellow wheel fairings, a flying dream. He landed and walked around the aircraft, instructing me on taxiing procedures and so on. I think he told me what to do. I think I just did not listen well enough.

I got in, buckled up, pulled the engines to life, and started taxiing down the field. Then I suddenly found myself at a heading ninety degrees off my planned path. I got the plane turned around and suddenly was going in the wrong direction again. Overanxious, I gave it too much throttle. In a second I was airborne! I assumed it would be easy once I got it up in the air, so I climbed, my legs vibrating with nervous fear. I tried a turn. I moved the stick and the Lazair banked the opposite way to what I had expected. Confused, I pushed the rudder pedal. Trying to think it out, I reached down and pulled back on the throttle. No! No! With more throttle now, I was going in a tighter and tighter circle. Desperately I moved the stick the opposite way. I was panicking, but as in all panic I did not recognize it. A huge tree loomed in front.

Instinctively I pulled back on the stick to clear the tree and screamed as I stalled into the trees on the other side.

Crash! One engine was still running. I was sitting straight and level. The left wing was hugging the trunk of a tall poplar. The right wing sat on top of a smaller tree. I shut off the engine and sat there not moving. For ten minutes I sat there, thirty-five feet in the air, not totally absorbed in the beauty of the fresh buds on the branches and the sweet spring song of red-winged blackbirds.

Too soon, Terry came crashing through the underbrush, yelling my name.

I called out to him, "I'm all right."

But the fact was I did not want to move. I just wanted to sit there and enjoy the spring from my birdlike perch. Also, I had absolutely no energy. None. Some other people came through the underbrush. I did not want to see them either. They were carrying a ladder and poked it toward me. The ladder was ten feet short. I jiggled the aircraft, to no avail. It was there solidly, a broken branch of the poplar hooked right through the leading edge of the left wing.

I looked down. The very top spike of a cedar was at my hand. I still did not want to move. The people on the ground were getting impatient and I was feeling more than a little embarrassed. I had only paid Terry half the money for the plane, so I made light of the situation and called to him that I had only smashed up my half and his half was still O.K. One of the people who brought the ladder called up, "We heard you scream over the engines as you went in." I don't remember that! No, that could not have been me!

Finally I made my Jell-O-like body start to work and attempted to clamber out of the seat and over to the poplar. I grabbed a branch. My hands had no grip. I had to concentrate just to hang on. It was probably the scariest thing I had ever attempted in my life. I finally got to the trunk of the poplar. It was straight as a telephone pole down to the top of the ladder, with no branches. Somehow I managed to hug it enough to lower myself to the ladder and get to the ground. Shaky, shaky. Terry drove me home, I had a stiff Scotch and went to bed for a few hours. I awoke at three a.m. thinking about how I was going to retrieve the bent Lazair from the treetops in the middle of a forest. Then I remembered a pair of old lineman's climbing spurs, the type used for climbing power poles. Flashlight in hand, in the middle of the night in the back of the shop, I rummaged through the considerable collection of odds and ends that I never throw out, and by seven a.m. I was back in the forest with two helpers. My climbing gear consisted of a block and tackle and the old swing seat from my Easy Riser. Within half an hour we had the Lazair lowered to the ground and carefully disassembled. A piece at a time, we carried it out of the bush and trucked it home.

I found another Lazair, brand new, but the engines had been stolen from it. The owner was desperate for money. I put together all the available funds I could muster and bought the Lazair at a bargain price. Within two weeks I had fitted the wings of the new riser on the fuselage of the crashed one, installed the old engines, and with the help of instruction from Jack Weber by two-way radio I was airborne, this time very carefully.

from A Lonely Kind of War
by Marshall Harrison

In Vietnam, the aircraft that could make the most noise got the most attention: Cobras, F-4s and loudest of all, the B-52s. Few observers noticed the waif-like lightplanes used by forward air controllers (FACs). Those pilots' job was to snoop around at treetop level, find the enemy and call in the noisemakers. It was a dangerous occupation, as Marshall Harrison's (1933–1998) first-hand account makes clear.

T he radio came alive with the flight leader's voice just as I saw them.

"Blade Flight, check in."

"Two."

"Three."

Sidewinder Two-one, this is Blade Lead. Are you up this frequency?"

"Blade Lead, this is Sidewinder Two-one," I replied. "I've got you loud and clear. Go ahead with your lineup."

"Rog, Sidewinder; Blade Flight is three F-100s, all loaded with snake and nape, plus a full load of twenty mike-mike."

With a grease pencil I copied this onto the Plexiglas of my canopy for reference during the strike. There weren't any surprises here; it was a standard load for preplanned strikes in-country. Snakes were retarded bombs and napes were napalm. Each plane also had a full load of 20mm cannon ammunition on board.

"Blade Flight, this is Sidewinder Two-one. The targets today are reported bunkers, although I haven't been able to pick them up. The elevation is about 650 feet. I've seen no ground fire, so I'd like you to run in on an east-west heading, with a left break off target. I'll be orbiting over the target at about 1,500 feet. The best bailout area is back toward home plate and I'll clear each pass. I want you to call the target and the FAC in sight before each pass. Any questions?" I wanted them to be particularly sure that they had the forward air controller (FAC) in sight. That was me.

"Blade Lead, negative. OK Blade Flight, take your positions; let's arm 'em up."

"Two."

"Three."

"Blade Lead, this is Sidewinder. I want 'em dropped in pairs with the snake first."

"Rog. Blade has you visually over the Testicles."

"OK, I also have you. The target is about five klicks north. I'm turning toward it now."

I watched over my shoulder as they dropped down to their perch altitude from which they would be rolling in to deliver the bombs. They moved into trail position as they descended over the rendezvous point, a prominent double oxbow in a slow-moving, dirty-looking river, charmingly nicknamed the Testicles. From 2,000 feet the countryside was a brilliant, verdant green that almost hurt the eyes. A true triple-canopy jungle with the tallest emergents thrusting out more than 200 feet in their search for sunlight. The green was broken only by several old bomb craters showing the nutrient-poor laterite beneath the luxuriant growth. From the air the green was deceptive. It looked so solid that you would have thought it impossible to move through it; however, the bomb craters gave away its secret. Looking diagonally down at the green, it was apparent that beneath the solid treetops was an almost parklike growth. The lack of sunlight beneath the branches discouraged any forest floor growth except for a few of the hardiest, shade-loving plants. Accurate map reading was impossible from the air or the ground, and some friendly long-range reconnaissance patrol

(LRRP) unit could be lurking down there in the bushes despite the fact that I had checked all known friendly locations before takeoff.

I glanced again at my map where I had marked the target on one of the one-kilometer grids, and I thought I was as close as I'd be able to get to it. I double-checked the area but still didn't see anything moving. I could only hope that if the friendlies were down there they'd have enough sense to try to contact someone when the bombs began falling around them. Except for a few dry streambeds, the map showed only solid green squares in every direction, indicating solid tree growth. One streambed to the west meandered toward the sluggish river, its bed now cracking into geometric patterns as the dry season became firmly entrenched in the countryside. The shape of the streambed didn't correspond to the bright blue line on my map. It probably changed courses several times a season, staying one step ahead of the mapmakers. I had only the roughest idea of where the target was supposed to be. I had tried to triangulate on any features I could find, but with the solid tree growth I wouldn't have bet on my accuracy. If there were indeed bunkers down there, they weren't visible from the air. For that matter they may have been ten years old and only recently resurrected from a moldy file by an intelligence officer hunting for some sort of target. Almost certainly, there would be no enemy troops in them. Their intelligence was normally better than that.

"OK, Blade Flight. Sidewinder is in for the marking pass." I put the stick over and rolled into a forty-degree dive. The lighted sight in the windscreen drifted over and settled near a prominent tree that I could use as a reference point during the air strike. With all the twisting and turning I'd be doing trying to keep track of the fighters, I'd need a good reference point. Since I didn't really know where the target was anyway, this tree was as good as any other. We were probably going to be making toothpicks out of perfectly good trees anyway. I armed one rocket pod and punched the firing button on the stick, then watched the rocket down to the ground. It wasn't bad—about twenty meters south of the trees. The smoke blossomed as the white phosphorous warhead detonated, the small white cloud standing out vividly against the wild green backdrop. It made a perfect target, although its usefulness would be short-lived as the smoke from the exploding bombs and their shock waves blended and mixed. No problem there though: my Bronco carried twenty-seven more marking rockets.

"Blade Lead, put your first bombs about twenty meters north of my smoke."

"Roger, Sidewinder. Twenty north of the smoke. Lead is in from the east with the FAC and target in sight."

"Blade Lead, this is Sidewinder. You're cleared in hot."

The first pair of bombs detonated about thirty meters south of the white ball of smoke.

"Pretty good, Lead," I said as I hauled the aircraft around in a tight, sixty-degree banked turn to face the number two aircraft already starting his dive. The marking smoke was already being blown away from the target, but now there were two bomb craters to use as a reference. I banked the Bronco quickly upon each wing, eyeballing the area exposed by the first pair of blasts. No bunkers were visible.

"Blade Two is in hot from the east, FAC and target in sight."

"Blade Lead is off left." His voice was fuzzy over the radio from the heavy g-force he was pulling.

"Blade Two, you're cleared in hot," I said. "Put 'em about thirty meters long on Lead's craters."

"Roger."

I flew directly at him until I was sure his run-in angle was good, and as he passed beneath me in his dive, I started a tight diving left turn to keep him in sight. Both bombs were good but they didn't uncover anything that looked promising.

"Blade Two is off to the left."

"Blade Three is in from the east with the FAC and target in sight." This one sounded nervous. Probably new in-country, which wasn't a crime. We all started there not too long ago. I'd have to watch him pretty closely though, for most new guys tried to press things a little beyond their capabilities. If he was a newbie he'd be all thumbs and elbows in the cockpit right about now, afraid he'd screw up.

"You're cleared in hot, Blade Three." Jesus Christ! As I spoke the words clearing him to start his bomb run, I saw two snake-eye bombs separate from his aircraft, at least 400 meters short of the target area. The explosions were more than a quarter mile on the far side of the dry streambed.

"Blade Flight, hold high and dry," I said as I banked my aircraft to stay out of his way. Well, no real damage done, since there were not supposed to be friendly troops anywhere in the area. It would probably be best not to make too big a deal out of it. But if there had been friendlies, I'd have fried his ass, new guy or not.

I tried to keep my voice light. "Blade Three, you were just a tad short there. Any problems?"

"Negative," he stammered, sounding very young.

"OK, Blade Three," I said. "No damage done. Let's see if we can't do some good bombing." We might as well let him practice a bit, I thought. Today's environment was hardly hostile, but his next flight might involve a troops-in-contact situation where a short bomb like he'd just delivered would be a disaster. We all had plenty of fuel and I had no pressing engagements for the next nine months.

"OK Lead, this is Sidewinder. Let's drop singles from now on. If you have me in sight you're cleared in hot." Maybe they'll buy me a drink the next time I'm at Bien Hoa, if I'm nice to them. We FACs are great at cadging drinks at the fighter clubs when we have the opportunity. Some blackmail is implied but unspoken in this, for we call in the results of their bombing, which, in turn, determines the scores of their fitness reports.

"Good idea, Sidewinder. Are you going to re-mark?" the lead pilot asked.

"Yeah, I'm in for the new mark now." I was almost directly over the target, so I rolled inverted and pulled through the horizon until I was headed down in an almost vertical dive. I had too many g's on the aircraft to shoot accurately, but what the hell? I didn't know what I was shooting at anyway. I punched off another rocket and watched the white smoke erupt from the tree canopy.

"Hit my smoke, Lead. If you have the target and the FAC, you're cleared in hot."

"Lead is in from the east, FAC and target in sight."

We played stateside gunnery range for the next few passes. The Lead pilot got into the spirit of things and began coaching his new wingman between his own runs. I took the part of the range officer, calling errors for number three by azimuth and distance. We'd all come to the same conclusion: There wasn't jackshit beneath those trees.

Blade Three pulled up sharply on his next pass; I didn't see any explosions.

"Three, this is Sidewinder. You must have had a dud. I didn't see anything go off."

"Negative, Sidewinder. I didn't release. I think somebody was shooting at me."

His voice was uncertain but it got everyone's attention. You could almost feel the tension increase over the radio. I slammed over into a vertical turn, pulling the stick back as hard as I dared.

"Blade Flight, hold high and dry. Three, where did it look like it was coming from?" Damn! I was supposed to be the one to see any ground fire, not some rookie pilot on his first in-country mission.

"It looked like tracers coming from those trees," he said, "just south of where I dropped those short bombs."

He was new and wouldn't know a lot about ground fire yet, but surely he'd know a tracer coming up at him if he saw it. Sometimes, though, they can be hard to see during the daylight on a 400-knot bombing run. Perhaps he'd seen the sun glint off a stream beneath the tree line; that sometimes looked like ground fire. Maybe he'd seen some debris from one of the other bomb blasts, which had been flung skyward. And maybe one day I'd be chief of staff. Actually I had already accepted the fact that he'd uncovered something with his wild-assed bombing. Maybe we'd never been in the right place to begin with. I sure wasn't that positive of having found the exact coordinates on my map. I checked to see that the fighters were holding in a racetrack pattern well above me and out of my way, then pushed the throttles forward and turned, toward the craters marking Blade Three's first bombing effort.

"Break, Sidewinder. They're hosing you down!"

I had already figured that. The left side panel of my canopy starred crazily from a small-caliber bullet. That concerned me but not as much as the two streams of green tracers drifting toward me. Without thinking, I again rolled inverted and dove for the treetops, which seemed to be the safest haven at the moment, since heavy-caliber weapon fire was sweeping the sky. It could be either a .50 caliber or a 12.7mm, either of which could be disastrous to an OV-10 Bronco doing 180 knots. Ten feet over the treetops I turned north and looked back at the tracers falling away. There was also the flash of small automatic weapons winking at me from beneath the tree line surrounding the bomb craters. I found I had instinctively hunched my shoulders and tightened my sphincter the way I always did when being fired upon. It doesn't do any good, but you feel like you're doing something.

Pulling the stick back sharply, I traded airspeed for altitude. At 5,000 feet, I leveled off and took stock. First, I had to admit to myself that I had made a serious mistake in judgment. No way should I have flown over that area without knowing a little something about what was going on. The round through the canopy was the only damage I could see. Some man with an AK-47 had almost put my eye out for me. I had gotten away luckier than I deserved. I became conscious of Blade Lead trying to reach me over the radio.

"Lead, this is Sidewinder. Just got a little careless and took one through the Plexiglas. No damage done. Blade Three was right though—they're down there. I don't know in what strength, but they're shooting mad. There are at least two heavy automatic weapons and I saw several AKs but didn't stick around to count them. What kind of ordnance do you have left?"

"We should each have one bomb and two napes left, plus the twenty mike-mike."

That wasn't very much to be going against those people. I berated myself for not keeping track of the remaining weapon load for that was part of my job. I had allowed myself to be lulled by what I thought was going to be a cakewalk. Carelessness got a lot of people killed over here.

"OK, Blade Flight. I'm going to come in from the north at 2,000 and mark from there. Since there are no friendlies around, you'll be cleared in on a heading of your choice. Break off the target is also your option, just let me know which way you're going so I can stay out of your way."

I swore at myself for having squandered the bombs. The napalm would be almost useless with this tree cover, since it would have to be delivered in a high-angle dive to get any sort of penetration through the trees. The normal flattened delivery allowed for a great deal of spread, but released from a more vertical dive the greatest danger was probably getting conked on the head by the canister. The 20mm. cannons ran into the same problem. The heavy tree canopy would deflect or destroy most of the rounds before they could penetrate to the ground. I'd better get some help lined up in case this turned out to be more than an isolated group of Indians.

"Blade Lead, Sidewinder is going off freq for one to see if there are any alert birds available."

"Roger that. We still have more than thirty minutes of loiter left."

"OK, I'll see you back on in one."

To enhance the OV-10 Bronco's role as a forward air control aircraft, its designers had put in a marvelous communications system. Using a simple row of toggle switches and a round wafer-selector switch, the pilot could simultaneously monitor two UHF radios, two FM radios, a VHF radio, an HF radio, a secure scrambler system, an FM homer, a Guard channel radio for use in emergencies, and assorted navigational gear. However, only one radio at a time could be used for transmissions. Unfortunately, no one else on any of the nets could do the same and therefore had no idea who else was trying to talk to the FAC. This jumble of voices breaking in on each other, each call more strident than the last as they competed for the FAC's attention, often became an audio nightmare. I turned my switches to talk to my control room on UHF.

"Sidewinder Control, this is Sidewinder Two-one. Call Division and see if they've got any spare fighters in the AO [*area of operations–ed.*]. I may be needing some more real soon. If they've got 'em, have them rendezvous with me over the Testicles. Keep 'em high and have them monitor my frequency in case I don't have time to do much briefing. You may have to do their briefing yourself, so stay alert to the situation and make sure you've got the big picture. Monitor me at all times and alert Brigade that we may have uncovered something sizable. You might also get the Duty FAC cranked up in case we need him."

"Yes sir, I've already done all of that except call for more fighters. I've been listening."

"Thanks, I'll get back to you. Out."

I switched back to the fighter frequency. If Bos said it was taken care of, it was. That rotund figure was as sharp as any two-striper I had ever seen.

"Blade Flight," I called, "I'm back with you and in for another marking round."

"Rog. Watch your ass."

He could bet money on it. This time I knew there were automatic weapons down there. I chose a high-angle dive to shoot the rocket, figuring they'd have less of my profile to aim at, and also I'd be in and out of the danger zone that much quicker. Luckily, I'd used only a few of my marking rockets while we'd been assing around before. Counting backward in my memory I figured I should have at least fifteen or so left.

I eased the stick back and let the nose rise as far above the horizon as it could without beginning to shudder with an approaching stall. I tried to keep the impact point I wanted fixed in my sight. Fortunately, the airplane was designed with a canopy that provided optimum viewing angles. Thanks to the bulbous, dragonfly-eye design, you could even see directly beneath the aircraft in level flight. As the stick began shaking, indicating the approaching stall, I eased it to one side of the cockpit, holding the rudder depressed to bring the nose almost straight down toward the target. The lighted sight pipper settled just under the target. I nudged the stick back slightly, adjusting the sight until it nestled over the point I wanted. Making sure that I had no pressure on any of the controls, I punched off another rocket. Without waiting to see its impact, I put the aircraft into a maximum-rate climb turn. The g-forces pulled my lower lip down toward my navel. Releasing some of the back pressure on the stick, and consequently some of the g-forces, I was again able to talk.

"Blade Lead, this is Sidewinder. All of you drop your snakes on this pass. Lead, you hit my smoke. Blade Two, if Lead uncovers anything, be ready to go with both your napes. If he doesn't find anything, we'll go with your bomb."

"Lead, rog."

"Two, rog."

"Blade Lead is in hot with the FAC and the target in sight."

The exploding bomb came from immediately under the slowly rising remnants of my smoke rocket.

"Good bomb, Lead. Blade Two, go through dry one time while I check it out."

I had been slowly turning the aircraft to keep the lead ship on my nose as he made his pass. As his bomb exploded, I let the plane drop rapidly, building up all the airspeed I could. OK, so even at top speed it wasn't all that much. Even so, the jokes were unnecessarily cruel about an OV-10 needing radar in its tail to prevent it from being overtaken by thunderstorms.

Leveling at 500 feet, I pointed myself at the impact area. Things very quickly became interesting. Rapidly moving my eyes about the area, I picked up the blinking of automatic weapon fire from the tree line surrounding the bomb blasts. I felt several rounds strike the aircraft and fancied that I could hear the firing of the larger guns, an obvious impossibility wearing my tightfitting ballistic helmet. The helmet was guaranteed to either stop or deflect a .30-caliber round. I didn't know if the claim was true, but like other FACs and helicopter pilots, I wanted to believe with the fervor of a disciple. Of course, if it didn't work, who would be able to complain about it?

The craters were shallow because we had been using instantaneous fusing on the bombs to blow down trees and open up the jungle. The giant hardwoods had been leveled in a large circle around each impact point. Around the lip of the shallow craters, several bodies were flung about in the uniquely grotesque postures achieved only by violent death. The movies have never been able to do justice to the position.

I bored straight ahead, shoving the nose down until I was just missing the tops of the taller trees. Clear of the hottest area, I pulled into a steep climbing turn to 1,500 feet.

"Blade Flight, it looks like we've gotten into an ants' nest down there. You've got some of them but there's still lots of automatic weapon fire. Blade Two, give me your bomb fifty meters into the tree line on any side of Lead's crater. You're cleared in hot if you have the FAC and target in sight."

"Roger, Blade Two is in hot from the east and I have the FAC and target in sight."

His bomb landed among the trees. Three strings of green tracers followed him from his dive. One stream was very close.

"Blade Two, Sidewinder. Are you OK?"

"Yeah, I think so. I felt something hit the aircraft, but I don't see any damage. They must have plinked me in the aft part of the fuselage."

"OK, Lead, do you want to take him out of the orbit and look him over while I finish up with Blade Three?"

"Rog. Come on Two, let's head over toward the river and I'll check you out."

Blade Three was too new for this. I was afraid we'd end up getting him hurt without anything to show for it. I had to let him go through for one last pass though, just so he wouldn't lose face with his flight.

"Blade Three, I want you to clear your racks on this pass. Call me and the target in sight and you'll be cleared in hot. Watch yourself on pullout because those guns are awfully active down there. Put everything just to the west of Two's smoke."

"Roger. In from the east, FAC and target in sight."

He bottomed out of his dive a little higher than normal, but it wasn't a bad bomb. The tracers had reached out again, trying to tickle his belly. I half-listened to Blade Lead checking over his wingman while I tried to decide whether or not to do another BDA (bomb damage assessment). There didn't appear to be any substantial damage to Blade Two. I decided against making another assessment.

The two F-100 pilots finished their caucus and announced they were ready to enter the fray once again. I directed them to clear all their remaining external stores on one last pass, scattering everything around the area.

"Before you leave me, Blade Flight, I'd like you each to give me a good long burst with your twenty mike-mike. I'm in for the mark now."

I'd been cruising at 1,500 feet, out of the range of the small arms fire from below. Letting the nose slip down below the horizon, I fired another marking round without losing much altitude. They wouldn't be aiming their cannon fire at a specific target anyway, so an accurate smoke rocket was unneeded. I watched each aircraft make a single firing pass, sloshing their fire around the jungle before they regrouped and headed south toward their home base.

"Good work, Blade Flight," I called. "I'm giving you 100 percent of your ordnance in the target area. You're going to have to wait a bit until I can get a BDA to you. I'll pass it back to your squadron just as soon as I can. I know for sure that you got some of them though." What the hell? Blade Three couldn't hit a bull in the ass with a bass fiddle, but it was his short bomb that had uncovered Mister Charley.

I watched them join into a tight formation and depart. Well, back to work.

"Sidewinder Control, this is Two-one. Do you have any more fighters inbound to me?"

"Sidewinder Two-one, this is Control. Affirmative. There's a flight of F-4s, call sign Fever, parked at 18,000 over the Testicles, and a flight of F-100s, call sign Blinky, coming up shortly to the same spot at 12,000."

"Good boy. Have they been briefed?"

"Affirmative, both flights have been briefed."

"You'll go far, lad. Fever Flight, are you up this freq?"

"That's correct, Sidewinder Two-one. We're up and briefed and we've been monitoring your festivities with Blade Flight, but you boys were having so much fun we didn't want to interrupt."

"Thank you, Fever. You're a charmer, you are. If you're ready to go to work, you can go ahead with your lineup."

"Roger, Fever Flight is three Fox-Fours. We've each got a full load of snake-eyes aboard. Negative guns."

"Way to go, Fever! The bombs are what we need for that crap down there. Stand by one while I check on another flight that's inbound. Blinky Flight, are you in the neighborhood yet?"

"Blinky reads you Sidewinder and we're coming on station now with three F-100s. All aircraft have a standard load."

Shit! More napalm. I needed bombs. Better than nothing though. The problem was that any fighters we got coming off the alert pads had to be configured to work in any part of the country. Napalm and guns were good for working down in the flat and almost treeless delta. In triple-canopy rain forest, they didn't work as well.

"This is Sidewinder Two-one. I'm going to use Fever Flight first. I want you to use three passes each for your external stores. You can run in from any heading, but call FAC and target in sight on each pass and call break off target with direction. You can expect ground fire any time on the run-in. Best bailout area looks as if it's going to be back toward the south. If you get hit or have any kind of a problem, try to let me know as soon as possible. I'll put the necessary wheels into motion. If I'm badly hit, call Sidewinder Control on this frequency and pass the word. We can have another FAC here within fifteen minutes. Any questions?"

"Fever Lead. Nope."

"Blinky Lead. Negative."

Announcing that I was in for the mark, I pushed the throttles on the Garrett engines to 100 percent power, rolled inverted, picked my spot, and rolled upright again but in a seventy-degree dive. The lighted sight in the windscreen drifted onto the target and I punched the button on the stick that fired the smoke rockets. From among the trees surrounding the blast areas, I saw the sparkle of automatic weapon fire begin once more. Tracers drifted toward me, then fell away rapidly, curving well behind the aircraft. An optical illusion. Unconsciously, I had scrunched into as small a ball as possible, my ass trying to bite chunks out of the seat cushion. Which way to turn? Most of us thought it was best to just plow straight ahead and not give the gunners any more belly than necessary. Everyone except headquarters agreed that treetop flying was about the safest place to be when taking ground fire. This reduced the gunner's tracking time tremendously. You couldn't be a pussy about it though; you really had to get down to where you were just clearing the trees or you had set yourself up to be blown from the sky.

As I was literally lifting over the taller trees, another small hole appeared in my lower left canopy. I wouldn't have noticed it except for the new stream of fresh air. It also erased forever some of the data I had written on the canopy in grease pencil. Things were happening quickly. I still had no clear idea of how many we were running against or how many larger weapons they had. The ground fire seemed to be coming from everywhere. Mentally, I revised my first estimate on the number of people down there. A VC company wouldn't have the kind of fire-power I was seeing. There were a lot of AK-47 muzzle blasts, but there was also a growing number of larger-caliber tracers beginning to flow again. It was puzzling that the force didn't try to break away the way they normally did, unless they were a larger unit that was prepared to stand and fight. Maybe we'd already killed the decision-makers. Highly unlikely that communist forces wouldn't have a disengagement plan, even if they lost their commanders. One thing for sure, the large caliber weapons made them NVA. But, how many? At least a company, probably larger.

Seeking the path of least resistance, I shoved the rudders from one limit to another, skidding the aircraft away from the areas of most intense ground fire. Finally reaching calm waters again, I pulled the stick back into my belly, trying to gain all the altitude that I could, as quickly as possible. Level at 4,000 feet. That should put me well above the AK fire. The larger guns would have no problem reaching me here, but I had a pretty good idea where they were and they couldn't get the angle on me in my present position. Fever Lead was shouting at me over the radio.

"Sidewinder, are you OK? There was crap all over the place down there. Do you want me to look you over?"

"Negative. I took a few hits I think, but I don't see anything dripping out. Let's get some." Nothing noble about it. We could have horsed around all day with him trying to slow down enough to formate on me.

"Fever Lead, hit anywhere within thirty meters of my smoke."

"Rog, Lead is in hot from the north with the FAC and target in sight."

"Fever Two, Sidewinder. Start your pass immediately from that position. Aim at Lead's explosions and let's get 'em as close together as we can. You're cleared in hot." There was little chance of him hitting exactly where the lead ship's bombs had gone. Some dispersion would happen, but we should still get a good concentration. Another voice broke in on the net.

"Sidewinder Two-one, this is Sidewinder Control."

"Go ahead Bos, this is Two-one."

"Roger, Big Boy wants you to come up TOC frequency."

Great. The army brigade I was attached to wanted to talk on their Tactical Operation Center radio. As I switched frequencies, I watched Fever Two's bombs impact. They looked good. Just about where I wanted them. The smoke from all the explosions was starting to rise and drift around the area, obscuring the visibility. It was those kinds of little things that they never told you about in FAC school. Or having to talk on three radios at a time. I made the call to the army.

"Big Boy Three, this is Sidewinder Two-one."

The response was immediate. They had obviously been waiting for my call. My radio operator in the control room sat only about ten feet from his army counterpart in the TOC. Between the two of them they generally knew what was happening around the brigade's area of operations (AO). This time, however, the call was returned by the brigade ops officer, a lieutenant colonel with whom I didn't get along too well. For that matter, no one got along with him too well, perhaps because of his job, which was a real ass-kicker. Or maybe he'd always been an asshole.

"Sidewinder, this is Big Boy Three. Can you adjust some arty on that position you're working?"

"I can try to do some adjusting between air strikes. Where will they be shooting from?"

"The battery out of Poppa Victor. Also, can you give me an estimate on the number of people down there?"

"Negative, not really. I'd guess that it's more than a company from the amount of ground fire we've been receiving, but I really don't have anything to back that up."

"Roger. I understand you're unable to make a good estimate at this time. Be advised that we're launching a Blue Team to be inserted on the november side of the blue line to your sierra. We're going to have them work november-whiskey."

I tried to decipher this bit of intelligence. I'm sure that Charley, if he were listening in, didn't have nearly as much trouble with it as I did.

"You mean you're going to put some troops in on the north bank of the river and have 'em move northwest?"

Long pause.

"Affirmative."

"OK, have the choppers orbit at 2,500 feet right over the river. Sidewinder out."

I tuned my other FM radio to the artillery battery at Phouc Vinh while I tried to figure out where to put the next bombs. Glancing quickly at my map I decided to work the artillery along a north-south line about two kilometers west of the target area. That should provide sufficient blocking fire to keep the . . . people from disengaging in that direction and to still provide a clear area in which to work the aircraft. I scribbled these numbers onto my canopy with my trusty grease pencil. By now there were so many figures scrawled there they were starting to reduce my visibility. I switched my radio back to the fighters.

"Fever Flight, I hate to do this to you but I'm going to have to restrict your run-in heading to either north or south, with an east break off target. We're going to have arty working about two klicks west of us." We tried to avoid a constant run-in heading if at all possible. Otherwise, after the first couple of passes the gunners didn't have to be graduates of Uncle Ho's military academy to realize that the next passes would probably be down the same tube.

"OK, Sidewinder. If we gotta', we gotta'." His voice betrayed no emotion at the news, still the same drawl affected by pilots everywhere to show how cool we really are. I knew he hated the idea, particularly now that we knew there was going to be a lot of ground fire. Too bad. Let him be an accountant if he didn't like this business.

"Lead, put 'em about twenty left of the heaviest smoke down there."

"Rog. Lead is in hot from the north. FAC and target in sight."

"You're cleared in hot, Lead."

The characteristically heavy black smoke trail of the F-4 made it easy to pick up as he turned onto his final run-in heading. He was moving fast as the bombs released. Before they detonated I was in toward the target, following his path but doing about one-fourth his speed. My aircraft pitched as the shock waves from the bomb's blast hit me. As quickly as I had the plane under control again, I corrected to put the sight on a new target area, slightly north of the bomb craters. I watched my rocket impact before I pulled hard back on the stick, partially losing my vision due to the g-forces. I relaxed enough back pressure to allow me to speak.

"Fever Two and Three, you're both cleared in hot. Put your bombs right and left of my new smoke. I'm going to have to leave you for one to talk to arty. Continue to make your calls and be sure that you have me in sight before you start your runs. And Lead, you were taking ground fire through most of your run. I saw at least two heavy calibers going after you. You all watch your butts while I'm off frequency."

"Fever Lead, roger."

I listened to Fever Two make his inbound call and then quickly switched to the artillery frequency, while continuing to monitor the calls of the other fighters over the other radio.

"Logger, this is Sidewinder Two-one. Fire mission."

"Sidewinder, this is Logger. Understand you have a fire mission. Pass us the coordinates."

There was an elaborate ritual that an artillery observer used, according to the Fort Sill School for Wayward Boys and Artillery Adjustment. Forward air controllers had discovered that the tube crews were as willing to dispense with it as we were, should the situation warrant that. Paring it to the bone, we could establish contact with them, pass the target coordinates, and tell them to start shooting. Unless there was some compelling reason to do otherwise, they usually did it. I passed the target coordinates to them.

"Sidewinder Two-one, this is Logger. We're ready to shoot."

"Let her go," I said, ignoring the standard terminology. I was in a hurry to get back to the fighters' frequency.

"Sidewinder, this is Logger. Shot. Out."

"Roger, Logger. Shot," I repeated. Their white phosphorous marking round was in the air. I turned toward the dry streambed to wait for the round's impact. I rotated the wafer switch to put me back on the fighters' frequency.

"Fever Flight, a willie pete arty round will be impacting momentarily to the west of your run-in line. I'm talking to the battery, so don't worry about it."

"Fever copies. Listen, Sidewinder, we're getting the shit shot out of us."

"Rog, I know. Tell you what let's do. On the next pass everyone clean your racks on my marker. You're all cleared in hot if you have me in sight. Maintain your assigned run-in headings after release and until you're clear of the area. I'm off frequency again to give the arty a quick adjustment."

"Logger, that looks real good," I told the artillery controller. "Work it at that distance, right and left 200 meters of that point. Fire for effect."

Another frequency shift back to the fighters. In only moments I watched the 105s begin to tear up the jungle west of the bombing area. It looked pretty good and should be enough to discourage Charley from breaking in that direction.

Time to mark again. This time I used a different sort of approach. Never do the same thing twice and maybe you'd stay alive. So, I was down to the treetops and boring in toward the target at low level; a quick pop-up, thumbing the button, then back to the treetops once more. A hard right turn when the most dangerous area was passed and a quick climb back to altitude. The OV-10 looked so slow and ungainly that the NVA gunners frequently made the same mistake as a novice duck hunter. They both forgot to lead their prey sufficiently, and most shots fell somewhere behind both the aircraft and the duck. Either that or they were laughing themselves silly at the appearance of Uncle Sam's newest efforts in counterinsurgency aircraft. My turn completed, I looked at my last mark. An overshoot; a common error when trying to fire from a low angle.

"Fever Flight, put everything you have about seventy-five meters due south of my smoke. I overshot it quite a bit."

"Sidewinder, this is Fever Lead. Do you think we could get you to put in a new mark a little closer to the target? There's so much smoke down there I'm not really sure which one I'm supposed to aim at."

Oh, sure. Why not? I'm going so slow that I have to map read across the target area, but I'll be glad to hang my bare ass out for you so that you can have your new mark. I'm tempted to tell the flight that I've changed my mind again and we'll have to drop their bombs in singles. That ought to increase his exposure time by about half an hour. Would you like that, Fever?

"Roger, Sidewinder in for the new mark."

I couldn't think of a real excuse not to do it, but I didn't want to. In fact, I would rather have done about anything else than stick my nose into that area again. At 2,500 feet I did a wing-over down toward the target. It's generally acknowledged that in attacking a hot target it's all for the best to just try to ignore the ground fire coming at you. There's nothing the pilot can do about it anyway. You might as well just look straight ahead and think pure thoughts. One friend advocated shouting poetry into his oxygen mask while on the bomb run. He swore that it bored him so much he forgot to be frightened.

The forward air controller unfortunately cannot do this. He must see as much of the target area as he can in order to place the bombs with maximum effectiveness. During this process, he also gets to see many unfriendly faces. In the fifteen seconds it took to dive and launch a new marking rocket, my eyes flicked painfully from point to point, dreading the sight of the tracers coming from all quadrants. Automatic weapons were twinkling from the tree lines surrounding the blast areas. I punched the rocket release on the stick and kicked hard left rudder, then fired again. Leveling at the treetops I "egressed" the area, as they like to say in military briefings.

"Fever Lead, hit the easternmost smoke. Fever Two and Three hit the westernmost mark."

A bright orange sheet of flames sprouted from the aft part of Fever Two's fuselage as he pulled out of his run. He was on fire from just behind his cockpit to the end of his tail. Something must have gotten a fuel cell and let the jet fuel pour out into the slipstream where it enveloped his aircraft.

"Get out, Two. You're on fire!"

It sounded like the voice of Fever Three. The lead ship wasn't in position to see his flaming wingman when he was hit. Unconsciously, I glanced quickly at the target, automatically registering the explosions of their bombs before turning my eyes back to the stricken fighter. The bombs looked good.

"Roger," Two's voice was tight and tense but under control. "I'm going to try to get to the other side of the river."

Good thinking. Charley probably wouldn't be too happy with one of the pilots who had just been bombing him. The pilot would be real lucky to even reach the ground alive aboard the old nylon elevator. It didn't really matter, for Fever Two suddenly exploded. One moment he was in a flying aircraft; the next he was in a close formation of junk metal, rapidly decelerating toward the ground. Most of the debris continued toward the river, clearing it to the far side.

"Fever Three, this is Lead. Let's set up an orbit over him. Did anyone see any chutes?"

I hated to be the bad guy, but that was what they were paying me for.

"Fever Flight, this is Sidewinder. Get your butts back where they belong. I'll decide whether we need a CAP or not. What are you plan-ning on using anyway? You're out of ordnance. I'll let you know if I need your help on the SAR. But I was looking at him and no one got out. I'm going to clear you both out of the area at this time. My control is listening in on this freq and I'm sure that he's already alerted the closest rescue birds. Isn't that right, Sidewinder Control?"

"Sidewinder Two-one, this is Sidewinder Control. That's affirmative, sir. We're in the process of diverting two Hueys right now. They ought to be at your location in about five." Good old Bos.

"We've got enough fuel to cap them until the choppers arrive," Fever Three cut in. He sounded combative. This thing had gone far enough.

"Negative, Fever Flight," I said. "No one got out. Now, rejoin your leader and clear the area to the north. We've still got a war going on here."

"Goddammit, Sidewinder. You don't know that no one's alive. It's possible that you missed it."

"Fever Flight, this is Sidewinder Two-one. Get your asses out of my AO immediately. We've got work to do here and your BDA will be passed to you. Out."

There would be no free drinks for me from that squadron. I switched to the artillery frequency, gave them a quick adjustment, and told them they were doing good work. Then, quickly, I switched to the chopper frequency.

"Rescue birds inbound to the Testicles, this is Sidewinder. What's your callsign?"

"This is Roach Four-eight and Roach Five-two. We're a slick and a Charley model. We've got the smoke from the air strike up ahead. Where did that fighter go in?"

"Most of it hit the south bank of the westernmost Testicle. Some of it may have gone into the river as well. I'm positive that no one got out but we ought to look the area over anyway. Be advised that I'll be working air strikes north of the river and arty is going in northwest of the crash site. I'd suggest that you stay as low as possible."

"You can count on it, Bro." I recognized the voice. It was a huge black warrant officer who flew the old model gunships. They were pretty lightly armed, but I hadn't seen any movement in the area of the crash, and if Charley was down there he'd more than likely didi out of the area after the burning fighter fell on him, knowing that rescue choppers would soon be overhead. It shouldn't take them long for I knew there were no living friendlies down there. I was sure the helicopter pilots would recognize that too as soon as they saw the wreckage.

"Sidewinder Two-one, this is Sidewinder Control. Got an update for you. You've got a flight of VNAF A-1s inbound to the Anthill [another nearby rendezvous point] and I told their controller to park them at 8,000. There's also a company-sized Blue Team just about airborne that ought to be in the insertion area in about ten. Two snake fire teams are en route to cover the insertion. I told all of them to head to the Anthill too, and that you'd get in touch with them as soon as you could. Nestor is the gunship call sip. Unknown on the VNAF."

"Unknown sounds about right. Did their controller have any idea what sort of ordnance they were carrying?"

"That's negative, Two-one. I had trouble understanding him at all."

"Not to worry, Bos. We'll figure something out. You're doing a good job. I may adopt you when I leave."

"Thank you, sir, but I'm already spoken for by a rich, elderly nymphomaniac back in Saginaw."

"Well, shit. Maybe you two could adopt me. Out."

"Blinky Lead, this is Sidewinder Two-one. Are you folks still with me?"

"Rog, Sidewinder, but I thought I was going to lose Two and Three when that Fox-Four went down. Those boys were ready to head back to the bar."

"Your ass," growled one of the wingmen.

Callous? Maybe. I found that everyone deals with tragedy in their own way. And you did have to learn how to deal with it.

I told the flight of F-100s to descend to orbit altitude and to stand by. Clamping my knees to the control stick to keep the wings level, I reached into the leg pocket of my flight suit and brought out a baby bottle of water. I had two more left. We used them because they would fit into the pocket and didn't leak. A canteen held more water, but we were upside down almost as much as we were straight and level, and didn't relish having a two-pound projectile loose in the cockpit. I drained the bottle in a single draught, then removed my helmet and gave my head a vigorous scratching, finishing up by toweling my face with the rolled sleeve of my flight suit. The suit was completely dark with sweat. The OV-10 was not air-conditioned, relying instead on two small ramair vents by the leg and one overhead in the canopy. The temperature in the cockpit was roughly the same as it was on the ground, possibly higher due to the sun beating down on the large canopy. Of course, I had the new, improved version with the AK-47 holes for additional cooling. Replacing my helmet, I heard Blinky Lead calling.

"Sidewinder, Blinky Flight is down to fifteen minutes loiter before we have to leave you."

"No problem, Blinky. I've got you in sight and we won't be making that many passes. You've probably heard that I'm going to have to restrict your run-in heading to north or south with an east pull-off. I'll be directly over the target at 2,000 feet. I want all your bombs on the first pass. Next pass, all of the nape. If you've got any time left after that we may try some twenty mike-mike sloshed around the area. They're getting pretty touchy, so let's try to make it in and out as quickly as we can. Keep your patterns as tight as possible and keep alert to the artillery working to the west of us. We've also got two army choppers inbound to the crash site, but they'll be working real low. Before we get started, did any of your flight happen to pick up a beeper on that F-4 that went in?"

"Negative. I've already checked with the rest of the flight. No one heard anything. We'll run from south to north with a right break off target. Let's arm 'em up, Blinky Flight."

"Sidewinder Two-one is in for the mark," I called. Turning hard left I put the nose of the Bronco down into a thirty-degree dive, flying a parabolic curve to the target. We had to stop most of the antiaircraft fire if we didn't want to lose someone else. I let the sight pipper ride through the target area to compensate for the g-forces of the turn, then fired another rocket. Continuing the turn, I looked back over my shoulder and watched the rocket impact in the jungle. The ground fire from light automatic weapons looked like a child's sparklers against the darkness beneath the trees. Dirty gray puffs blossomed beneath my right wing. Not too accurate, but it put things into a different perspective. It was probably a .37mm tracking me. That meant that I could no longer stay over the target at 4,000 feet with immunity from the fire coming from below. That baby could be aimed accurately up to 15,000 feet. Obviously, there was no way I was going to be able to get over it and still work the target. I'd have to dazzle them with my low animal cunning by staying too low for them to be able to track me properly. I'd have to keep some trees between the .37mm and me. That thing had to go immediately, and I hoped they didn't have another one. The heavy machine guns were bad enough. Mentally, I marked its location, figuring an azimuth and distance from my last marker. I went back to the fighters.

"Blinky Lead, you've got some heavy stuff about fifty meters west of my smoke, just inside that tree line by the westernmost crater. I want your entire flight to scatter the snakes in that area. Keep 'em jinking because he was really after me that time. There's lots of AK fire down there too."

"Rog, we saw that. Blinky Lead is in hot. FAC and target in sight."

An unintelligible singsong of Vietnamese broke in on the radio. Obviously, the flight of VNAF A-1s that Bos had told me about had arrived. Unless a pilot's diction is good, it's very hard to understand him over the radio. In this instance it was impossible. I couldn't even tell if they were trying to speak English.

"Blinky Lead, you'd better hold your flight high and dry until we can get this sorted out. It seems our comrades from the VNAF have joined us. Try to stay out of their way and they'll probably be finished in a few minutes."

"Roger that," he replied with some feeling. A midair collision can ruin your whole day.

I went through the briefing spiel with them, not having a clue as to whether or not they understood any of it. I didn't even know where they were, for that matter.

That question was answered when a bomb suddenly erupted in the target area. None of the F-100s had even been close to it. As usual, the Vietnamese Air Force seemed to prefer the direct approach. They took off, they flew to what they thought might be the target area; they dropped their bombs on it; they went home. Life was really very simple for them, but it did cause some complications in ours. They knew how to bomb with those old A-1s, though. They flew over the target, rolled the nose nearly vertical into a dive, and came straight down with those huge dive brakes hanging out to slow them down. They usually dumped everything on one pass, and the effect, if they were on the correct target, could be devastating. Any of their old aircraft could carry its own weight in bombs. This time was no exception. All three loads hit within twenty meters of each other. It was still fifty meters away from my smoke, but it was in the right area and must have done some good. Smoke from their explosions completely obscured the target area for a few moments.

A new voice broke in on my helmet: "FAC working north of the Testicles, this is Big Boy Six. Over." Absolutely charming! The brigade commander had decided to join us. This made a perfect day. He was a prickly old fart who completely dominated a communications net once he got on it. He was ferried daily around the brigade's AO by whatever hapless Huey crew drew the black bean. I tried to sort my communications problem in my mind before I answered him. Let's see, I would have the brigade commander dominating one of the FM radios; the artillery would be on the other FM; the command-ship pilot would want to be in contact on the VHF radio, unheard by his passenger; the fighters and my control room would be on UHF; when the Blues arrived they'd be working VHF; and God knows where the VNAF would be.

"Big Boy Six, this is Sidewinder Two-one. What's your position, please? I've got artillery going in on a 400-meter line, fronting that dry streamed to the west, and a flight of VNAF fighters are now engaging in the target area with no control."

The colonel began his usual tirade over the airways, almost as if he were thinking aloud. The command-ship pilot spoke to me over the VHF radio, unknown to the colonel, who continued to voice his views ad nauseam.

"Where do you want us, Sidewinder?" He was wisely concerned about being pinched between the artillery on one side and the air strikes on the other.

Rotating the radio wafer switch to get on his channel, I suggested the safest area would probably be about a klick west of the smoke over the target. He would have to keep his turns tight and find some altitude that would keep him clear of the ground fire as well as the jets coming off target.

I was still talking when my windscreen was filled with the shiny, olive drab HU-1B that the army aviation battalion provided their VIP passengers. I pulled back the control stick as hard as I could and the earth rapidly rotated around me. While still inverted in the top half of a loop, I swiveled my head until I picked up the chopper, then nudged the rudder so that I could complete the maneuver away from him.

Still on the helicopter pilot's frequency, I said, "That was close. Another three feet and I'd have been wearing you." I was pretty steamed, but I couldn't blame the pilot too much. I knew that he was flying where the colonel directed, and it would have taken a lot of balls to tell him that he wouldn't.

"Roger that," he said. His voice was tight but calm. "We're going to try to get out of your way." The colonel continued to rave, unaware how close he had been to being a dead colonel.

Another burst of Vietnamese announced that they had either completed their bombing or were going to attack the helicopter. I'd seen no more bombs or rockets from them and assumed they were leaving. I tried to find them, but the rising smoke from the bombs and my smoke rockets had substantially reduced the visibility.

"Sidewinder, Blinky Lead here. It looks like our gallant allies are departing to the south. We're going to have to go to work pretty quick. We're all approaching bingo fuel."

"No problem, Blinky. We'll put you right in. Be advised that we've now got a C and C chopper orbiting between the target and that line of arty fire. I'll try to keep everyone clear, but try to keep an eye in that direction in case he strays. You'll be cleared in hot just as soon as you see my new mark."

After he started his run-in he'd be lucky to spare a glance in that direction, for the smoke was drifting badly and he'd be coming down the tube at about 500 knots.

Playing it safe, I lowered the nose and fired another smoke rocket from 1,500 feet. After this pass, I'd have to do another assessment run over the target. I was already dreading it.

"Hit anywhere in the vicinity of my smoke, Lead. Two and Three, I'm going to make a BDA after Lead's pass. Be ready for a quick change of targets. Also, acknowledge that you have the info about the chopper working west of the target."

They dutifully acknowledged and I watched the lead aircraft being tracked by long trails of green tracers and several puffs of gray flak. The bombs missed them, for they continued to track the jet as he broke off target. I decided to delay the BDA until we'd put away the gun.

"Blinky Two and Three. Change of plans. You're both cleared in hot, in sequence. Both of you put your bombs about fifty meters north of Lead's last explosions."

The colonel continued to natter on the FM radio. Screw him. I watched Two pull off the target, jinking wildly. Three was already halfway down his run. Both sets of bombs were good—about thirty meters or so from where I had wanted them, but good enough. Damned good under the circumstances.

"Where are you guys from? That was good stuff.

"Thanks, neighbor. We're out of Tuy Hoa," the leader replied in a corn-pone accent. "We thank you for the compliment, but I think I might have dumped something other than bombs on that pass. My flight suit sure does feel heavy."

"I know what you mean," I replied. "Now if I could get a pair of you to make simultaneous gun runs from the north, about a hundred meters east and west of the last target, I'll try to sneak in between you and go down to see if we've done anything. After that, I'll clear you from the area."

"You heard the man, Blinky Two. You take the east and I'll take the west. Three, you hold high and dry and keep your eye on Sidewinder while he dazzles us with his feats of daring and airmanship. Just let us know when you're ready, Sidewinder."

Very funny. "OK, let's go." My strategy was simple enough. I planned to fly directly at the attacking fighters but at a slightly higher altitude. Just before I reached their spread formation, I would roll the Bronco inverted and change directions completely, using the dive to increase my airspeed. If I timed it right I would complete the course reversal at low level, going in their direction, and be able to use the cover of their strafing run to survive should there be more heavy guns down there.

It almost worked. I relaxed the g-forces and leveled out above the trees, peering ahead in the smoke for the fighters. They were already by me though, bumping their rudders to disperse their cannon fire. I had misjudged the speed differential between their aircraft and mine. They simply had too much for me. They disappeared into the smoke; moments later I saw the sun glint on their wings as they made sharp pullouts from over the target. I was just getting into the target area.

Initially, there was little ground fire. The NVA were probably trying to get their brains back in gear after the cannon run. Either that or they couldn't believe what they were seeing. Here was the answer to the prayer of every frustrated Viet gunner who had been bombed, strafed, and generally harassed by aircraft every step of the way down the long Ho Chi Minh Trail. Here was meat on the hoof. A Yankee plane at low level, put-putting its way across the sky. I felt as naked as the day I was born. My eyes darted back and forth across the blast-cleared area. The jungle was mangled. The huge but shallow-rooted trees had been blown aside. Tiny human stick figures lay tumbled about the periphery of the blast zone. More of them were sprawled well up into the tree line as far as I could see into its darkness. There was nothing recognizable closer to the blasts except the remains of a crew-served antiaircraft gun, now on its side. Hopefully, this was the one that had been so active a little earlier. Maybe we really got them, I thought. Maybe I can just fly around here and count the pieces and this thing will be over.

Automatic weapon fire suddenly erupted from beneath the tree line and the now-familiar green tracers began to track me. They began flying at me from both sides and straight ahead. Good Christ, which way to go? I sawed at the rudders and ailerons in uncoordinated flight. The hair on my neck bristled and I tried to squeeze my shoulders into my crash helmet. Panic was only a breath away. I felt like a high-speed driver on an icy road just before he loses control. I stared straight ahead, slamming the stick from one side to the other, accomplishing nothing. My brain stem registered the impact of the rounds as they slammed into the aircraft, but the lobes were frozen. Suddenly, the bottom of the instrument panel blew into my lap. I could see the tops of the trees through the hole. At least two more holes were in the canopy; the one directly in front of me was long and jagged. Then as suddenly as it began, the ground fire stopped and there was nothing but unsullied rain forest in front of me again. I continued straight ahead until my brain took over from my reflexes, then made a slow climbing turn back to altitude. I forced my head left and then right to assess the damage. The air coming through the new hole in the instrument panel felt nice. Maybe I should petition the Air Force to install holes like that in all the OV-10s.

Ignoring the radio squawking at me, I took inventory. Aside from the instrument panel and the new holes in the canopy, there were several jagged holes visible in the wings and fuselage. The tanks were self-sealing up to a point. I didn't know if I had exceeded that point or not, but I didn't see anything flowing out. I took that as a good sign; I was more frightened of a fire in an aircraft than anything else that could happen. There also seemed to be a piece missing from the right wing tip, although I could see nothing dribbling out of the hole. The engines seemed to be running well, whining away with the normal screech of the turboprop. What engine instruments I had left on my instrument panel confirmed that they were pulling full power. Angling the mirror toward my face, I saw several deep scratches in my helmet's sun visor.

As I ran my hand over the front of my helmet, I felt several small pieces of metal and glass embedded there, undoubtedly the result of the instrument panel's demise. Arms. Legs. Head. Torso. Everything seemed to be as good as it was before. I pushed the mike button and tried to talk, but couldn't. My mouth had dried so much that I could hardly part my lips. Pulling another baby bottle of water from my pocket, I gulped it down. Like an opera singer warming up, I experimentally warbled a few notes until my voice sounded almost normal.

"Blinky Lead, this is Sidewinder. We got a bunch of them, but there are plenty still full of fight. I'm going to clear you out of the area now 'cause we've got some gunships inbound. You guys did damned good work and I'll be sure to get a BDA up to you as soon as I can. I'll look you up sometime. So long."

"Roger, Sidewinder," the slow drawl came back. "It's been a pleasure doing business with you. We can stretch the fuel a bit more if you'd like. I'm sure we can stay until someone else gets into the area. You look like you were hit mighty hard on that last BDA."

"Naw, I think everything's OK. It kinda' shook me up for a minute but I'm all right now. Thanks for the offer, though. The choppers ought to be up here shortly."

"OK, Buddy. If you ever get up to Tuy Hoa, the drinks are on me."

"I'll take you up on that. Adios."

From my relatively safe perch I watched the three graceful aircraft join into a loose formation and turn northward, climbing quickly out of sight. To the south I could see the two army helicopters hovering around the wreckage of the downed F-4. They began to slowly quarter the area, apparently not finding anything to pick up. In that position they shouldn't be in anyone's way, although they could be in the way of the Blue Team's insertion. Let them figure it out. I was too tired. My hand that was holding the control stick seemed too heavy to keep in place. Some of my fatigue may be shock, I thought. Maybe some dehydration too. I'd drunk two of my baby bottles but had probably sweated twenty times that much. Using my left hand, I reached over and squeezed the right sleeve of my flight suit. Liquid dribbled out in a steady stream, as if it were being wrung from a wet dishcloth. Grabbing the stick with my knees, I raised my visor, unclipped my chin strap, and removed my helmet again. I leaned my head back against the ejection seat headrest and idly rubbed my gloved hand over the helmet, dislodging the shards of glass and metal that had been blown into it. I checked my face in the mirror; it was flaming red with heat and sweat but no cuts. Luck had been with me so far. I removed my last baby bottle and poured the water down my parched throat. It didn't come close to satisfying my thirst. I replaced and buckled my helmet just in time to hear the brigade commander swearing at me over the radio.

"Goddammit, Sidewinder Two-one. Do you read me? This is Big Boy Six."

"Go ahead Six, this is Sidewinder Two-one."

"What the hell is going on over there? Are there any dinks or are you people just pissing in the wind?"

I felt like telling him to get just a little closer and he'd find out for himself. But I didn't. Instead, I briefed him on the situation as I saw it. I explained that we had expended four flights of fighters in the area and that I could get more if he wanted. What I suggested, though, was that the artillery be adjusted onto the target. Additional alert birds would be standing by on the pads at Bien Hoa, only some fifteen minutes away and available for the Blue's insertion, should he want them.

Most of the ground commanders would accept the FAC's advice concerning aircraft employment, but they were mighty touchy if they thought you were straying from your area of expertise. Most of them knew that they didn't know any more about employing bombs than I did about running an infantry battalion. Some, like old numbnuts now circling the area, wanted to run the whole show. He also wanted to play platoon leader, recalling his glory years as a second lieutenant in the Ardennes. More times than I liked to remember, I had seen him circling above some hapless grunt platoon, giving directions to its harried young commander, who already had more than his share of problems humping in the bush.

He jumped at the opportunity to bring in the artillery. That way he could claim most of the KIAs (killed in action) as being done in by arty. He would have preferred that all of them be killed by his infantry, but this was difficult to achieve with bodies ripped asunder by high explosives. In his view, credit to the artillery would be better than letting the Air Force get away with destroying the enemy in his AO. He could claim them all as victims of his personal .45 for all I cared.

I watched the command helicopter ease cautiously toward the target area. The commander was an asshole, but not a fainthearted asshole. If any of those big guns were left in there, that Huey was going to die.

"Big Boy Six, Sidewinder. Best remain clear of that area. There still may be some big guns working down there." As I spoke, another string of tracers lifted toward the helicopter. It swiftly banked toward the west, clearing the hot area.

"Six, this is Sidewinder. If you can take over the arty adjustment, I'll see if there's anything airborne that we can put in quickly before the Blues get here."

"OK, Sidewinder. We'll take over the adjustment and we'll keep it clear of your area until you can get your damned planes in and out."

Gracious sod. I called Bos at the control room again. "Sidewinder Control, this is Two-one. I hope you've been monitoring. Is there anything we can use anywhere close to us?"

"Roger," he responded immediately. "Roscoe Flight; three F-4s inbound to you now. They've got a full load of iron bombs and they've already been briefed. They should be up this frequency now." Good old Bos!

"Thanks, Control. Roscoe Lead, are you up this freq?"

"Roger, Sidewinder. We're approaching the Testicles now. Can you give us some smoke?"

"Rog, Roscoe. Smoker is coming on now."

I put the Bronco into a shallow turn and pulled the toggle switch, which dumped oil into the hot exhaust ports, creating a dense white smoke like that used by skywriters. The smoke was very helpful in making a rendezvous with the fighters. Few know how difficult it is for one aircraft to see another aircraft in flight, despite Hollywood's insistence that an eagle-eyed hero can spot his prey miles away. In real life, aircraft routinely pass within yards of one another with no one being the wiser.

"OK, Sidewinder, Roscoe Flight has you in sight. We're at your eight o'clock, descending through 14,000 feet."

Peering over my left shoulder, I let go of the smoke switch. I saw the sun glinting off the F-4s' wings as the planes spread into attack formation.

"Roscoe Flight, Sidewinder. We'll make one pass and haul ass. OK? Dump it all because we're in a hurry here. Make your runs north to south with an east break off target. Call FAC and target in sight. I'm in for the mark now."

I handled the OV-10 very gently as I rolled in to shoot one of my few remaining rockets. I didn't know how much damage the aircraft had sustained, and I didn't want to take more chances than necessary. I watched the white smoke billow from the rocket, just about where I had last seen the tracers erupting. There was not nearly as much ground fire this time, and I saw nothing of the larger guns. Most of the stuff coming up was AK-47.

"Roscoe Lead, hit my smoke, and on pullout continue your easterly heading coming off target. Be advised we're still taking some small arms fire from the area. Roscoe Two, hit fifty meters west of my smoke. Roscoe Three, hit fifty meters east. If you have me in sight, you're all cleared in hot, in sequence. Watch yourself, everyone. We've already lost one F-4 in the area this morning."

"OK, Sidewinder. Understand one pass and haul ass. Lead's in hot."

Roscoe Two and Three called inbound shortly. The havoc created by a planeload of bombs dropped at once was impressive. All three runs looked good. I was already limping across the target at 500 feet before the smoke had cleared from the last explosion. The destruction to the rain forest had been awesome.

From one of the far blast areas, a lone AK-47 winked at me from the tree line. Quickly I flicked the arming switches to my four machine guns and, without using the sight, pulled the trigger on the control stick. I slewed the nose of the aircraft with the rudders toward the source of the fire. I wasn't trying to hit him. I just wanted to keep his head down until I was out of the area. Pulling gingerly on the stick, I crept back to safe altitude and made a last call to Roscoe Flight, now leaving the area. I promised to forward their BDA as soon as I could.

Nestor, the helicopter gunships inbound to cover the troop insertion, were calling on the VHF. I looked toward the Anthill and picked up the flight of six.

"Nestor, this is Sidewinder Two-one. I've got you in sight. Suggest you conserve your ordnance for the Blue Team's insertion. I've only got a couple of willie petes left, but I'll put one in where we were taking most of the ground fire. I think we've pretty well taken care of it though, except for an isolated AK here and there. God knows how many are down there. You might try calling Big Boy Six, who's orbiting west of the area between that smoke and the dry streambed out there. I'm sure he'll be glad to mark the area he wants you to hit."

"Sounds good, Sidewinder. I'm leaving freq to talk to Big Boy."

I listened to the remainder of his flight acknowledge the frequency shift and then heard the gunship leader come up on the command frequency. As they discussed the planned insertion, I rolled in gently once more and fired my next-to-last rocket, then pointed the nose of the Bronco to the south. Over the river, I saw that the rescue attempt had been abandoned and the choppers had left unnoticed. Over the command net, the colonel sounded pleased to have a more active role. I waited for a break in the radio traffic to tell them I was leaving, carefully checking the one fuel gauge left on my instrument panel. The other one was in my lap. If the functional one was anywhere near accurate, it was going to be close on fuel. The youthful exuberance of the fire team leader was frightening. Most of the Cobra pilots seemed to be about eighteen years old, with all the fearlessness and the belief in their own immortality of that age group. Most of them had the judgment of a load of bricks. If the pilots could be controlled, they were great to have around. If left on their own, they were a hazard to every living thing in the area. I finally broke in for one last transmission.

"Big Boy Six, this is Sidewinder. I'm going to have to leave the area now. Another FAC will be up shortly in case you need any more fast movers. I'm departing to the south."

"Sidewinder, this is Six. Thanks, that was a good job. I'd like you to pass along my compliments to the pilots."

The old fart was actually being gracious.

One last chore. "Sidewinder Control, this is Two-one. Call the hootch and get the Duty FAC airborne. Have him take a good look at the situation map in the TOC before he takes off and then have him head to the Testicles and orbit. The Blues are inbound and the CO might change the insertion coordinates. Also, give Bien Hoa a call and tell them we're going to need another aircraft. This one is all used up until they can get it repaired. They'd better send a sheet-metal man too, so they can fix this one enough to fly back. They'll also need someone who can OK a one-time flight for it down there."

"Roger, Two-one. Are you going to try to got in hem or head on back to Bien Hoa?"

I knew what he was saying. Lai Khe had only a minimum of crash equipment for the airstrip, whereas Bien Hoa was like a stateside base, with big fire trucks and firemen in asbestos suits. Bien Hoa also had the capability to foam the runway if I couldn't get my landing gear down and had to belly it in. In that event, the foam went a long way in suppressing any fire caused by the friction of the aircraft skin against the hard surface of the runway. At Lai Khe they'd probably just walk over and try to beat out the flames with their entrenching tools.

"Negative, I'm coming back to home plate. I shouldn't have any trouble getting in. Besides, I don't think I've got enough fuel to go to Bien Hoa."

"Roger. Be advised that Sidewinder Two-five is airborne in your vicinity if you want him to look you over before landing."

"That's good, Bos. Tell him to come up this frequency and I'll be heading on slowly toward the house."

"Two-one, this is Two-five. I've been monitoring your frequency. Give me a shot of smoke, jefe."

My arms were so tired they felt numb. I could hardly reach the smoker switch. I glanced at the clock and saw that I had been airborne for almost four hours.

"Got you now, Two-one," Paco said. "Just keep her going toward home and I'll join up."

I looked behind me until I found the other OV-10 coming up on my left side, overtaking me rapidly. He brought his aircraft snugly in behind my left wing, then moved gently into a trail formation, then onto the right wing.

"You've got a lot of damage, but I can't see anything that would keep you from landing all right. Are you hurt?"

"Negative, I'm OK. And thanks, Paco, but you'd better head on in in case I tie up the runway."

"Naw. I got nothing better to do. I think I'll just practice some formation flying. I'm getting pretty rusty."

"Suit yourself." He was lying and we both knew it, but I was appreciative of the company. I heard the Duty FAC call airborne. He must have been primed and ready to go to get off that quickly. He called me.

"Sidewinder Two-one, this is Two-seven. I've been listening to your strikes in the control room with Bos. If we have to put in any more strikes, you got any idea where's the best place to put them?"

"The way they're shooting today, I'd suggest Des Moines," I said wearily. "If the dinks are smart, they'll be heading east because I think they're pretty well blocked in the other direction. Which means they'll probably do just the opposite of what I said. Whatever you do, watch your butt. They've got some gunners down there today."

"No sweat. I'll be the soul of discretion. See you later, boss." Yeah, the soul of discretion. If I knew him he'd be down in the treetops before the fighters ever got there, gunning with everything he had.

Lassitude crept over me like someone was pouring it from a bucket.

I wiggled my toes vigorously in my jungle boots, tying to pump myself up for the landing. I leaned my face down toward the fresh air flowing through the shell hole in the instrument panel. It helped dry some of the sweat dribbling from under my close-fitting helmet. I loosened my shoulder straps and slid my pistol out of the position where it had been digging into my ribs. Suddenly, everything was uncomfortable. My mouth had dried out again, but I had nothing left to drink. I turned my helmet back and forth on my head, trying to find a comfortable position for my ears, which seemed to have grown in the last few hours.

Minutes later, the rubber plantation surrounding the Lai Khe airstrip came into view. The pockmarked runway wasn't visible until I was nearly upon it. The approach had to be made down a cleared lane through the rubber trees. I called the tower—a GI sitting on top of a sandbagged bunker—and announced my intentions to land straight in rather than flying the prescribed pattern. The landing gear came down just as advertised, and was verified by the green lights on the panel. I was delighted. At least the enemy rounds seemed to have missed my hydraulic system, which meant the brakes should also work. The landing was terrible, but I didn't care.

Between the holes in the canopy, the grease-pencil markings on my windscreen, and the deep scratches on my visor from the exploding instrument panel, I could hardly follow Butch's marshaling signals. I taxied slowly into the sandbagged revetment and shut down the engines. It was steaming in the cockpit, but I didn't have the strength to raise the canopy. Butch stood shirtless and scowling at me, red hair plastered to his head with sweat. He turned his head slowly as he looked at his aircraft, the scowl deepening at the sight. His eyes came back to me. I stared at him goggle-eyed, breathing like a derby loser. His features smoothed a little as he continued to watch me. Then he walked slowly to the side of the aircraft and opened the canopy with the external handle. I gasped at him as though I was giving birth to a whale.

He crawled up the steps and unlocked my parachute harness. Seeing that I hadn't safed my ejection seat, he reached into my leg pocket and pulled out the safety pins. Carefully, he installed them and then grasped my arm and gently urged me from the cockpit. I half-fell and half-crawled down to the pierced steel planking (PSP) ramp and sat heavily against one of the main tires. The rest of the ground crew stared at me, then at the aircraft. Butch walked to the Conex box that served as his maintenance storage area. Dixie, the black armorer, knelt and removed my helmet, then slid my parachute harness and survival vest from my torso. I think he thought I was wounded. Butch returned with two hot beers, opened them both with his sheath knife, and handed them to me silently. Two swallows and they were both gone.

"How was it, Major?" Butch finally spoke.

"Fine, just fine," I croaked.

As I felt the liquid giving life back to my body, I watched Butch walk slowly around the Bronco, shaking his head and muttering mechanical incantations. Dixie placed my gear in the duty jeep as I staggered over to it. Absentmindedly, I noticed that the Duty FAC, now airborne, had again forgotten to lock the chain around the steering wheel. If that continued unchecked, some grunt would more than likely steal the jeep from us. That would be discouraging considering all the trouble we had taken to steal it from them. I made a mental note to speak to the Duty FAC about it later.

I drove slowly back to the FAC hootch. The roads were covered with six inches of red dust, constantly being churned by the passing vehicles. I should have gone by the brigade TOC for debriefing, but I was too exhausted to even think straight. As I parked in front of the sandbagged hootch, one of the new guys burst through the door and ran toward me.

"Hey, Maj. They've got a real one going on up there where you were. I've been monitoring it over the radio. The Blues got the crap shot out of them on insertion, and we've already lost one slick and one gunship. Don took your place and has already put in three more sets of fighters. Shit hot, huh?"

"Yeah, shit hot," I replied. "How about calling up the TOC for me and telling them I'll be over later to debrief. I doubt if they've got time to talk to me now, anyway. Also, call the division TACP and let the air liaison officer know what's going on."

"No sweat. I was on my way to the TOC anyway. See you later, boss."

I walked to my bunk and placed my gear in my locker. The smell of mildew was strong as I opened the locker door. Wearily, I lay back on the bunk and shut my eyes. My brain was going too fast to turn off, though, and I could feel my eyes flickering wildly beneath the closed lids. Later, I heard some of the pilots gathering in what we laughingly called the "dayroom." Paco's voice, more strident than the others, hammered its way into my consciousness. We had, it seemed, been responsible for more than 300 KBAs—killed by air—so far in today's activities. The count was incomplete but still rising as the ground sweep continued. Not that different from many other days. It was my sixty-seventh day in the Republic of South Vietnam, and so far 1969 had been a hell of a year.

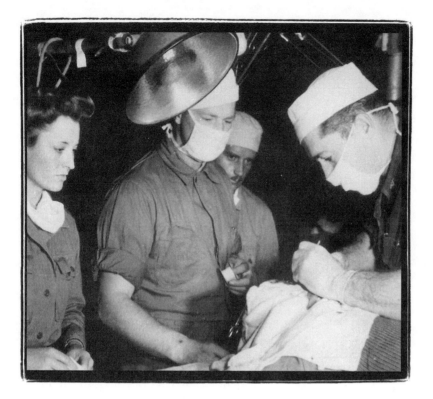

The Price of Fire

by Martha Gellhorn

The phrase "go down in flames" is no mere metaphor for pilots, especially in wartime. Novelist and reporter Martha Gellhorn (1908-1998) filed this report on her visit to a Royal Air Force burn center during World War II. The piece ran in Collier's *magazine in May 1944.*

T he ward is a long, wide, cold room with bright green curtains at the windows. There are yellow and mauve potted chrysanthemums on the table down the center of the room, and a black iron coal stove at either end. Wicker chairs and a table covered with magazines stand in front of the far stove, and this is where the patients, wearing Royal Air Force uniforms, gather. Five or six men are lying in the white-painted beds.

The ward has the casual, cheerful, faintly bored feeling of any place where men are convalescing. But this ward is not like other wards, because no one here has a real face, and many of the patients have hands that are not much good, either. These men are members of the air crews who crashed in planes or were thrown clear or dragged from the burning wreckage—but not quite soon enough.

The men around the stove interrupted their conversation to talk to one of the patients in bed. The wagon that will carry him to the operating room is drawn up alongside the bed, and a nurse is helping him onto it.

"What's it to be today, Bill?"

"Eyebrows!"

"Won't he be pretty!"

Then there is a chorus of "Cheerios," and the operating-room trolley rolls away. There was no special feeling about this, because eyebrows aren't bad. The boy had been through so many operations and was so close to having a face again that this little extra pain did not worry him. Besides, men have been wheeled in and out of this ward all day long, day after day, and each man, alone, has learned how to wait for and endure these trips.

In a bed farther down, another boy is waiting. His turn will come after the eyebrows are made. He is going to get a nose. For weeks, he has been growing the skin for his nose in a narrow sausage-shaped pedicle attached to the unharmed skin of his shoulder. His face is incredible, and one hand is entirely gone.

There is no expression in these burned and scarred faces; all the expression is in the eyes and in the voice. You cannot tell age. Fire takes that away, too. The boy has light brown, tufty hair and good, laughing eyes and a good voice and a dreadful face that will soon, at least, have a nose. He was twenty-one, though you could only know this if you were told. He had been a chauffeur before the war, driving for the squire of his village.

The welfare officer had arranged to get him an industrial job when he would have enough of a face, but he did not want it. He wanted to go back with one hand and that face and be a chauffeur again in his village. Because the village is "home" and what he loves. His people are there. The village is a recognizable world.

In fact, they would all like to go back to what was before—before the war and before the flames got them.

Around the stove, there are now four boys gossiping together. One has just come from London, and they are asking him about his trip.

He is going to be operated on tomorrow and, after that, he will return to flying and he is very happy. He is an American from Columbus, Ohio, and he crashed in a Hurricane.

His face, they say, was simply pushed back two inches inside his head. Now his nose is very flattened, and the skin around his eyes is odd, but by contrast with the others, he looks fine. He feels fine, too, because what he likes is to fly and he will be doing that again.

The others will not fly. They are talking easily and generously about his squadron, and neither you nor they nor anyone looks at the curled claws of hands of the 19-year-old Canadian or at the melted stump that the 21-year-old English boy has, or at the stiff, reddish, solidified fingers of a boy who always worked on a farm in Canada and who would like to again. Maybe some day his hands will bend just enough to let him do it.

The 19-year-old Canadian with the claw hands wants to be a boat builder. He is a darling with a lively brain, but one half of his face is hardened, twisted, reddish meat, and the other half is fairly okay, so that you can see what a nice-looking kid he was. He thought he'd lost his left eye after he was pulled out of the wrecked plane because he couldn't see out of that eye. He was a gunner, and his pal, the navigator, pulled him out, and he said to his pal, "Where's my eye? I have lost my eye somewhere here."

So his pal said: "Well, we'll look for, it, then." And they crawled around on the grass dazed and burned, looking for the eye.

This story, you may not instantly guess, produces roars of laughter from everyone, because it just goes to show how dopey a guy can be.

There is a wonderful man on the staff of this hospital, a former schoolteacher, now a flight sergeant, who lives with these wounded boys and whose job it is to see that they make the hard and lonely adjustment to their disfigurement that they must make if they are to live. He is their friend and confidant and he knows as much about them as one man can know about another. He treats them with a matter-of-factness which is essential and, in the beginning, startling to an outsider.

He said casually, "Pete, show your hand. He's got a real bad hand."

And there was the hand, or rather the non-hand, and there above it was the serious, hesitant face of the 21-year-old Englishman. We looked at his hand as if it belonged to someone else and we were only interested to see what fire could do to a hand. His face was fairly good, but the sides of his head had been burned flat and a head is strange without ears. This boy had been a talented pilot. He completed his operational tour, which means thirty separate missions against the enemy. Then, as a rest, he was sent to be an instructor. it happened that his student crashed the training plane when he was flying with him, and the pilot got these burns trying to pull the student out of the wreckage. But this is just bad luck, you see.

The saline baths, which are the essential basis of burn treatment, are in rooms alongside the ward. We went in to see the baths, and there was a boy sitting in the deep tub in the chilly white room. The attendants were keeping his face dampened and under the water. He was patiently flexing his purplish hands. He was being cheered on by a sergeant who is in charge of the baths and who loves the baths only less than he loves the boys he is saving.

"Come on!" the sergeant said. "You can bend them more than that." Then, not to be too hard on this child, who had been here only three days, he said, "You see yourself how good they are. Your face is fine, too. We'll have you out of here in no time."

The boy answered, but you could not understand what he said. His skin was burned so tight that he could scarcely move his mouth, and the words came out in a shy mumble. The face was absolutely expressionless, so set that it looked dead, and yet the shape of it was still intact. Two bright blue eyes stared out of the scarred face and watched the stiff hands that bent ever so slightly under water. The rest of him was the fragile tender body of a very young boy, for, after all, nineteen is a very young boy.

"Come on, now," the sergeant said. "Come on. Bend them."

The boy had been opening and shutting his fingers the distance of a quarter of an inch for two hours and he would go on doing that for more days than one wanted to think about. But in the end, he would move his hands, and his face would be fixed, and then he would fly again.

They were having tea in the reception office, This is a wonderful hospital, in which the staff and patients call one another by their first names and nicknames, and the patients feel as at home as if they were guests at a summer camp and they have all been together so often or so long that they have permanent jokes, and they have all got such guts that there is no place for pity.

In the office, there was a pretty blond girl in khaki who is a chauffeur now and who drives these boys to the village pub or to a neighboring football field where the hospital team plays an army team or to the train or the movies or wherever they want to go. Another pretty girl, who wears a Saint John's black uniform, is the secretary, and there were a few interns getting a quick cup of tea during a lull in the operating room. There was also a girl wearing a blue silk bandanna handkerchief over her hair, and a polo coat. She was tiny and pink-cheeked and absurdly young-looking to be a married woman. But she was married, and her husband was sitting beside her, and he was very young, too, and tall. He was blind now. Beneath the bandage over his eyes, you could see the familiar drawn, burned face.

The girl had come to this hospital on the first day her husband arrived and she had not left him since. He was new to being blind and very awkward about it. She managed so that her husband should not feel his awkwardness. The blind soldier talked happily and easily, with the confidence his wife had given him. He was teasing the girl chauffeur about the football team that she lugged all over the countryside: What sort of football team was she sponsoring anyhow? They had been beaten everywhere since she started driving them.

This hospital is one of four Royal Air Force burn centers and it was planned as a wartime hospital. But there will be five or seven years' work after the war, not counting the men now prisoners in Germany who will need this sort of care. The average hospitalization is from six to eight weeks; but these bad burn cases take two years, at a minimum, to be repaired.

Not only R.A.F. cases are treated here. There are bomb wounds where the face has been torn apart, and sailors who have been burned and rescued from the sea, and men of all services who have been terribly damaged in accidents. But the largest group are the boys in Air Force blue, and the oldest among them is twenty-nine.

The hospital is a marvel. The men have unbounded confidence in the surgeons. This confidence is based on observation. They see with their own eyes the slow, patient miracles performed by Doctor Archibald McIndoe. He works with them tirelessly, operating three or five days a week, sometimes from ten in the morning until ten at night. But he does more than surgery, and that is why the hospital is a marvel. You would never see a more delicate and unpretentious job of lifesaving than goes on here.

Mac believes that, with sufficient time, he can fix a man's face "so that it will not cause comment." This is what he tells them, promising nothing more and delivering nothing less. When these burned boys arrive, they see others like themselves, and the rubber in the human soul is so resilient that they always see someone who looks worse than they look. Mirrors are handy. The men are not allowed to become afraid of facing their present disfigurement.

Since they will be in and out of this hospital regularly for years, they do not wear hospital uniforms. As soon as they can walk, they are given their R.A.F. uniforms and shipped off to the village to mingle with people and get used to living in the daily world. The local people are accustomed to them. They are not stared at, and this first adjustment is fairly easy. After this, they are encouraged to go to London, mainly to see and be seen. They are apt to go in pairs and keep each other company, but the job of making them accept themselves without self-consciousness is so well done that this initial contact with strangers appears to come off successfully every time.

Mac has abandoned the basket-weaving school of occupational therapy. He feels it is silly. These are men vitally concerned in the war effort, and there is an industrial workshop at the hospital which makes small airplane parts. The work is voluntary, and they know that they are doing something useful. When Mac is through with a patient for a time, feeling that he has had all the operations he can take, the patient is sent away to work at a job or, if the disability is too serious, the patient is sent to a rest home which is also a limited factory and training school. The men are not permitted to become idle or to feel that they have lost all chance of fitting into an average life during the long years of treatment.

Mac says that the worst disability is blindness, but after that comes the loss of hands. Fortunately, total loss of both hands is rare, and it is amazing what these boys can learn to do with a hook for a hand or by using the stumps of fingers. And when they come back to the hospital—as they must—they build up an affection for the staff. They find old friends in the wards and, due to Mac, there is no hospital gloom, none of that excessive starched hospital discipline, and the men are really very cheerful about their return visits.

They have a club called the Guinea Pig Club, which gives a bang-up dinner in the village once a year, and all the old patients come as if they were attending a school reunion. It is a great enough achievement to repair these damaged faces, but to keep the minds behind the faces so sound and so self-reliant is a triumph.

There are some things which even Mac cannot handle, and they are not talked of especially. There is the heartbreak of parents when they first see their children come back like this. There is the tragedy of the wives who cannot take it. One doesn't talk of this, and the losses are cut and life goes on.

There is something else, perhaps worse and deeper. It is the fear of these very young men that, after the war, they will never really be able to compete with whole men and that they will not find a decent job and will not be able to provide properly for themselves or their families. So they make a joke of disaster and form a beggars' union.

It is natural that these boys should not be thinking much about the peace and how to prevent the Germans from ever starting another war. They have done their share. They have paid for the safety of world in advance.

from Ironclaw: A Navy Carrier
Pilot's Gulf War Experience
by Sherman Baldwin

Those who have done it say that landing a jet on a rolling, heaving aircraft carrier at night is a frightening experience. As Sherman Baldwin (born 1964) knows, it's worse when you are a green pilot and your career as well as your life is at stake.

The jet blast deflector began to lower as the steam from the freshly fired catapult swirled around outside the cockpit. My eyes strained in the blackness of the night to watch the vanishing glow of the F/A-18 Hornet's engines, which just seconds ago had been on the catapult only a few feet in front of us. Now it was our turn. I slammed the parking brake handle in to free the wheels of the 57,000-pound EA-6B Prowler, allowing it to roll toward one of the USS *Midway*'s two steam-powered catapults. The steel wall that had protected us from the blast of the Hornet's engines was now being lowered by six sturdy hydraulically powered steel arms. As soon as it was flush with the flight deck, the Prowler's nosewheel tentatively rolled across it toward the catapult's shuttle. The steam still obscured my view of the yellow-shirted aircraft director. Unable to see his signals, I stopped the jet and swore under my breath.

"They're showing me a fifty-seven-thousand-pound weight board, and I'm rogering it," said Cave as he made a circular signal with his flashlight, informing the blue-shirted sailor ten feet below us on the flight deck that he had correctly guessed our jet's gross weight. *Cave* was short for "Caveman," which seemed to be an appropriate call sign for the man sitting next to me. His dark hair was closely cropped in a traditional crew cut, and his square jaw seemed to pull his ruddy skin tightly over his face. His medium build was muscular but not excessively so. Most important, he was an experienced and competent Electronic Countermeasures Officer (ECMO) trained extensively in the arts of navigation and electronic combat. ECMOs did not have pilot training, but Cave had the calm temperament necessary to help a first-cruise pilot like myself, known in the air wing as a "nugget," adjust to the intensity of fleet carrier options.

The catapult's billowing white steam cloud finally subsided and the yellowshirt reappeared like a magician from the midst of a cloud of smoke. He gave us the wingspread signal followed by a frantic hand signal for me to start taxiing the jet faster toward the catapult. I felt rushed and my brain was reaching task saturation. Simply stated, my bucket was full.

"Spread the wings," I said over the intercom system, but Cave was way ahead of me. I glanced in the rearview mirror and saw the wings unfolding and spreading to the extended and locked position.

"Spread and locked, no flag on the right," said Cave. "Go dirty." "No flag on the left," I responded as my hand moved the flap lever. I could barely see the flaps and slats moving in the darkness. "Going dirty."

"Call 'em when you got 'em," said Cave.

"Flaps thirty, stab shifted, slats out, and boards are in. Checks complete," I said. My breathing was labored and sweat was cascading down my face into my eyes.

Like a blind man following his long tapping cane, I maneuvered the Prowler forward as its nosewheel launch bar searched for its home in the shuttle that would connect the jet to the catapult. The yellowshirt's motions became slower and more precise as the launch bar approached the shuttle. I followed his hand signals explicitly, and now instead of a full arm signal, he signaled me with just a nod of his head.

A nod to the left and then a nod to the right was all it took before I felt the comforting thump of the launch bar sliding into the shuttle. The yellowshirt now backed away from the jet to a safe distance and signaled me to continue my forward progress. I advanced the throttles so that the Prowler was straining slightly against the holdback fitting of the catapult. The holdback was designed to keep the Prowler stationary until the catapult generated 53,000 pounds of force. At that magical moment the holdback would snap and the jet would accelerate from a standstill to 150 miles per hour in less than two seconds. With approval from the catapult officer, the yellowshirt jumped in the air and flung his left arm forward parallel to the deck and cocked his bent right arm toward the pitch-black night. He looked just like a quarterback preparing to throw a deep pass.

In response to the yellowshirt's signal, my left arm jammed the throttles forward to full power. "I'm in tension," my ritual litany began, "my feet are to the deck, I have a visual on the stab, the controls are free and easy, engine instruments are good, no warning lights. My lights are coming on." My left thumb flicked the external lights master switch, and instantly the Prowler was transformed from a dark-gray machine into an eerie glowing mixture of red and green lights. The jet was straining against the holdback fitting that restrained the two powerful Pratt & Whitney engines roaring at full power beneath me. As soon as the lights came on, the catapult officer knelt down and touched the flight deck, giving the signal to the catapult shooter. The final safety check was done and the launch button was pushed. Our fate was sealed.

My head slammed against the ejection seat's headrest, and I groaned audibly over the intercom as I strained against the rapid onset of G forces from the catapult shot. The instruments looked fuzzy as my eyeballs compressed into the back of their sockets, and the jet shook violently as it rattled down the catapult track toward the pitch-black abyss. By the end of the catapult stroke I was able to focus again. The numbers *130* and *120* were ingrained in my brain. My eyes began to search for them in fear of the actions these numbers represented. Before the catapult shot I had set a marker on the airspeed indicator at 130 knots. If the indicator's needle pointed at an airspeed less than 130 knots at the end of the stroke, I would be forced to jettison all of my external stores, lightening the jet by 7,400 pounds, enabling it to fly away safely. If I saw less than 120 knots, I would instantly command eject the Prowler's four-man crew out of the jet, because no matter what happened, we did not have sufficient airspeed to fly. Thankfully, I saw the indicator's needle passing through 145 knots and said over the intercom, "Good airspeed, good shot," as the blackness of the night engulfed us. My instruments showed us climbing, and I hoped they were right. There was no horizon and I could not see anything outside of the cockpit. My left arm was locked at the elbow, and my entire body was tensed against the throttles, squeezing every last bit of thrust out of the two large engines that lay only a few feet below me.

"You can raise the gear now," chuckled Cave.

"Roger," I gasped as we passed 1,500 feet. I should have raised the gear immediately after the cat shot in order to reduce drag, but my eyes were locked onto the instruments and shaken by the violence and uncertainty of the night catapult shot. I quickly lifted the landing gear handle and waited for the proper indication. "I've got three up and locked, waiting for one eighty-five," I announced, letting my crew know that I would not raise the flaps until the Prowler had accelerated past 185 knots, the minimum flap retraction speed for the aircraft. "Passing one eighty-five, flaps are moving on the left," I said as I watched the slats retract in one of the cockpit's rearview mirrors.

"Moving on the right," said Cave.

"I'm up, clean, and isolated," I said, referring to the aircraft's configuration and the status of the hydraulic system isolation valve.

What pilots hate about night catapult shots is the lack of control. You are launched into the night, praying that the catapult has given the jet enough airspeed to fly when it reaches the end of the deck. In the daytime your eyes can see the acceleration and they signal your brain, saying that this catapult shot looks good. However, at night all the visual cues are gone and all that you have are your instruments. You still feel the violent onset of G forces, yet there are no visual cues, so you focus on your airspeed indicator and pray that it does not lie.

"Ironclaw 605 is passing 2.5," said Cave, referring to our altitude as he followed the departure procedures to the letter. Each squadron had a radio call sign; for our squadron it was *Ironclaw.* I liked our call sign because it sounded tough, and on an aircraft carrier, tough is good. Cave had several cruises under his belt and so did his flight boots. They were so old and worn that you could see the faint white salt stains on the tongues of the boots where his sweat had permeated the once-shiny and supple black leather. As a "nugget" pilot it was comforting for me to be with an experienced ECMO like Cave.

At seven miles I turned to intercept a ten-mile arc around the *Midway.* I circled the carrier until we were flying on a northwesterly heading of 330 degrees. "Departure, Ironclaw 605 is kilo, switching," said Cave telling the *Midway*'s departure controller that we were mission capable and switching to the strike-control frequency. We needed to switch radio frequencies from the departure controller to the strike controller before eventually starting our mission. Each controller was responsible for different air space around the carrier. "Strike, Ironclaw 605 is up for Parrot India checks." Cave was ensuring that Strike's air traffic controllers had an accurate readout of our jet's position on their radar scopes. The Prowler's Identification Friend or Foe system would reply to the carrier's radar interrogation with a discrete signal and altitude readout. In peacetime this discrete signal would allow the controllers to monitor our mission and tell us of any conflicting traffic. In wartime this system helped the carrier's controllers tell the good guys from the bad guys.

"Ironclaw 605, Strike holds you sweet and sweet, you are cleared to proceed."

"Switching," said Cave as he quickly twisted the knob on the radio to give us the proper radio frequency for the E-2C Hawkeye, an aircraft that acted as an airborne controller monitoring our mission and keeping us clear of any conflicting air traffic. The Hawkeye had launched fifteen minutes earlier in order to establish an air "picture" of the entire operating area for the mission.

"Liberty, Ironclaw 605 is up for ESM."

"Ironclaw 605, Liberty, roger," said the voice of the Hawkeye controller, acknowledging our jet's presence on his radar scope.

"One thousand to go," I said over the intercom, announcing the fact that we had just passed 19,000 feet climbing toward our final altitude of 20,000 feet. I gradually reduced the jet's rate of climb, pulling back on the throttles and lowering the nose slightly. The level-off was smooth, and I smiled under my oxygen mask. I desperately wanted to give the ECMOs confidence in my airmanship.

Tonight Cave was in the front seat with me, while Face and Bhagwan were the two ECMOs in the backseat of our Prowler. Face was called *Face* because he liked women and believed they liked him. He had a deep, dark, permanent Mediterranean tan which was fitting for his image. Bhagwan, in contrast, was a short, stocky, and feisty bulldog of a man. His call sign was *Bhagwan* because we thought that if you wrapped a turban around his head, he would look convincingly like a Bedouin with a name like Bhagwan.

Our mission tonight was officially Electronic Surveillance Measures, and we would use the Prowler's sophisticated electronic receivers to detect and locate possible hostile radar emitters in the Gulf of Oman. Face and Bhagwan would search for electronic signals that could be linked to enemy radars that, in turn, would identify an enemy position. The *Midway* was sailing several hundred miles south of the Strait of Hormuz, the narrow body of water that connects the Persian Gulf with the Gulf of Oman, so we did not expect to identify any threats tonight. Actually, the real but unstated mission of the flight was to update the currency of my night-landing qualification, and to see how I would stack up in the constant competition among my fellow pilots that surrounds carrier landings.

It had been fifty-three days since my last night carrier landing in training and I was more than a little nervous. The navy's regulation stated that nugget pilots were allowed a maximum of twenty days between their last night trap in training and their first night trap in their new squadron, if their squadron was at sea. However, the political situation was tense in the Persian Gulf and my squadron needed a new pilot, so the commander of Air Wing Five (known as the CAG, a holdover from when his title was Commander of the Air Group) on the *Midway* had waived this regulation for me. I was glad to be trusted, but that did not make me any less nervous.

Only ten days ago I had completed my shore-based training at Naval Air Station Whidbey Island, Washington, just north of Seattle. Now, on December 10, 1990, I found myself at Saddam Hussein's doorstep four months after the Iraqi Army had invaded Kuwait on August 2. I faced an incredibly steep learning curve. Knowing that the *Midway* would be in the thick of any combat action, I had requested this assignment, but now I was feeling overwhelmed and unsure of myself. At the completion of my two and a half years of flight training I had made a total of twenty daytime carrier landings and only six at night. Not only did I feel inexperienced and awkward in the fast-paced environment of fleet-carrier operations, but there now existed a high probability of combat in the near future. In order to be "combat ready," I knew I needed to increase my pilot proficiency level rapidly, if I hoped to survive. In aviation a pilot's proficiency is perishable over time, meaning that if a pilot does not fly frequently, his skills quickly deteriorate. The great pilots are always a step ahead of every situation in the cockpit and use good judgment to choose among various courses of action. They are proactive, rather than reactive. Being ahead of the aircraft comes from experience and practice. Tonight, being inexperienced and out of practice, I felt slow and reactive, behind the aircraft rather than ahead of it. It was not a good feeling.

"Nav is tight," said Cave as he diligently updated the navigation solution using the Prowler's ground-mapping radar to send position updates to the jet's Inertial Navigation System.

"Roger that," I said. "Hydraulics are good, oil is good, and we're looking at fifteen thousand pounds of gas." We had another forty-five minutes to go until our recovery, when my rusty landing skills would be put to the test. Right now I felt comfortably above my fuel ladder calculations. Projecting forward at the current fuel-flow setting that I had chosen, we would have 11,400 pounds of fuel when the recovery began. That was ample. The Prowler was limited by structural design to a maximum of 8,800 pounds for a carrier landing, so I figured that we might even have to dump some fuel. Fuel is every navy pilot's major worry when the only place to land is on a ship in the middle of the ocean. I began to feel more relaxed. I realized that I was finally starting to think ahead of the aircraft, anticipating the possible sequence of events.

Fortunately, tonight we were within range of a small airfield called Seeb in the United Arab Emirates. The UAE had given the *Midway* permission to use the field for emergencies only. We had been briefed that Seeb was a last-ditch divert airfield because it was a short field without arresting gear to stop our jet, and we were all unfamiliar with it. Since we were roughly one hundred miles from Seeb, it would be a 3.5 bingo. This meant that if we had not landed on the carrier by the time we reached 3,500 pounds of fuel, then we would immediately turn toward Seeb, and commit ourselves to landing with a low fuel caution light at an unfamiliar field. This was a thought that nobody in the crew was excited about. The three ECMOs in my crew all realized that this was my first night trap in the squadron. I'm sure they hoped that I would be able to get aboard without any difficulty, but they also knew that nuggets were unpredictable and often had a rough time with night landings when they first arrived in a fleet squadron. In turn, my crew was ready for anything. During the preflight brief Bhagwan had produced his toothbrush and a clean pair of underwear as testament to the fact that he was prepared in case I was unable to land back aboard the carrier tonight and we were forced to divert to Seeb.

We had flown north for thirty minutes toward the Iranian coast, trying to identify any signals of interest that were being emitted by the Iranian air defense forces. Face and Bhagwan were operating the Prowler's ALQ-99 surveillance system, which had extremely sensitive receivers able to identify a vast range of electronic signals. The ESM mission was focused primarily on the backseaters. Cave and I were responsible for navigating a specific course that would place us in the optimum position to receive signals intelligence, while Face and Bhagwan worked the system to pick up as many signals as possible. They were probably chatting back and forth about what they were seeing on the system, but I could not hear a word of it because they had the front seat deselected from the intercom so as not to disturb my dialogue with Cave in the front seat regarding the navigation of the mission.

The Prowler's Internal Communications System (ICS) was quite complicated. Usually on missions the backseaters would do most of their talking to each other about the electronic countermeasures (jamming enemy radars) or electronic surveillance (listening to enemy radars) that they were doing. They would normally set up their ICS in the backseat so that they could also hear everything that the frontseaters were saying, but they would need to press a switch to talk to us in the front seat. This created an environment where an insecure pilot might always be wondering what his backseaters were saying about the way he was flying. It did not usually even cross my mind, but I was now the new guy in the squadron, hoping to make a good impression. I could not help wondering what Face and Bhagwan might be saying about me in the backseat. Perhaps they were betting on the odds of my being able to land back onboard the *Midway* tonight. I tried to push such thoughts out of my head and keep my confidence up as we continued to fly through the darkness. "We are showing hardly any activity on the system," said Face.

"Well, keep looking," said Cave. We flew our preplanned route without incident, and about twenty minutes later, I finally heard Cave's voice say in my ear, "We might as well head back to the ship." I nodded in agreement and turned inbound to the ship as Cave began to orchestrate our return. The Tactical Air Navigation (TACAN) system indicated that we were ninety-five miles northeast of the *Midway*. I immediately began to think about the upcoming landing. On our departure from the carrier, we had flown through several layers of clouds at lower altitudes that would be extremely disorienting during the approach to the carrier. Flying in and out of clouds at night was never fun and I was not looking forward to it. After a few minutes of flight toward the carrier, Cave made the first of many standard radio calls. "Strike, Ironclaw 605 is fifty miles to the northeast, state is base plus 8.6." By using the base number from the kneeboard card of the day, which today was four, the ship would know that we had 12,600 pounds of gas.

"Ironclaw 605, Strike, roger. Case III recovery marshal radial is the 090. You're cleared inbound and cleared to switch marshal." I still found the radio dance somewhat confusing and was glad to have Cave, who quickly switched to the marshal frequency where we would be given our holding instructions and other pertinent information about the recovery from the controller aboard the *Midway*. As soon as the frequency was dialed into our radio, we heard some familiar chatter from the other air wing aircraft airborne, preparing for this recovery. There were eight squadrons in the *Midway*'s air wing: three Hornet, two Intruder, one Prowler, one Hawkeye, and one helicopter squadron, for a total of more than sixty aircraft. Because of the small size of the *Midway*'s deck we did not have any F-14 Tomcats or S-3 Vikings in our air wing. We liked to think that our air wing's composition of predominantly Hornets, Intruders, and Prowlers made us the premier attack air wing in the US Navy.

"Marshal, Eagle 510 is checking in, state is 9.0," said the A-6 Intruder's bombardier/navigator (BN), meaning he had nine thousand pounds of gas.

"Eagle 510, marshal, you're cleared to marshal on the 090 radial, angels 13, expect approach time 59, altimeter 30.10." As soon as the BN had read back his aircraft's holding instructions Cave jumped on the frequency. "Marshal, Ironclaw 605 is checking in; state is 12.6."

"Ironclaw 605, marshal, you're cleared to marshal on the 090 radial, angels 14, expect approach time 00, altimeter 30.10."

Cave read back the instructions verbatim as I started a descending turn toward our assigned holding point 29 miles due east of the carrier at 14,000 feet. Before long, nine aircraft were stacked neatly from 6,000 feet all the way up to 14,000 feet due east of the *Midway*. Each aircraft was separated by 1,000 feet and the holding points were determined by adding the number 15 to the given holding altitude. I was holding at angels 14, or 14,000 feet, so my holding point was 29 miles away from the ship. The lowest aircraft in the stack would fly the first approach starting at time 2152, followed by the aircraft 1,000 feet above him at time 2153, and so on. The aircraft in the marshal stack would continue to fly approaches to the carrier in this way until those of us at the top of the stack had trapped on the carrier's deck.

"Time in fifteen seconds will be 46," said the marshal controller. There was a brief pause and then his voice returned. "Five, four, three, two, one, mark time 46," said the voice of the marshal controller, ensuring that each of the nine aircraft in the marshal holding stack had the correct time so that their approaches would be synchronized. As each aircraft checked in the marshal controller would give them their assigned position in the stack.

Each aircraft was expected to commence its approach from the holding point plus or minus five seconds of the given approach time. If you started your approach either earlier or later than five seconds either side of the given time, you were expected to confess over the radio and publicly embarrass yourself. The confession helped the controllers to sequence the jets and ensure that the minimum amount of separation was maintained. The confession also served as a severe form of motivation to the pilots who, to a man, feared nothing more than looking bad in front of their fellow aviators.

Tonight the recovery started out smoothly. The lowest jet in the stack was an F/A-18 Hornet at 6,000 feet. At 2152 I heard, "Dragon 307, commencing, altimeter 30.10." We had eight minutes to go until we would commence our approach to the carrier. The Prowler's holding speed was 250 knots. The technique I used in order to hit the holding point on time was to fly the jet in a six-minute racetrack pattern. At 250 knots and 22 degrees angle of bank, it took the Prowler two minutes to turn 180 degrees. So if I could set myself up heading inbound at the holding point with six minutes to go, then I could fly a two-minute outboard turn, a one-minute outbound leg, a two-minute turn inbound, and then a final one-minute inbound leg, which would place the jet at the holding point exactly on time. The length of the outbound leg could easily be adjusted, depending on how much time was remaining. There were now six minutes and thirty-five seconds remaining until the approach time of 2200, and I was on the 090 radial at thirty-two miles. Aside from the timing problem there was also a fuel concern; I still had 11,500 pounds of gas. Flying the approach would require about 800 pounds of gas, so when I commenced my approach in seven minutes, I wanted to have no more than 9,600 pounds in order to land with the maximum allowable limit of 8,800, according to the stress limits of the jet's fuel tanks. I needed to dump gas quickly. "I'm going to dump about two thousand pounds," I announced to my crew, letting them know that I was ahead of the jet. I turned the dumps on as the DME (mileage) indicator in the TACAN read twenty-nine miles, and I commenced my 22-degree angle of bank outbound turn. The clock showed that there were five minutes and forty seconds remaining until my approach time. That translated into a fifty-second outbound leg in order to hit the holding point on time. Cave led me through the challenge-and-reply descent and approach to landing checklists. He turned on the Automatic Carrier Landing System (ACLS) and the Instrument Landing System (ILS), testing each one for proper operation. Both systems seemed to be operating normally, but we would not really know until we were on our final approach.

The word *automatic* in the ACLS system was truly a misnomer. For the Prowler, there was nothing automatic about landing on the *Midway*. On the larger nuclear-powered carriers, some fleet aircraft could be landed, using this system without the pilot touching the controls throughout the approach. However, the combination of the Prowler's older automatic flight-control system, the *Midway*'s small deck, and its minimal hook to ramp clearance of only ten feet made it a completely manual process for the pilot. Even if it was not truly automatic, the ACLS was still invaluable to all of the *Midway*'s pilots. ACLS was an interactive system between the *Midway* and each aircraft as it flew its approach. The ACLS radar on the carrier could lock on to a jet's radar beacon and then send continuously updated azimuth and glide-slope information to the jet's cockpit. The information was then displayed to the pilot in the form of a vertical and horizontal needle as a background to a small-aircraft symbol. The horizontal needle displayed glide slope and the vertical needle azimuth. The pilot's job was to fly the jet so that the small-aircraft symbol was directly superimposed on the crosshairs formed by the two needles.

"Checks are complete and I'm securing the dumps. One minute to push and we've got 9,600 pounds of gas. We're in good shape," I said as I smiled under my mask. Everything was going smoothly.

"Delta, delta, all aircraft stand by for new approach times," said the voice of the marshal controller.

"Shit," said Cave. The delta call signaled a delay in the recovery and as a result, a delay in our approach time. I wished there were a way to bring back the gas I had just so carefully dumped. The controller now started asking each aircraft its fuel state. "Eagle 510, say your state."

"Eagle 510 is level angels 11, state is 7.0," said the Intruder BN ahead of us at 11,000 feet. He had already started his approach to the ship when the delta had been called, so according to procedures, he had leveled off at the next odd altitude after he heard the delta call.

"Ironclaw 605, say your state," said the controller.

"605, state 9.6," came Cave's terse response. Everyone's thoughts turned to gas. For the moment we were fine, but one could never tell how long the delay might be. "There's no Texaco tonight, but there is an Iron Maiden. Its call sign is Mako 12, at angels 24," said Cave. I cringed. Texaco was the navy term for the carrier-based A-6 tankers which I had learned to tank from in flight training. Many A-6 pilots on the *Midway* wore Texaco patches on their flight jackets because they provided the air wing with gas. Iron Maiden, on the other hand, was our squadron's nickname for an air force KC-135 tanker. The KC-135 was a converted air force cargo plane that was truly a gas station in the sky. The tanker had earned its nickname because tanking off it was a cruel form of torture that had already broken dozens of our air wing's refueling probes.

"We still have lots of gas to play with," I said cheerfully.

"Yeah, we should be fine," Cave replied. "Don't break out your toothbrush yet, Bhagwan."

It had now been six minutes since the marshal controller had given us the delta call and we were back at our holding point. The weather was disorienting at our holding altitude. There was no discernible horizon, yet I could tell that we were flying in and out of the clouds because of the varying intensity of the reflection of the Prowler's anticollision strobe lights. Delays in a recovery could be caused by a number of different situations. The frustrating aspect of it was that the carrier never seemed to tell you the nature of the delay. *It could be that a few jets had boltered, missing all three of the* Midway's *wires, and the landing pattern around the carrier was now full. Or it could be that a jet has just crashed into the back end of the boat,* I said to myself. I smiled under my oxygen mask, realizing that I had already adopted the naval aviator's habit of referring to the ship as a boat, the stem as the back end, and the bow as the pointy end. It was language used by aviators to annoy the officers in the Surface Warfare community who were cut from the more traditional naval cloth.

The back end of the boat was also called the ramp. When an aircraft crashed into the ramp, it was called a ramp strike. They were rare, but everyone had heard stories of the massive fireballs that would light up the dark night. The ramp at night became the type of a monster that lived in every pilot's nightmares. All navy pilots have had at least one close call with the ramp that they would prefer to forget. The pilots who learned from the encounter forevermore flew on the high side of the glide slope—and those who didn't learn—well, it was just a matter of time. The ramp monster began to creep into my thoughts as we waited to learn our new approach time. My eyes glanced repeatedly at our fuel gauge as it kept getting lower and lower.

Once again the marshal controller asked each aircraft to say his fuel state. And once again we heard, "Eagle 510, state 5.5."

"Ironclaw 605, state 8.0," said Cave. In another ten minutes we would be below our ramp fuel of 7.0, which was the target fuel that

Prowlers were expected to land with, according to our air wing's standard operating procedure. As long as we stayed above 4,700 pounds, I would be happy. At 4,700 pounds or less we would be sent to the Iron Maiden, and I really wanted to avoid that at all costs.

After what seemed an eternity, we heard the controller's voice again: "Standby for expected approach times."

"Great," I said. We would be fine if we pushed in the next ten minutes. The time was now 2210.

The controller's voice came over the radio: "Acknowledge your approach time with fuel states. Eagle 510, expect approach time 16."

"510, approach time 16, state is 4.5," repeated the Intruder's BN, who was now getting quite low on gas. It was time to land. Time was becoming critical.

"Ironclaw 605, expect approach time 17."

"Ironclaw 605, approach time 17, state is 7.0" said Cave. "Another six minutes to our approach time. We should call the ball with about 5.8. That's plenty, no problem," said Cave.

"Calling the ball" happened at three quarters of a mile behind the carrier when the pilot transitioned from an instrument approach to a visual approach. It was the most critical part of a night carrier landing. It would take about twenty seconds to fly that final three quarters of a mile. Those twenty seconds were infused with the purest form of survival instinct. Night carrier landings were the practice of overcoming the fear of death that lingered in the back of every pilot's mind.

"The ball" or "meatball" was the nickname given to the navy's Fresnel lens system that offered pilots a visual reference to help them fly a constant glide slope from three quarters of a mile all the way to landing. Five specially cut rectangular lenses of light were stacked vertically in the middle of a horizontal row of green circular lights. The vertical stack of cells projected a yellow "meatball" of light toward an incoming jet. The top four cells were yellow and the bottom cell was red. If a pilot saw the yellow "meatball" higher than the horizontal row of green lights, then his jet was high. If the yellow "meatball" appeared below the row of green lights, then his jet was low. If the "meatball" turned red, then the pilot knew he was dangerously below glide slope and would hit the ramp if he did not make an aggressive power addition. Flying the ball was more of a philosophy or an art than a science. Pilots attached a Zen-like aura to those few who had truly mastered the art.

Tonight I did not feel as if I had the requisite Zen. I was nervous and I prayed that I would not bolter. Bolters were embarrassing, and I was determined not to be embarrassed tonight. However, I realized that boltering was a distinct possibility, and I wanted to have enough gas so that if I did bolter, I could go around again without being forced to go to the Iron Maiden. Bottom line: I needed to land before my jet's fuel gauge indicated 4,700 pounds. As my mind wandered and worried, our expected approach time drew closer. I needed to focus on the job at hand, which was to hit my holding point on time so that I would get a good start to my approach.

"Two minutes to go," said Cave, as we both closely monitored our progress in the holding pattern. We had ninety degrees of turn left and then we would have a fifty-second inbound leg. The timing problem seemed on track, but I continued to focus on our fuel situation. The gauge indicated about 6,600 pounds, which was about 3,000 pounds less than what I would have liked to have. It would have to be enough. *No bolter tonight*, I told myself.

At time 2216 we heard, "Eagle 510, pushing, altimeter 30.10." The Intruder below us was on his way and we would soon follow in less than a minute. As I rolled out wings level on the inbound course, the timing looked good. The INS indicated a ground speed of 240 knots, and there were four miles to go. I was going to be right on time.

"Ironclaw 605, pushing, altimeter 30.10," said Cave as the second hand passed through the twelve.

"Ironclaw 605, I show you at 29 DME switch button 18," said the marshal controller.

"Switching," said Cave, as I eased back on the throttles to 75 percent RPM, lowered the Prowler's nose ten degrees below the horizon, and extended the speed brakes, which increased the drag on the aircraft and enabled a rapid descent. This maneuver quickly gave the Prowler a 5,000-feet-per-minute rate of descent toward the water below. I felt the rush of speed when I saw with my peripheral vision layers of clouds whipping by the cockpit as we plunged downward. The analog hand of the altimeter unwound quickly as I scanned my instruments to ensure that all systems were normal.

"Approach, Ironclaw 605, checking in at twenty-seven miles."

"Ironclaw 605, continue CV1 approach, cleared to angels 1.2," said the new voice on the radio. The large heavy nose of the Prowler naturally sought the water. The altimeter kept spinning at a quick rate until we passed 5,000 feet and the preset radar altimeter started beeping, warning me to reduce my rate of descent. My thumb pushed the speed-brake switch in, and the Prowler's wingtip speed brakes on both sides closed flush like hands joined at the palms closing together. I then pulled back on the stick in order to reduce my closure with the ocean below.

"Ironclaw 605, platform," said Cave, making the next mandatory radio call as our jet passed through 5,000. Having adjusted my rate of descent, I started to concentrate on the level off.

"One thousand to go," I said over the intercom as I gradually added power and pulled the nose up even farther, easing the descent to 1,200 feet. At fourteen miles from the *Midway* we were now flying straight and level toward the ramp at 250 knots.

"Ironclaw 605, stay clean through ten, I'll call your dirty up," said the approach controller.

"605," said Cave, acknowledging the call. The normal procedure was to transition to the landing configuration at ten miles, but because the Intruder ahead of us had pushed from a lower altitude than normal, there was a bigger gap between us. The controller wanted me to keep my speed up until eight miles so as to close this gap and expedite the recovery. The transition from 250 knots clean to 130 knots with the landing gear down and the flaps down was a major transition. Eight miles was considered the minimum distance to make a smooth transition.

"Delta, delta," said the voice of the approach controller. "Ironclaw 605, discontinue your approach. Take angels 2 and continue inbound." Our fuel gauge now indicated 6,000 and it seemed to be decreasing as I glanced at it.

"We have a foul deck for at least ten minutes. Ironclaw 605 estimate state on the ball at time 2230," said the controller.

"Stand by," said Cave.

"Ten minutes at this altitude will be about eight hundred pounds plus the fuel for the approach another eight hundred. We will be at 4.6." I grimaced as I said this figure because it was below 4.7.

"Approach, Ironclaw 605, estimating 4.6 on the ball at time 2230," said Cave matter of factly.

"Ironclaw 605, approach, copy 4.6. Your signal is tank. Mako 12 is overhead at angels 24."

"Damn," I said, as I rammed the throttles to full power to give me the most fuel efficient climb to 24,000 feet. The two Pratt & Whitney P408A engines roared, and the Prowler responded as if it were an angry horse that I had just kicked with the spurs on my boots. We quickly accelerated to .7 indicated mach airspeed, the Prowler's most efficient climb airspeed. *That damned Intruder ahead of us must have broken down in the landing area,* I said to myself. At 16,000 feet the haze layer disappeared below us and visibility drastically improved. The stars were out, and I struggled to pick out the tanker's white light amid the field of constellations. "One thousand feet to go," I said as the altimeter passed through 22,500. "I'll level off at 23,500 until we have the tanker in sight, and then I'll climb to rendezvous."

"Traffic at two o'clock a little high," said Cave. I cranked the jet around to the right to put the nose onto the possible tanker. Off to the right of the nose I saw a white strobe and agreed that it must be the tanker. The trick to any rendezvous is figuring out the aspect and closure rate with the other aircraft. At night, without a fighter's sophisticated air-to-air radar, the Prowler was at a distinct disadvantage. By turning nose to the tanker, I hoped to be able to develop a picture of the relative motion of the tanker to my jet. The white strobe began slowly to track from right to left across my windscreen. That was good. It was best to join up on the tanker from the inside of its left-hand racetrack pattern. I let the nose of my jet lag behind the white strobe light. This lag increased the rate at which the light passed across my windscreen. I then added power and climbed the final 500 feet to be co-altitude with the Iron Maiden. My airspeed was 350 knots and I expected Mako to be at the standard rendezvous speed of 250.

I was now facing the common tanking dilemma; if the rendezvous was not expeditious, then the length of time would run me short on fuel. Yet, if I was too aggressive in expediting the rendezvous, that too might run us out of fuel because of the high power settings required for maneuvering. I did not want to divert, so I needed to time the rendezvous just right. I now held an aggressive 100 knots of closure on the tanker and knew that I had to be careful. Such a high closure rate at night could easily get out of control. I increased my angle of bank to the left, now putting my jet's nose in front of the tanker. By leading the tanker in this way I was also increasing my closure rate. Afraid of too high a closure rate, I began to ease back on the throttles and decelerate. Now, with a slower airspeed of 300 knots, I felt much more comfortable, yet a left-turn rendezvous was never truly comfortable in the Prowler. The jet's side-by-side seating design, with the pilot on the left, made it incredibly difficult for me to see the tanker on my right side while I was in a left-hand turn. I strained my neck to see the KC-135 over the Prowler's canopy rail on Cave's side of the cockpit.

"Too much closure," said Cave anxiously. The tanker was getting very large very quickly. I pulled the throttles to idle, extended the speed brakes, and lowered the nose to make sure that we did not have a collision. I arrested the closure rate just in time, and, even though it was not a pretty rendezvous, we were now flying off the tanker's left wing.

"Ironclaw 605, port observation, nose cold, switches safe, looking for 5.0," said Cave, who had tanked off the KC-135s many times before and knew what to expect. We ran through the refueling checklist quickly and I selected air-to-air on the Prowler's refueling panel.

"Ironclaw 605, you're cleared in for 5.0," said the tanker pilot.

"Do you want to lower your seat?" asked Cave, knowing that every other pilot in the squadron had learned through experience that it made tanking off the Iron Maiden a lot easier if you lowered your seat.

"No, I'll just leave it like it is," I said with a mild tone of resentment. *Who does he think he is anyway? I'm the pilot, damn it,* I said to myself. I pulled the throttles back and maneuvered the Prowler behind the tanker and took a look at the Iron Maiden's basket for the first time. Our gas gauge now read 4.8, and my flight gloves were soaked with sweat. The leather palms of the Nomex flight gloves felt slippery on the stick's hard black plastic grip. My fingers were clenched around the grip, squeezing it tightly. I needed to relax, but too many things were happening tonight that I had never seen before. I was feeling the stress and knew my crew could tell that I was. If I could not tank successfully, we would have to fly to Seeb. What a nightmare; the embarrassment of not being able to hack it was too great to contemplate. I could imagine Face and Bhagwan taking out their approach plates and control frequencies for the divert field in anticipation of my failure. As a nugget, my every move was watched by everyone in the squadron. If I were to fly in combat, then I would have to be able to tank off these KC-135s at night routinely. I needed to prove myself reliable. I needed to hack it.

The KC-135's refueling basket had a hard steel rim illuminated by small orange lights. The basket was only thirty-six inches in diameter and was connected to a stiff nine-foot reinforced rubber hose by a metal ball joint that swiveled, depending on the position of the basket. The only "night" tanking I had ever done was off an A-6 tanker in training at Naval Air Station Whidbey Island. It had been done one minute after official sunset, and at twenty thousand feet it was still quite light out. At that time my instructor said, "I guarantee you that the first time you tank at night in the fleet it will be pitch black and you will really need the gas." I smiled wryly as I realized how right he had been. From talking to the other pilots in the squadron I knew that there were two obstacles I needed to overcome to tank successfully off the Iron Maiden. The first was the boom operator and the second was bending the hose.

The KC-135, being an air force aircraft, was designed to refuel air force tactical jets and had to be reconfigured to fuel navy jets. In the infinite wisdom of the Department of Defense, the navy and air force accomplish air-to-air refueling with completely contradictory philosophies. In the navy, the receiving aircraft positions itself aft of the tanker's refueling basket and the receiving aircraft's pilot then maneuvers his aircraft's refueling probe into the tanker's basket. In the air force, the receiving aircraft positions itself aft of the tanker and the tanker extends its refueling probe. While the receiving aircraft maintains its position, the tanker's boom operator will fly the tanker's refueling probe into a small basket that is located on the top of the receiving aircraft. On a KC-135 tanker reconfigured for use with navy jets, the tanker's refueling probe is replaced by a basket so that the navy jets can use their refueling probe to "plug" the basket. Problems arise when a navy pilot tries to "plug" the basket and a well-intentioned air force boom operator attempts to guide the basket onto the jet's refueling probe. The result is similar to what happens when one person in a group drops a coin on the floor and two people bend over to pick it up and smack their heads together. Even though both people are trying to accomplish the same thing, they are not coordinated. In the end, one person will bend over and pick up the coin. I hoped that the boom operator would simply let me "pick up the coin" and plug the basket without trying to be too helpful.

The second obstacle was staying in the basket long enough to receive five thousand pounds of gas. The A-6 tanker package had a much longer and more flexible hose that allowed the receiving aircraft to maneuver more freely behind the tanker. The other pilots in the squadron had described how it was necessary to bend the KC-135's hose into an S shape that would allow the pilot to control the swiveling ball joint of the basket. If the hose was not bent properly, then the swiveling ball joint could violently twist around the jet's refueling probe and possibly damage it so that further refueling was impossible. If the hose twisted quickly, then the best course of action was to disengage. However, on disengagement there was always the possibility that the basket's large steel rim could slam down on the nose of the receiving aircraft. With these thoughts swirling in my brain and my palms drenched with sweat, my stomach knotted with fear, I started my approach toward the thirty-six-inch basket.

The Prowler's refueling probe was illuminated by a small red light that was directed upward from the base of the jet's windscreen. My hands felt as if they were shaking, but they were simply making the minute movements necessary to keep the probe moving slowly toward the basket. The basket was now ten feet in front of the probe's tip, and as the distance decreased I watched the basket start to move. Was it my own poor technique or was it the friendly boom operator trying to be helpful? I couldn't tell. I added more power and continued to close on the basket. It began to move to the left and I made the necessary correction. I was almost there when the basket suddenly moved down. The probe tip hit the basket just inside the top of its rim and bent the swivel joint upward. Instead of sliding into the basket, the probe slipped over the top of its rim and the steel basket snapped down and smashed into the nose of the Prowler. "Damn it," I swore over the intercom system. I pulled back on the throttles and winced. I slid back twenty feet behind the Iron Maiden and looked at the nose of my jet.

"No harm done," I said.

"The probe looks all right," said Cave. "Well, let's give it another try." His calm voice belied the fact that our fuel gauge now indicated 4.2. I needed to get in the basket and stay in the basket. After a deep breath and unclenching my fingers several times, I began my second approach. My left hand gently pushed the throttles forward, creating the necessary closure on the basket. Once again the basket stayed steady until the probe was only a few feet away. Now I began to doubt myself. The boom operator was probably doing nothing. Was it just my poor technique that was preventing me from getting into the basket? The frenetic minor corrections I was making to chase the basket were getting smaller and smaller as the probe got closer and closer. At the last instant, the basket started to move down again. I added a handful of power and lowered the nose. The probe slammed home in the center of the basket and the swivel joint whipped the hose around the top of the probe. *Bend the hose, bend the hose,* I told myself. The hose turned and twisted wildly as I tried to stabilize my position and create the bend in the hose that was required. My hands jerked crazily as if I were being electrocuted.

The problem was that I could barely see the basket. The Prowler's canopy has almost as much steel as glass. Since I hadn't lowered my seat, I was forced to lean forward and awkwardly stretch my neck and roll my eyes upward in order to keep sight of the basket and the probe tip. I was leaning so far forward that my chest was right on top of the stick, so it was difficult to make the necessary corrections to keep the probe in the basket. The KC-135 had just reached the end of its holding pattern's straightaway and it started to turn. The angle of bank swung the boom out to the side, and as I tried to make the necessary recorrection my chest got in the way. The oscillations started to become too great. As I leaned back to allow more room for stick movement, I lost sight of the basket behind the canopy's steel frame. I pulled back on the throttles too quickly and could not recorrect in time. The Iron Maiden spit out the probe, and once again I found myself with more sweat and less fuel than I had had a few minutes earlier.

"Let's give it one more try and then we'll divert to Seeb. Our bingo fuel from here is 3.5 and right now we've got 3.8," said Cave.

"Concur. I'm going to lower my seat," I said, recalling Cave's sage advice given fifteen minutes earlier. I could just imagine the twinkle in Cave's eye and the grin on his lips.

The boom swung gently as the lumbering KC-135 continued its turn. I rested and breathed deeply as the tanker turned. It would be much easier to plug and stay plugged once the tanker rolled out of the turn, so I decided to wait. As the tanker rolled out I looked at the gas gauge; the needle wavered at 3.7. This was definitely the last chance I would have. The perspective was different now that I had lowered my seat. I felt my neck muscles relax as I was now able to look up comfortably at the basket while I added power and began to close the gap. The new seat position also gave me renewed confidence. The basket started to move again as I closed within ten feet. I pulled some power and stopped the closure. My hands kept moving and I wiggled my toes, which had always helped to relax me in the past. A warm rush of adrenaline pulsed through my veins as I added power. The basket stabilized and the probe struck the center of the basket. The hose quickly bent into an *S* shape, and now that I could see the basket easily, I knew that I could maintain this position.

"We've got good flow," said Cave. My hands kept up the frenetic pace of correction and recorrection. Each power addition would bend the hose more, and each power reduction would bring me closer to losing control of the bend and having the hose wrap wildly around my refueling probe and possibly spit me out again. Finally, after several minutes of torture, the fuel gauge indicated 8.5. "We've got all we need. Great job," said Cave. I knew he was trying to build my confidence because he knew as well as I did that the hard part of the flight was still ahead. I now had to land on the smallest carrier in the fleet.

"Mako 12, Ironclaw 605, thanks for the gas, we're switching," said Cave.

"605, you're cleared to detach. Have a good night," said the cheerfully relaxed voice of the air force tanker pilot, who knew he would be landing on a ten-thousand-foot-long stationary runway at the end of his mission. In contrast, I was planning to land on the pitching and rolling deck of an aircraft carrier that was less than a thousand feet long. As I turned the Prowler toward the *Midway,* I wondered how much the deck would be moving tonight. This carrier was infamous for rocking and rolling, and every *Midway* pilot had a good story about a scary night landing.

Her keel was laid in 1943, during the height of World War II, and for the first decade of the *Midway*'s service she was the largest warship in the world. Forty-seven years later, the *Midway* was now the oldest and smallest carrier in the US Navy. Her hull was originally designed for a cruiser, which made the *Midway* a nimble ship compared with the newer and larger aircraft carriers. In the late 1960s the *Midway* was decommissioned and brought into the yards for extensive renovations in order to extend the ship's service life and enable it to handle the navy's new high-performance jets. One major aspect of the renovation was the addition of an enlarged steel, angled flight deck. The new larger deck surface, combined with the ship's small cruiser-type hull, made the ship topheavy and therefore extremely unstable in heavy seas. Not being pilots, the naval engineers did not appreciate the importance of having a stable deck on which to land high-performance jet aircraft. The navy made several attempts to stabilize the *Midway*, but she quickly developed a reputation as being the toughest ship to land on in the fleet. The *Midway*'s roll angle occasionally exceeded twenty-four degrees, and the pitch angle was so bad that pilots on final approach had seen the ship's propellers breach the surface of the water. Another part of the problem was that the larger, more modern aircraft carriers in the fleet had four arresting wires to catch their jets, whereas the *Midway* had only three.

My mind was brought back to flying by Cave's voice. "Marshal, Ironclaw 605 is tank complete, state 8.5."

"Ironclaw 605, Marshal, we have a ready deck. These will be vectors to a manual push. Take heading 090, descend and maintain angels 1.2, altimeter 30.10."

"Marshal, Ironclaw 605 heading 090, descending to angels 1.2, altimeter 30.10," said Cave. Cave quickly reviewed the approach to landing checklist and tested the ILS and ACLS boxes, ensuring these instrument landing aids would be working properly. Everything seemed to be operating normally.

The good news about a manual push and a ready deck was that I would get spoon-fed the approach information and would not have to go through the hassle of setting up a holding pattern in order to hit my holding point on time. The bad news was that because it had taken me so long to tank, all the other jets had already recovered. Now the entire air wing was sitting comfortably in their ready room chairs waiting to watch me fly my approach on the carrier's closed-circuit television. The Pilot

Landing Aid Television (PLAT) was on channel seven, and it was probably the most watched channel of the four or five channels available,
which included a movie channel, a news channel offering taped delay
CNN, a weather channel, and an educational channel. The PLAT picture on the screen was produced by a small flush-mounted video camera lens installed on the centerline of the carrier's landing area. The
PLAT recorded every approach and landing made on the carrier.

Superimposed on the lens were crosshairs that projected a rough
estimation of the proper glide slope and lineup that a jet needed to fly
in order to land safely. The favorite pastime for aviators who were not
flying was being a "PLAT LSO." LSO stood for Landing Signals Officer,
and they were the pilots onboard the carrier who were responsible for
the safe and expeditious recovery of the air wing's aircraft. They controlled the recoveries and also evaluated every pilot by grading every
landing made on the *Midway*. The expression "Everyone's a critic" was
probably developed on an aircraft carrier. Every night the squadron
ready rooms around the ship were packed with aviators criticizing their
comrades' approaches. The banter was always fast and furious.

"He came down like a ton of shit," one aviator would say.

"If I were the LSO, I would have waved him off," another would
respond.

"That was really ugly," would say the first and then they both would
nod and prepare to critique the next approach on the TV, knowing full
well that the next night it would be their turn to fly the approach and
someone else would be criticizing their performance. The PLAT
offered everyone on board the carrier a chance to tease a pilot if he
boltered or flew a particularly poor approach.

The professional critics, the air wing's LSOs, were actually on the
flight deck only a few feet away from the jets as they landed. Teams of
five or six LSOs would write down descriptive comments concerning
the deviations from glide slope, lineup, and airspeed on every
approach and then assign a grade. The meticulous grading of each
landing allowed the air wing to monitor its pilots' performance. The
consequences of poor performance were too severe to let substandard

landings continue for very long. As a result, any pilot with consistently poor landing grades would face a board of inquiry and risk losing his wings. The pressure to make safe landings was real and intense, especially for the nuggets, like myself, who were being watched very closely.

Thinking about the several thousand eyeballs that were going to be watching my approach did not help me relax as the altimeter unwound past five thousand feet. The radalt started beeping and I retracted the speed brakes and pulled back on the stick to reduce my rate of descent.

"Marshal, Ironclaw six zero five, platform," said Cave.

"Radalt is reset to three thousand feet," I said.

"New final bearing one seven five," said the approach controller. The radar altimeter started beeping again as we descended through three thousand feet.

"Radalt is reset, at a thousand feet." The TACAN indicated that the ship was only twelve miles away.

"Ironclaw 605, stay clean through ten, I'll call your dirty," said the approach controller. A minute passed. "Ironclaw 605, at eight miles, dirty up," said the approach controller.

My left hand pulled back on the throttles and then lowered the landing gear handle and moved the flap lever to the down position. As the Prowler started the clumsy transition to the slower airspeed, my right hand pulled the hook release lever, lowering the tailhook. As soon as I could see all the proper indications, I blurted out the landing checklist: "Gear one, two three down and locked, flaps thirty degrees, stab shifted, slats out, hook's down, harness set, holding the boards, pressure's normal and on speed will be one twenty-eight knots with 7.8 on the gas." My thumb began to move at a feverish pace adjusting the electric trim button on top of the control stick in an attempt to "trim out" any extraneous stick forces so that the jet would fly smoothly through the night down the glide slope once we hit the tipover point at three miles. Night carrier landings are like nightmares—but worse. At least in nightmares one has the luxury of being able to escape one's fate simply by waking up. During a night landing, one's eyes are wide open and one's senses are on full alert, as the jet approaches the stern of the pitching and rolling carrier. During those last twenty seconds of the approach as the deck gets closer and closer, it is a pure survival instinct that guides the pilot's hands through the wakeful nightmare.

"Ironclaw 605, at four and one half miles, ACLS lock on, call your needles."

"Fly up and right," I said, hoping that the controller would concur.

"Concur, 605, this will be a Mode II approach," said the approach controller, meaning that I would get voice calls from the controller from three miles to three quarters of a mile, telling me my glide slope and azimuth status. Inside the cockpit I would listen to these calls but would be focused primarily on my ACLS needles, which would give me the same information in a more timely fashion. The first call had confirmed that the needles on my instrument panel's gyro were giving me accurate azimuth and glide-slope information. I was not flying the jet precisely enough. Fortunately, there was still time to correct. My instrument scan felt slow. My eyes were sluggish with exhaustion and were not darting around the cockpit's instruments quickly enough. Every pilot develops his own personal instrument scan pattern, his own way of looking at his instruments and absorbing all of the information presented by them. The quicker the instrument scan, the better the pilot.

The miniature aircraft symbol on the gyro was to the left of the vertical needle, so I needed to fly to the right. Maintaining twelve hundred feet, I turned to the right until the vertical needle was centered on the aircraft symbol. The horizontal needle now started down rapidly, indicating that the jet had intercepted the glide slope and that I needed to begin my descent. "Boards are out, landing checks complete," I stated, as I nervously squirmed in my ejection seat.

After establishing a steady rate of descent, I looked up over the instrument panel and saw a faint yellow light in the distance, which was all I could see of the *Midway*. *Great, I'm going to land on a faint yellow light,* I said to myself. Immediately, my eyes were back inside the cockpit scanning the instruments, my hands twitching as they made minor movements with the stick and throttles. The toughest aspect of a night carrier landing was the visual transition that occurred at three quarters of a mile. At that point, I would transition from an instrument scan inside the cockpit to a visual scan outside the cockpit for the last twenty seconds before landing. I would have to leave my instruments and refocus my eyes outside the cockpit on three critical parameters: the "meatball" for glide-slope information; the deck's lighted center-line for lineup information; and the jet's angle of attack (AOA) for air-speed information. Controlling these three parameters was the juggling act that I needed to perform in order to land safely.

If I flew low I would hit the ramp and would be swallowed instantly by the ensuing fireball. If I flew high I would miss all the wires and bolter. If I drifted right my wingtip might slice the nose of a parked jet on the crowded deck, and if I drifted left I might go over the edge for an unwanted swim. I would also need to maintain a constant airspeed so that my tailhook would be in the proper position to catch one of the three arresting wires when I landed. The jet's AOA indicator was located on the far left side of the cockpit above the instrument panel. Its location allowed me to use peripheral vision to see it as I scanned the meatball and centerline outside the cockpit. The AOA indicator would display an amber circle or "doughnut" if I maintained the proper airspeed for the jet's given gross weight, plus or minus one knot. If the jet accelerated, the indicator would display a red chevron, and it would make the jet prone to bolter because of the nose down, hook up, landing attitude of the aircraft. If the jet decelerated, the indicator would display a green chevron, telling me that the jet was close to stall airspeed. These instrument lights in the cockpit were wired to and repeated on the external nosewheel landing gear door, which was clearly visible to the LSOs standing near the ramp, telling them whether the jet was fast, slow, or on speed. Each one of the three para-meters of the approach was critical, and all three needed to be within strict limits in order to make a safe landing. If there was any significant deviation to any one of these three parameters, the LSOs would turn on the red waveoff lights, and I would be forced to abort the approach.

"Ironclaw 605, you're lined up left and on glide slope at three quar-ters of a mile, call the ball," said the controller.

"605, Prowler ball, 7.5," said Cave. My eyes now came up from the instruments and I shifted my focus to the landing area and the meatball which was now less than three quarters of a mile away. I dipped the right wing to correct for the lineup deviation, but did not add enough power to compensate for the wing movement.

"Don't settle," came the call from the LSO. I added power but the "meatball" still appeared to be centered, so I went back to looking at lineup. Lineup was now good. My heart was pounding, and I was hyperventilating. The faint yellow light in the distance was now a huge floating piece of steel. Only a few more seconds to go.

"You're low," said the annoyed voice of the LSO. "Power." My eyes flashed back to the meatball and I saw that he was right. The meatball was now below the horizontal datum lights. My left hand shot forward adding lots of power. It was too big a correction, and the meatball began to rise rapidly.

"Easy with it," said the LSO in a softer voice. "You're overpowered." In the periphery I saw the red chevron of the ADA indicator and knew that I was now high and fast. I pulled back on the throttles and the engines started to spool down. "Right for lineup," said the LSO, then followed quickly by a crescendoing call, "Power! *Power!*"

I had drifted to the left and gave a big right-wing dip to correct, but I neglected to add power for the lineup correction. I was horrified to see the meatball start a rapid descent and within an instant it changed colors to red. Ramp strike was all I could think as I rammed the throttles to the stops. Terror coursing through my veins, I was unsure whether or not I would clear the ramp. The Prowler careened onto the carrier's flight deck. My body was hurled forward violently as the tailhook grabbed the *Midway*'s first wire. After two seconds and 195 feet of roll out on the flight deck, the jet had gone from 128 knots to a standstill. My left arm was locked at the elbow and my knees were trembling. Above the sound of my heart pounding in my chest and my hyperventilating I heard a calm voice, that of the air boss looking down at me from the tower, say, "It's OK, 605, we've got you now, throttle back, and turn off your lights." We had made it. Bhagwan wouldn't need his toothbrush after all, but I smiled with the thought that he might need that clean pair of underwear.

I quickly pulled the throttles to idle, turned off my lights, and raised the flaps and slats lever. The terror of seeing the meatball turn red still had me shaking. Once the flaps and slats were retracted, Cave was able to fold the wings so that we could taxi around the crowded flight deck. The outboard ten feet of each wing was raised and folded across the jet's back in order to reduce the Prowler's wingspan, making it easier to avoid the many obstacles around the carrier's flight deck. I taxied toward the bow, following the signals of the yellowshirt. My legs were still shaking from the combination of utter fear and adrenaline from the landing. Pilots called it "sewing machine leg," and it was actually humorous to look down and see my legs bobbing up and down uncontrollably on the rudder pedals.

"It looks like we're going to do the bow dance," said Cave. I reluctantly followed the yellowshirt's signals toward the bow of the carrier. If the engineers at Grumman had ever done a "bow dance" on a carrier at night, they would have designed the Prowler differently. The two front seats in the Prowler are six feet in front of the nosewheel. As a result, it is possible for the nosewheel to be within inches of the edge of the deck and the two aircrew in the front cockpit actually to be sitting over the water. In my mind, it was reminiscent of the pirate's tradition of forcing people to "walk the plank." After a stressful night landing, doing the bow dance is an absolutely awful way to end a flight. I taxied up the starboard side feeling helpless. We were completely at the mercy of the yellowshirt. It was a black night and I could barely see the edge of the deck. The yellowshirt was now slightly behind my left shoulder, still signaling me to taxi forward. I knew that the nosewheel must have been within a foot of the edge of the deck. If I stopped the momentum of the jet then it would be much harder to make the left turn into the parking spot they had reserved for me, but if I kept rolling, I was sure that I would go right over the edge of the deck. Finally, the yellowshirt signaled me to turn left and my shaky left leg pushed the rudder pedal to the floorboard. Since my right thumb had engaged the nosewheel steering switch on the stick, the nosewheel started to swing to the left. Soon my body was back over the deck and I started to relax. Moments later I pulled out the parking brake and our mission was complete. "They're tying us down here. Let's safe our seats," I said over the intercom, reminding my crew of the importance of securing the two ejection handles on each seat before leaving the aircraft.

The yellowshirt passed control of the jet to my squadron's plane captain, who signaled me to shut down the engines. As the second engine spooled down, I asked Cave if he was clear of the canopy. Cave responded with a thumbs up, and I raised the canopy.

The cool sea air rushed into the cockpit, and all of the tension and stress began to ebb. A feeling of exhilaration took hold of me and I smiled, realizing that even though it had not been pretty, I had gotten the job done.

In the darkness, my hands instinctively reached for the fittings that bound me to the ejection seat. Within seconds I released all six fittings and began to pull myself out of the jet. The salty breeze felt refreshing on my sweaty face as I grabbed the familiar handgrip that was welded to the inside of the canopy's frame. The Prowler's forward cockpit was extremely difficult to access and it required the flexibility of a contortionist to make the awkward motions necessary to enter and exit the jet. Once out of the cockpit, I perched on the small boarding platform waiting for Bhagwan to clear the ladder that would take me down to the flight deck. Face had already exited on the other side.

Once my feet touched the deck I was surrounded by the maintenance crew. The first face was a young third-class petty officer named Clement. The face of this young avionics technician was smeared with oil and grease that had been baked into his skin after a long day on the flight deck, working next to the burning-hot jet exhaust. He was a slender kid who wore a permanent smile that some might call a smirk. He had probably been far to bright for his high school and his boredom had helped him develop his mischievous smirk.

"How'd she fly, sir?" he asked. He was starting the standard interrogation of the pilot to discover any serious problems with the jet so that they could start working right away, in the hope that the problem could be corrected before the first morning launch.

"Just fine, I don't have any major gripes," I said.

"Did you tank?" asked Clement.

"Yes, we took about five thousand pounds of gas."

After asking me several more specific systems questions, he finally released me. "Great, sir thanks a lot." Clement turned to Chief Ross, our squadron's flight deck coordinator, and gave him a thumbs up, meaning that the jet was good to go for the first launch of the next day. I saw the chief start talking on his headset microphone built into his protective helmet, telling flight deck control that they could park this Prowler in a "go spot" tonight. Clement and the other maintenance experts who had gathered around me all dispersed and started working on the routine maintenance and checks that needed to be done after every flight. The oldest one among them was probably twenty-five. They were all good, but Clement had been selected to be the troubleshooter, the one maintenance man who would interact with the pilots when there were problems. He had an excellent knowledge of the aircraft and more important, a calm and friendly personality. Without fail, he knew how to reassure even the most senior pilots that their aircraft looked good and were ready to fly. He was special and our squadron was lucky to have such a good troubleshooter. He seemed to have endless energy, which is exactly what he needed.

The normally hectic pace of the flight deck was now more relaxed. The deafening noise of jet engines was gone and, now that flight operations for the night were finished, the troops on the deck seemed to work at a calmer pace. The flight deck at night was like a field filled with fireflies. All of the yellowshirts were now using their flashlights to signal to the blueshirts who were driving the tractors that towed the jets around the flight deck. The jets were being pushed and pulled around the deck, being respotted for the first launch of the next day. The Aircraft Handling Officer, otherwise known as "The Handler," was the man responsible for all of the jets' movement on the flight and hangar deck. His job was to solve this complex jigsaw puzzle every day, so that the carrier could launch and recover aircraft in the most efficient manner. The tight spaces on the flight deck forced the jets to be parked within inches of each other all over the deck. Moving so many jets in such a tight space was a mishap waiting to happen, but fortunately, the *Midway*'s handler was a puzzle master.

I joined the ranks of the fireflies by taking my flashlight from my survival vest and using it to make my presence known so that no tractor would run me over in the darkness. My crew was already off the deck not waiting for me to finish the maintenance debrief. It did not bother me that they did not wait. I would do the same thing in their shoes. The flight deck was not a place to linger. The flight deck always made me nervous. There were simply too many things that could go wrong, too many ways to get injured. My flashlight illuminated the dark ladder that led off the carrier's deck onto the catwalk that lined most of the carrier's deck edge. The steps led me to a large watertight hatch that needed a strong shove to loosen the lever that bolted the hatch shut. Once through the hatch, I entered into the midst of our maintenance control office, the heart and soul of every squadron.

"So, did you break my jet, lieutenant?" asked the senior chief, a bear of a man with a bushy black mustache, who ran our squadron's maintenance effort.

"Not tonight, senior chief, the jet flew well. I have no gripes."

"Well, that's good," he said, happy to know that there weren't lots of complaints about the jet that would keep his people working throughout the night.

"It looked like you were trying to get some extra flight time tonight," said another voice from the other side of the small office. It was the voice of our Maintenance Material Control Officer, who had the endearing nickname of Beast. His barrel chest and two sinewy arms said, "Don't tread on me," but his gruff exterior belied the warmth of the man. If one looked closely, one could see an irreverent twinkle in his eyes. He was teasing me about my approach and informing me that the PLAT LSOs in maintenance control thought I had been lucky not to bolter on my approach, because I had gotten so high in the middle.

"No, thanks, I had plenty of flight time tonight," I said, grateful that I had been able to catch a wire. The senior chief would have come up with another sarcastic comment, but I did not give him the chance, as I walked through maintenance control and into the equipment room where all of our flight gear was kept. Upon my arrival, our entire crew of four was standing in the cramped space trying to shed the forty-plus pounds of personal survival gear that we wore on every flight.

"That was a pretty big settle at the ramp," said Cave, a master of understatement.

"Yeah, I took off too much power to correct for the high in close," I said, grudgingly, accepting Cave's unsolicited comments. It had not been a great approach, but I hoped that people would refrain from commenting on my efforts. It had been a long night, and my body desperately needed a shower and a good night's sleep.

The first person I met when I entered the ready room was our squadron's senior LSO. His large, lanky frame seemed to comfortably fit his call sign of Horse. "Pretty dark night out there," he said, managing a smile. Horse was a natural pilot; there were a few of them around. The movement of the stick and throttles came instinctively to him, where I and many other pilots needed to consciously consider what we were doing in the air. His dad had been a navy pilot, so it was in his blood. He had grown up on the beaches of Pensacola, Florida, the cradle of naval aviation. He had watched the Blue Angels, the navy's elite flight demonstration team, regularly fly overhead, and so from an early age Horse was hooked. He knew all along that when he grew up he wanted to fly navy jets.

"It was black," I said. I finally thought I had a sympathetic audience and was hoping that Horse would give me a few words of encouragement or perhaps even a pat on the back.

"If you can't be smooth, be high. Welcome to the fleet," said Horse with a chuckle as he walked away. So much for sympathy. Our crew gathered in the back of the ready room to debrief the flight. Before we had finished talking about the departure from the ship we were interrupted by the grand entrance of the air wing LSOs. Generally speaking, the LSOs were selected from among the best pilots in the air wing, and I desperately wanted to be one. The senior air wing LSO was a feisty A-6 Intruder pilot whose call sign was Mad Dog. His title of CAG LSO meant that he was one of two lieutenant commanders who represented the commander of the air wing and who organized and trained the air wing's LSO teams. He walked briskly into the ready room and quickly picked out my face as the face of a nugget pilot after a scary night landing. "Hi, I'm Mad Dog, the senior CAG LSO." We shook hands, and I stood to face the judgment of this senior respected LSO and fellow aviator.

Mad Dog looked into the book filled with grades and comments for every single approach that had been flown that day. His finger moved down the columns of numbers and names until he found mine. "Settle on start, too much power on the come-on in the middle, high in close, fly through down on lineup at the ramp, for a no grade taxi-one wire," barked Mad Dog. "If you had pulled off much more power correcting for that high in close, you might have hit the ramp. Remember, you must never recenter the high ball in close." This was a rule to live by, literally, and I had heard it thousands of times throughout my training. The comments and the grade for this approach were below average, and I was mad at myself for flying so poorly. A taxi-one wire was very bad. It meant that I had landed significantly short of the first wire and had in effect "taxied" the jet into the wire. I had been dangerously low.

Mad Dog continued his lecture. "If you didn't see a red meatball when you crossed the ramp, then you must have been spotting the deck." "Spotting the deck" was a cardinal sin and also extremely dangerous. It meant that the pilot tried to land by looking at the deck without looking at the meatball. It was a risky technique, since at night, almost all of one's visual cues are gone and one's senses can easily be fooled. I hoped that I was not already developing bad habits in my landings. "Just concentrate on scanning the meatball all the way to touchdown," said Mad Dog.

"Yes, sir, ahh . . . ahh . . . I did see a red meatball at the ramp," I said glumly, not pleased with my performance.

"Don't let the jet go low like that again. Just fly the ball and you'll do fine. Welcome to the fleet," said Mad Dog with a smile as he slugged me in the shoulder. He turned to leave, leading the traveling troupe of LSOs out of our ready room in search of the next pilot to debrief. I must have looked terrible. I had worked so hard and done so poorly. At least I was alive and in the fleet. I was in "the show" now.

from The Sky Beyond
by Sir Gordon Taylor

Sir Gordon Taylor left Australia in 1916 to join England's Royal Flying Corps and fight the Germans. Taught to obey his superiors without question, Taylor almost at once found himself in a terrible jam.

E arly in the morning of August 5, 1914, groups of boys crowded round the newspaper stands in the school library. The dramatic news was there in the staring headlines. England had declared war on Germany.

I was one of those boys, with still another year at school before I would be old enough to go. Our picture of war was a glorious affair in those times—a terrific adventure of drums and flags and soldiers charging into battle, routing the enemy. It was by pure chance that I happened to join the Royal Flying Corps, and to become a fighter pilot on the western front in France.

I was reading the *Strand Magazine,* coming home in the train for the holidays. There was a story of British aircraft bombing the Zeppelin hangars at Cuxhafen, with illustrations of the Avros diving on the great sheds which housed the German airships. It all seemed exciting and adventurous. This, I thought, was obviously the way to go to war.

So, in 1916, after discovering that the recently formed Australian Flying Corps was not at that time enlisting people for training as pilots, I went to England and joined the Royal Flying Corps. I did not realize that the ease with which I got into the R.F.C. was partly due to the very heavy casualties being inflicted by new German aircraft upon the crews of the obsolete types with which the R.F.C. was very largely equipped.

I passed through a course of ground instruction at Reading, was posted to Netheravon elementary flying training school on Salisbury Plain, and the adventure of the air was before me. After more lectures on aircraft and some frustrating days of waiting around the hangars for flying training to begin, I was suddenly confronted by a rather morose instructor who, with few words, launched me abruptly into my first experience of flight.

"You Taylor?"

"Yes, sir."

"Had any instruction yet?"

"No, I haven't, sir."

"All right, I'll give you some landings."

With these brief words he walked off towards a Maurice Farman standing on the tarmac and I followed him in a somewhat confused state of mind. This wasn't exactly what I had expected for the beginning of my flying training. I had pictured some sort of orderly approach to the thing: a talk with the instructor before my first flight, and some idea of how to control the airplane. Instead, I climbed up after him into the rear seat of a thing about the size and shape of a bathtub, slung between the wings of a biplane held together by many wires and struts and having the engine with a pusher airscrew located immediately behind the place where I was sitting. Though I was charged with enthusiasm for the great adventure which was about to begin, I couldn't help noting that the engine was conveniently located to come right through the back of my neck in the event of a crash dislodging it from its mountings.

But there was little time for speculation. A mechanic swung the propeller, the pilot ran up the engine, waved away the chocks, and we were away out onto the grassy ridge of the airfield. My instructor said nothing. I sat in the back confronted with what looked like the handle of a large pair of scissors on the top end of a control column, and a rudder bar on which I didn't know whether or not to put my feet. Having received no instructions I thought it best not to touch anything; so I kept my hands and feet off the controls.

We swung round into wind, the sound of the engine rose to a roar behind me and the machine started to move off over the surface. In what seemed to me to be a very short distance the rattling of the under-carriage on the grassy surface subsided and stopped and I realized that we were flying. Rather than having any sensation of climbing I felt that the ground was sinking away from the airplane and a new landscape invisible from below was spreading out around us. I waited in excited anticipation for some words from the instructor; but none came.

Instead, the airplane turned up on a wing, circled the airfield, and faced up in the direction in which we had taken off. Quite suddenly the roar of the engine ceased, the nose went down, and we were gliding steeply for the earth. I sat back keeping clear of everything and won-dered whether this was a normal approach to the ground or something had gone wrong and we were just going to crash. The earth rushed up at us, the airplane flattened quite smoothly out of its steep glide, and in a few moments I again felt the rattling of the wheels on the grass.

Now, I thought, we shall stop and I shall be told how to do it. But no, again. Before the machine had come to rest the engine came on with a roar and we were away again, and into the air. We went into the same close circuit of the airdrome, flew downwind, and round, to line up for the approach to land. The engine was throttled back, the nose went down, and a shout came from the instructor in the front seat, "You land it!"

The shock of this remark caused a physical reaction almost before my mind had grasped the enormity of its meaning. My hands shot out to the scissors handles in front of me and my feet to the rudder bar on the floor. Instinctively I imagined that unless I took the controls instantly the airplane might fall out of control to the ground. I knew nothing. Nothing beyond the absurdity of the demand that I should land the airplane. Then the first spark of hostility was ignited in the panic that threatened to engulf me in this ridiculous situation. This man was in the airplane with me. Even if he was mad enough to expect me to land it with no instruction he would probably be sane enough to stop me from crashing it.

I tried to hold the controls steady so that the machine continued on down in the glide he had set as he handed over to me. I daren't in fact move them much because I had no idea of the effect of movement of controls. Somehow I managed to keep the old Rumpety going on down. There wasn't much height to lose anyway: only about two hundred feet. Very soon the earth was visibly rushing up to meet us and I realized that something would have to be done before we dived into the ground. I drew back on the control column, much over-controlling of course, and the airplane began to swoop up again. The engine came on, the controls were snatched out of my hands and a savage shout came back to me from the instructor, "Bloody awful!"

Again we climbed away, went sweeping round the circuit and in for another landing. I tried mentally to anticipate the next demand, but none came and I just sat there, out of the picture, feeling utterly confused and ineffectual. The grass was coming up again and another landing was upon us. The machine began to flatten out, swept low over the surface and the now familiar clatter of the wheels told me we were on the ground once more. Visibly acknowledging my existence for the first time, the instructor turned slightly and announced in a more conciliatory tone, "That's better."

"What's better?" I thought. Then the impact of his meaning hit me, and with it a surge of fear about this whole mad act. I hadn't touched the controls. I still have no idea how the airplane was landed that day. I wanted to get out of it now: out, onto the ground, away from this man, and his flying machine.

But before I could utter a word in protest the engine at the back of my neck shattered all coherent thought with another blast of urgent power, the propeller thrust the machine forward, and we were away again. I mentally clung to the sides of the airplane, torn now between a conviction that I must somehow get out of this the next time we touched the ground, and a shocked impression of the consequences from such a flagrant breach of military discipline. Thoroughly shaken now by this conflict, and with the threat of disaster dominating all my reactions, I shirked my decision, and with the last shreds of morale which were left to me waited for the next move.

It surprised me. Instead of another mad circus performance round the airfield we climbed steadily and flew away over Salisbury Plain.

I was now given some brief instruction in how to fly the airplane straight and level, and found, with a returning sense of inspiration, that this was fairly easy. The instructor also seemed to have settled down and I felt for the first time some reasonable sort of human contact between us.

After about twenty minutes' practice in the most elementary control in level flight the airplane was again snatched out of my hands without comment, and we went soaring round and back for the field. Obviously we were going to land again, and with that realization all the warning signals went up again. Was I to land it? Was he? What should I do? The machine banked into a turn and the engine stopped. We were already in the final glide. Too late to say or do anything. I resigned myself, and waited.

The instructor did the landing, and, to my very great relief, turned the airplane and taxied in for the hangars. On the tarmac he switched off the engine, climbed out of the nacelle, jumped down to the ground, and walked away.

So this was learning to fly.

I sat for a few moments, taking stock. Then I too got out of the airplane and went down to the quarters. I badly needed some thought and some advice about this whole affair. Having absorbed a strong traditional sense of military service and the sanctity of military discipline from recent experience at school where I was an officer in the Cadet Corps and senior prefect of the school, I had instinctive respect for authority and an inclination to accept and obey an order from a senior officer without question even in my mind. This instructor was of course senior in rank to me: a captain, against my recently acquired status in the Royal Flying Corps as a temporary second lieutenant on probation.

Beneath all this was a fundamental sense of injustice and resentment at so disillusioning and untidy an experience for my first flight in an airplane. I had come twelve thousand miles from Australia, with high hopes and inspiration to fly and fight in the service of the Royal Flying Corps. I knew I could sail a boat, ride a horse, run, swim, play football, and do most of the things I had been asked about as physical qualifications for service as a pilot in the R.F.C. I didn't believe I was such a fool as this instructor seemed to think. But I was confused and frustrated with conflicting thoughts and emotions after this wretched beginning to my career as a pilot

That evening I had a good talk with "Anzac" Whiteman, a Rhodes scholar from Perth in Western Australia. Whiteman and I had gone through ground school together at Reading. We had teamed up as friends, and formed the idea of trying to go right on through to a squadron in France. I felt better after a talk with Anzac: decided to turn up for flying the next day without any approach to the instructor, and have the situation out with him in the airplane if things went the same way.

On the tarmac he was perfectly friendly, even cordial, as we went out to the machine. But as soon as we were in our seats and our belts fastened he started the engine and went off without explanation or any indication of what we were going to do.

In the air we did a few very gentle turns in which I had a somewhat indefinite part, not knowing really whether he, or I, was flying the airplane: a few minutes straight and level again; and then, with mixed emotions and a "this is it" feeling, I realized that landings were upon us again.

This time I was told to do the landing: a shout from the front, with no details. I had discovered that if you let the nose of this airplane go down beyond a certain speed you could not pull it out; also that if you didn't put it down far enough it would stall and crash. So I took the controls and really concentrated on the critical action of keeping the airplane in the correct glide, of easing her out, and touching the wheels down on the grass. I could feel the instructor also on the controls, creating an uncertainty in opposition to my movements; and in this way we went on down, both landing the airplane. In some intangible fashion the landing turned out to be quite a good one; but I had had enough. I was afraid and angry, and determined now to have a showdown with this man before another take-off.

He didn't give me a chance. To my utter astonishment he got up out of his seat, climbed over the side and down, to stand on the grass of the airfield. Then he looked up and called to me, "You can bloody well go solo now."

For the moment the shock froze me into a state of inaction. I couldn't believe he was serious. Then he started to walk away. This was it. I had to make a decision, for better or worse. I put my hand over the side of the nacelle, felt for the switch, and stopped the engine.

The instructor turned and came back, shouting at me, "What's the matter with you? Why did you stop the engine?"

Horror-stricken momentarily by the implications of my decision, I hit back at him. "I am not going solo."

I expected, and was quite prepared, to be instantly placed under arrest for refusing to obey an order. I knew I couldn't fly the airplane. I had never done a take-off, nor a landing without interference, and in the total of one hour and thirty minutes of this nightmare experience had briefly flown the machine straight and level alone. I felt hostile now; not horrified by fear of the consequences any more. I hadn't come all the way from my home in Australia to kill myself at the orders of this lunatic. But I was shaken and desperately unhappy about it. I waited for the blast I expected would be forthcoming. But this man was completely unpredictable. He called up to me, in an almost friendly voice, "What do you want to do?"

What *did* I want to do? A quick, instinctive thought shot out of my mind as an innocent statement of fact. "I want to fly with another instructor."

"Very well then; we'll taxi in and I'll see if I can arrange it for you." There was even a note of relief in his voice. Was I as bad as all that?

In at the hangar I was handed over to a long, genial instructor. His name was Prallé. Lieutenant Prallé. I see his name now, signed in my logbook. He wasted no time. "I believe you're having some trouble with your flying, Taylor?"

"Well, not exactly, sir. I just don't know how to fly, that's all."

"All right. Come on out and we'll start from scratch."

From that moment I knew I was on the way. Prallé gave me another two hours' concise and friendly instruction: take-offs, climb, straight and level flight, gentle and medium turns, glide with engine off, and landings: and a firm warning not to let the Rumpety's nose down below the angle of glide and speed he had shown me.

I went off solo keyed up to the realization of flight alone, where nobody could help me but myself, but confident; and in a few more days finished my time on Rumpetys and went on for advanced training at the Central Flying School, a few miles away at Upavon.

But Anzac Whiteman was killed; on his first solo he got the nose down and flew into the ground.

Some time afterwards I heard the story behind my first instructor. He had been a good pilot, with a fine record in France; but finally cracked up under the stress of flying an airplane of poor performance and ineffective armament against the new German fighters. Sent home for a rest, he was put on instructing, but was a nervous wreck for flying of any kind.

from Enduring Love
by Ian McEwan

This passage from Ian McEwan's (born 1948) 1998 novel is about some of the ways that things go wrong on the ground or in the air: weather changes, communications break down, people lose courage. The principal characters include a child in a hot air balloon, his would-be rescuers and the wind.

The beginning is simple to mark. We were in sunlight under a turkey oak, partly protected from a strong, gusty wind. I was kneeling on the grass with a corkscrew in my hand, and Clarissa was passing me the bottle—a 1987 Daumas Gassac. This was the moment, this was the pinprick on the time map: I was stretching out my hand, and as the cool neck and the black foil touched my palm, we heard a man's shout. We turned to look across the field and saw the danger. Next thing, I was running toward it. The transformation was absolute: I don't recall dropping the corkscrew, or getting to my feet, or making a decision, or hearing the caution Clarissa called after me. What idiocy, to be racing into this story and its labyrinths, sprinting away from our happiness among the fresh spring grasses by the oak. There was the shout again, and a child's cry, enfeebled by the wind that roared in the tall trees along the hedgerows. I ran faster. And there, suddenly, from different points around the field, four other men were converging on the scene, running like me.

I see us from two hundred feet up, through the eyes of the buzzard we had watched earlier, soaring, circling, and dipping in the tumult of currents: five men running silently toward the center of a hundred-acre field. I approached from the southeast, with the wind at my back. About two hundred yards to my left two men ran side by side. They were farm laborers who had been repairing the fence along the field's southern edge where it skirts the road. The same distance beyond them was the motorist, John Logan, whose car was banked on the grass verge with its door, or doors, wide open. Knowing what I know now, it's odd to evoke the figure of Jed Parry directly ahead of me, emerging from a line of beeches on the far side of the field a quarter of a mile away, running into the wind. To the buzzard, Parry and I were tiny forms, our white shirts brilliant against the green, rushing toward each other like lovers, innocent of the grief this entanglement would bring. The encounter that would unhinge us was minutes away, its enormity disguised from us not only by the barrier of time but by the colossus in the center of the field, which drew us in with the power of a terrible ratio that set fabulous magnitude against the puny human distress at its base.

What was Clarissa doing? She said she walked quickly toward the center of the field. I don't know how she resisted the urge to run. By the time it happened, the event I am about to describe—the fall—she had almost caught us up and was well placed as an observer, unencumbered by participation, by the ropes and the shouting, and by our fatal lack of cooperation. What I describe is shaped by what Clarissa saw too, by what we told each other in the time of obsessive reexamination that followed: the aftermath, an appropriate term for what happened in a field waiting for its early summer mowing. The aftermath, the second crop, the growth promoted by that first cut in May.

I'm holding back, delaying the information. I'm lingering in the prior moment because it was a time when other outcomes were still possible; the convergence of six figures in a flat green space has a comforting geometry from the buzzard's perspective, the knowable, limited plane of the snooker table. The initial conditions, the force and the direction of the force, define all the consequent pathways, all the angles of collision and return, and the glow of the overhead light bathes the field, the baize and all its moving bodies, in reassuring clarity. I think that while we were still converging, before we made contact, we were in a state of mathematical grace. I linger on our dispositions, the relative distances and the compass point—because as far as these occurrences were concerned, this was the last time I understood anything clearly at all.

What were we running toward? I don't think any of us would ever know fully. But superficially the answer was a balloon. Not the nominal space that encloses a cartoon character's speech or thought, or, by analogy, the kind that's driven by mere hot air. It was an enormous balloon filled with helium, that elemental gas forged from hydrogen in the nuclear furnace of the stars, first step along the way in the generation of multiplicity and variety of matter in the universe, including our selves and all our thoughts.

We were running toward a catastrophe, which itself was a kind of furnace in whose heat identities and fates would buckle into new shapes. At the base of the balloon was a basket in which there was a boy, and by the basket, clinging to a rope, was a man in need of help. . .

What we saw when we stood from our picnic was this: a huge gray balloon, the size of a house, the shape of a teardrop, had come down in the field. The pilot must have been halfway out of the passenger basket as it touched the ground. His leg had become entangled in a rope that was attached to an anchor. Now, as the wind gusted and pushed and lifted the balloon toward the escarpment, he was being half dragged, half carried across the field. In the basket was a child, a boy of about ten. In a sudden lull, the man was on his feet, clutching at the basket, or at the boy. Then there was another gust, and the pilot was on his back, bumping over the rough ground, trying to dig his feet in for purchase or lunging for the anchor behind him in order to secure it in

the earth. Even if he had been able, he would not have dared disen-
tangle himself from the anchor rope. He needed his weight to keep the
balloon on the ground, and the wind could have snatched the rope
from his hands.

As I ran I heard him shouting at the boy, urging him to leap clear of
the basket. But the boy was tossed from one side to another as the balloon lurched across the field. He regained his balance and got a leg
over the edge of the basket. The balloon rose and fell, thumping into a
hummock, and the boy dropped backward out of sight. Then he was
up again, arms stretched out toward the man and shouting something
in return—words or inarticulate fear, I couldn't tell.

I must have been a hundred yards away when the situation came
under control. The wind had dropped; the man was on his feet, bending over the anchor as he drove it into the ground. He had unlooped
the rope from his leg. For some reason—complacency, exhaustion, or
simply because he was doing what he was told—the boy remained
where he was. The towering balloon wavered and tilted and tugged, but
the beast was tamed. I slowed my pace, though I did not stop. As the
man straightened, he saw us—or at least the farmworkers and me—
and he waved us on. He still needed help, but I was glad to slow to a
brisk walk. The farm laborers were also walking now. One of them was
coughing loudly. But the man with the car, John Logan, knew something we didn't and kept on running. As for Jed Parry, my view of him
was blocked by the balloon that lay between us.

The wind renewed its rage in the treetops just before I felt its
force on my back. Then it struck the balloon, which ceased its innocent, comical wagging and was suddenly stilled. Its only motion was
a shimmer of strain that rippled out across its ridged surface as the
contained energy accumulated. It broke free, the anchor flew up in
a spray of dirt, and balloon and basket rose ten feet in the air. The
boy was thrown back, out of sight. The pilot had the rope in his
hands and was lifted two feet clear off the ground. If Logan had not
reached him and taken hold of one of the many dangling lines, the
balloon would have carried the boy away. Instead, both men were

now being pulled across the field, and the farmworkers and I were running again.

I got there before them. When I took a rope, the basket was above head height. The boy inside it was screaming. Despite the wind, I caught the smell of urine. Jed Parry was on a rope seconds after me, and the two farmworkers, Joseph Lacey and Toby Greene, caught hold just after him. Greene was having a coughing fit, but he kept his grip. The pilot was shouting instructions at us, but too frantically, and no one was listening. He had been struggling too long, and now he was exhausted and emotionally out of control. With five of us on the lines the balloon was secured. We simply had to keep steady on our feet and pull hand over hand to bring the basket down, and this, despite whatever the pilot was shouting, was what we began to do.

By this time we were standing on the escarpment. The ground dropped away sharply at a gradient of about twenty-five percent and then leveled out into a gentle slope toward the bottom. In winter this is a favorite tobogganing spot for local kids. We were all talking at once. Two of us, myself and the motorist, wanted to walk the balloon away from the edge. Someone thought the priority was to get the boy out. Someone else was calling for the balloon to be pulled down so that we could anchor it firmly. I saw no contradiction, for we could be pulling the balloon down as we moved back into the field. But the second opinion was prevailing. The pilot had a fourth idea, but no one knew or cared what it was.

I should make something clear. There may have been a vague communality of purpose, but we were never a team. There was no chance, no time. Coincidences of time and place, a predisposition to help, had brought us together under the balloon. No one was in charge—or everyone was, and we were in a shouting match. The pilot, red-faced, bawling, and sweating, we ignored. Incompetence came off him like heat. But we were beginning to bawl our own instructions too. I know that if I had been uncontested leader, the tragedy would not have happened. Later I heard some of the others say the same thing about themselves. But there was not time, no opportunity for force of character to show. Any leader, any firm plan, would have been preferable to none. No human society, from the hunter-gatherer to the postindustrial, has come to the attention of anthropologists that did not have its leaders and the led; and no emergency was ever dealt with effectively by democratic process.

It was not so difficult to bring the passenger basket down low enough for us to see inside. We had a new problem. The boy was curled up on the floor. His arms covered his face and he was gripping his hair tightly. "What's his name?" we said to the red-faced man.

"Harry."

"Harry!" we shouted. "Come on, Harry. Harry! Take my hand, Harry. Get out of there, Harry!"

But Harry curled up tighter. He flinched each time we said his name. Our words were like stones thrown down at his body. He was in paralysis of will, a state known as learned helplessness, often noted in laboratory animals subjected to unusual stress; all impulses to problem-solving disappear, all instinct for survival drains away. We pulled the basket down to the ground and managed to keep it there, and we were just leaning in to try and lift the boy out when the pilot shouldered us aside and attempted to climb in. He said later that he told us what he was trying to do. We heard nothing for our own shouting and swearing. What he was doing seemed ridiculous, but his intentions, it turned out, were completely sensible. He wanted to deflate the balloon by pulling a cord that was tangled in the basket.

"Yer great pillock!" Lacey shouted. "Help us reach the lad out."

I heard what was coming two seconds before it reached us. It was as though an express train were traversing the treetops, hurtling toward us. An airy, whining, whooshing sound grew to full volume in half a second. At the inquest, the Met office figures for wind speeds that day were part of the evidence, and there were some gusts, it was said, of seventy miles an hour. This must have been one, but before I let it reach us, let me freeze the frame—there's a security in stillness—to describe our circle.

To my right the ground dropped away. Immediately to my left was

John Logan, a family doctor from Oxford, forty-two years old, married to a historian, with two children. He was not the youngest of our group, but he was the fittest. He played tennis to county level and belonged to a mountaineering club. He had done a stint with a mountain rescue team in the western Highlands. Logan was a mild, reticent man, apparently, otherwise he might have been able to force himself usefully on us as a leader. To his left was Joseph Lacey, sixty-three, farm laborer, odd-job man, captain of his local bowls team. He lived with his wife in Watlington, a small town at the foot of the escarpment. On his left was his mate, Toby Greene, fifty-eight, also a farm laborer, unmarried, living with his mother at Russell's Water. Both men worked for the Stonor estate. Greene was the one with the smoker's cough. Next around the circle, trying to get into the basket, was the pilot, James Gadd, fifty-five, an executive in a small advertising company who lived in Reading with his wife and one of their grownup children, who was mentally handicapped. At the inquest, Gadd was found to have breached half a dozen basic safety procedures, which the coroner listed tonelessly. Gadd's ballooning license was withdrawn. The boy in the basket was Harry Gadd, his grandson, ten years old, from Camberwell, London. Facing me, with the ground sloping away to his left, was Jed Parry. He was twenty-eight, unemployed, living on an inheritance in Hampstead.

This was the crew. As far as we were concerned, the pilot had abdicated his authority. We were breathless, excited, determined on our separate plans, while the boy was beyond participating in his own survival. He lay in a heap, blocking out the world with his forearms. Lacey, Greene, and I were attempting to fish him out, and now Gadd was climbing over the top of us. Logan and Parry were calling out their own suggestions. Gadd had placed one foot by his grandson's head and Greene was cussing him when it happened. A mighty fist socked the balloon in two rapid blows, one-two, the second more vicious than the first. And the first was vicious. It jerked Gadd right out of the basket onto the ground, and it lifted the balloon five feet or so, straight into the air. Gadd's considerable weight was removed from the equation.

The rope ran through my grip, scorching my palms, but I managed to keep hold, with two feet of line spare. The others kept hold too. The basket was right above our heads now, and we stood with arms upraised like Sunday bell ringers. Into our amazed silence, before the shouting could resume, the second punch came and knocked the balloon up and westward. Suddenly we were treading the air with all our weight in the grip of our fists.

Those one or two ungrounded seconds occupy as much space in memory as might a long journey up an uncharted river. My first impulse was to hang on in order to keep the balloon weighted down. The child was incapable, and was about to be borne away. Two miles to the west were high-voltage power lines. A child alone and needing help. It was my duty to hang on, and I thought we would all do the same.

Almost simultaneous with the desire to stay on the rope and save the boy, barely a neuronal pulse later, came other thoughts, in which fear and instant calculations of logarithmic complexity were fused. We were rising, and the ground was dropping away as the balloon was pushed westward. I knew I had to get my legs and feet locked around the rope. But the end of the line barely reached below my waist, and my grip was slipping. My legs flailed in the empty air. Every fraction of a second that passed increased the drop, and the point must come when to let go would be impossible or fatal. And compared with me, Harry was safe, curled up in the basket. The balloon might well come down safely at the bottom of the hill. And perhaps my impulse to hang on was nothing more than a continuation of what I had been attempting moments before, simply a failure to adjust quickly.

And again, less than one adrenally incensed heartbeat later, another variable was added to the equation: someone let go, and the balloon and its hangers-on lurched upward another several feet.

I didn't know, nor have I ever discovered, who let go first. I'm not prepared to accept that it was me. But everyone claims not to have been first. What is certain is that if we had not broken ranks, our collective weight would have brought the balloon to earth a quarter of the way down the slope as the gust subsided a few seconds later. But as I've said, there was no team, there was no plan, no agreement to be broken. No failure. So can we accept that it was right, every man for himself? Were we all happy afterward that this was a reasonable course? We never had that comfort, for there was a deeper covenant, ancient and automatic, written in our nature. Cooperation—the basis of our earliest hunting successes, the force behind our evolving capacity for language, the glue of our social cohesion. Our misery in the aftermath was proof that we knew we had failed ourselves. But letting go was in our nature too. Selfishness is also written on our hearts. This is our mammalian conflict: what to give to the others and what to keep for yourself. Treading that line, keeping the others in check and being kept in check by them, is what we call morality. Hanging a few feet above the Chilterns escarpment, our crew enacted morality's ancient, irresolvable dilemma: us, or me.

Someone said *me*, and then there was nothing to be gained by saying *us*. Mostly, we are good when it makes sense. A good society is one that makes sense of being good. Suddenly, hanging there below the basket, we were a bad society, we were disintegrating. Suddenly the sensible choice was to look out for yourself. The child was not my child, and I was not going to die for it. The moment I glimpsed a body falling away—but whose?—and I felt the balloon lurch upward, the matter was settled; altruism had no place. Being good made no sense. I let go and fell, I reckon, about twelve feet. I landed heavily on my side; I got away with a bruised thigh. Around me—before or after, I'm not so sure—bodies were thumping to the ground. Jed Parry was unhurt. Toby Greene broke his ankle. Joseph Lacey, the oldest, who had done his National Service with a paratroop regiment, did no more than wind himself.

By the time I got to my feet, the balloon was fifty yards away and one man was still dangling by his rope. In John Logan, husband, father, doctor, and mountain rescue worker, the flame of altruism must have burned a little stronger. It didn't need much. When four of us let go, the balloon, with six hundred pounds shed, must have surged upward. A delay of one second would have been enough to close his options. When I stood up and saw him, he was a hundred feet up and rising, just where the ground itself was falling. He wasn't struggling, he wasn't kicking or trying to claw his way up. He hung perfectly still along the line of the rope, all his energies concentrated in his weakening grip. He was already a tiny figure, almost black against the sky. There was no sight of the boy. The balloon and its basket lifted away and westward, and the smaller Logan became, the more terrible it was, so terrible it was funny, it was a stunt, a joke, a cartoon, and a frightened laugh heaved out of my chest. For this was preposterous, the kind of thing that happened to Bugs Bunny or Tom or Jerry, and for an instant I thought it wasn't true, and that only I could see right through the joke, and that my utter disbelief would set reality straight and see Dr. Logan safely to the ground.

I don't know whether the others were standing or sprawling. Toby Greene was probably doubled up over his ankle. But I do remember the silence into which I laughed. No exclamations, no shouted instructions as before. Mute helplessness. He was two hundred yards away now, and perhaps three hundred feet above the ground. Our silence was a kind of acceptance, a death warrant. Or it was horrified shame, because the wind had dropped, and barely stirred against our backs. He had been on the rope so long that I began to think he might stay there until the balloon drifted down or the boy came to his senses and found the valve that released the gas, or until some beam, or god, or some other impossible cartoon thing, came and gathered him up. Even as I had that hope, we saw him slip down right to the end of the rope. And still he hung there. For two seconds, three, four. And then he let go. Even then, there was a fraction of time when he barely fell, and I still thought there was a chance that a freak physical law, a furious thermal, some phenomenon no more astonishing than the one we were witnessing, would intervene and bear him up. We watched him drop. You could see the acceleration. No forgiveness, no special dispensation for flesh, or bravery, or kindness. Only ruthless gravity. And from somewhere, perhaps from him, perhaps from some indifferent crow, a thin squawk cut through the stilled air. He fell as he had hung, a stiff little black stick. I've never seen such a terrible thing as that falling man.

from Wind, Sand and Stars
by Antoine de Saint-Exupéry

Frenchman Antoine de Saint-Exupéry (1900–1944) wrote with extraordinary grace about the perils and the rewards of flight. In Patagonia before World War II, he flew directly into a cyclone.

When Joseph Conrad described a typhoon he said very little about towering waves, or darkness, or the whistling of the wind in the shrouds. He knew better. Instead, he took his reader down into the hold of the vessel, packed with emigrant coolies, where the rolling and the pitching of the ship had ripped up and scattered their bags and bundles, burst open their boxes, and flung their humble belongings into a crazy heap. Family treasures painfully collected in a lifetime of poverty, pitiful mementoes so alike that nobody but their owners could have told them apart, had lost their identity and lapsed into chaos, into anonymity, into an amorphous magma. It was this human drama that Conrad described when he painted a typhoon.

Every airline pilot has flown through cyclonic storms, has returned out of them to the fold—to the little restaurant in Toulouse where we sat in peace under the watchful eye of the waitress—and there, recognizing his powerlessness to convey what he has been through, has given up the idea of describing hell. His descriptions, his gestures, his big words would have made the rest of us smile as if we were listening to a little boy bragging. And necessarily so. The cyclone of which I am about to speak was, physically, much the most brutal and overwhelming experience I ever underwent; and yet beyond a certain point I do not know how to convey its violence except by piling one adjective on another, so that in the end I should convey no impression at all— unless perhaps that of an embarrassing taste for exaggeration.

It took me some time to grasp the fundamental reason for this powerlessness, which is simply that I should be trying to describe a catastrophe that never took place. The reason why writers fail when they attempt to evoke horror is that horror is something invented after the fact, when one is re-creating the experience over again in the memory. Horror does not manifest itself in the world of reality. And so, in beginning my story of a revolt of the elements which I myself lived through I have no feeling that I shall write something which you will find dramatic.

I had taken off from the field at Trelew and was flying down to Comodoro-Rivadavia, in the Patagonian Argentine. Here the crust of the earth is as dented as an old boiler. The high-pressure regions over the Pacific send the winds past a gap in the Andes into a corridor fifty miles wide through which they rush to the Atlantic in a strangled and accelerated buffeting that scrapes the surface of everything in their path. The sole vegetation visible in this barren landscape is a plantation of oil derricks looking like the after-effects of a forest fire. Towering over the round hills on which the winds have left a residue of stony gravel, there rises a chain of prow-shaped, saw-toothed, razor-edged mountains stripped by the elements down to the bare rock.

For three months of the year the speed of these winds at ground level is up to a hundred miles an hour. We who flew the route knew that once we had crossed the marshes of Trelew and had reached the threshold of the zone they swept, we should recognize the winds from afar by a grey-blue tint in the atmosphere at the sight of which we would tighten our belts and shoulder-straps in preparation for what was coming. From then on we had an hour of stiff fighting and of stumbling again and again into invisible ditches of air. This was manual labor, and our muscles felt it pretty much as if we had been carrying a longshoreman's load. But it lasted only an hour. Our machines stood up under it. We had no fear of wings suddenly dropping off. Visibility was generally good, and not a problem. This section of the line was a stint, yes; it was certainly not a drama.

But on this particular day I did not like the color of the sky.

The sky was blue. Pure blue. Too pure. A hard blue sky that shone over the scraped and barren world while the fleshless vertebrae of the mountain chain flashed in the sunlight. Not a cloud. The blue sky glittered like a new-honed knife. I felt in advance the vague distaste that accompanies the prospect of physical exertion. The purity of the sky upset me. Give me a good black storm in which the enemy is plainly visible. I can measure its extent and prepare myself for its attack. I can get my hands on my adversary. But when you are flying very high in clear weather the shock of a blue storm is as disturbing as if something collapsed that had been holding up your ship in the air. It is the only time when a pilot feels that there is a gulf beneath his ship.

Another thing bothered me. I could see on a level with the mountain peaks not a haze, not a mist, not a sandy fog, but a sort of ash-colored streamer in the sky. I did not like the look of that scarf of filings scraped off the surface of the earth and borne out to sea by the wind. I tightened my leather harness as far as it would go and I steered the ship with one hand while with the other I hung on to the longéron that ran alongside my seat. I was still flying in remarkably calm air.

Very soon came a slight tremor. As every pilot knows, there are secret little quiverings that foretell your real storm. No rolling, no pitching. No swing to speak of. The flight continues horizontal and rectilinear. But you have felt a warning drum on the wings of your plane, little intermittent rappings scarcely audible and infinitely brief, little cracklings from time to time as if there were traces of gunpowder in the air.

And then everything round me blew up.

Concerning the next couple of minutes I have nothing to say. All that I can find in my memory is a few rudimentary notions, fragments of thoughts, direct observations. I cannot compose them into a dramatic recital because there was no drama. The best I can do is to line them up in a kind of chronological order.

In the first place, I was standing still. Having banked right in order to correct a sudden drift, I saw the landscape freeze abruptly where it was and remain jiggling on the same spot. I was making no headway. My wings had ceased to nibble into the outline of the earth. I could see the earth buckle, pivot—but it stayed put. The plane was skidding as if on a toothless cogwheel.

Meanwhile I had the absurd feeling that I had exposed myself completely to the enemy. All those peaks, those crests, those teeth that were cutting into the wind and unleashing its gusts in my direction, seemed to me so many guns pointed straight at my defenseless person. I was slow to think, but the thought did come to me that I ought to give up altitude and make for one of the neighboring valleys where I might take shelter against a mountainside. As a matter of fact, whether I liked it or not I was being helplessly sucked down towards the earth.

Trapped this way in the first breaking waves of a cyclone about which I learned, twenty minutes later, that at sea level it was blowing at the fantastic rate of one hundred and fifty miles an hour, I certainly had no impression of tragedy. Now, as I write, if I shut my eyes, if I forget the plane and the flight and try to express the plain truth about what was happening to me, I find that I felt weighed down, I felt like a porter carrying a slippery load, grabbing one object in a jerky movement that sent another slithering down, so that, overcome by exasperation, the porter is tempted to let the whole load drop. There is a kind of law of the shortest distance to the image, a psychological law by which the event to which one is subjected is visualized in a symbol that represents its swiftest summing up: I was a man who, carrying a pile of plates, had slipped on a waxed floor and let his scaffolding of porcelain crash.

I found myself imprisoned in a valley. My discomfort was not less, it was greater. I grant you that a down current has never killed anybody, that the expression "flattened out by a down current" belongs to journalism and not to the language of flyers. How could air possibly pierce the ground? But here I was in a valley at the wheel of a ship that was three-quarters out of my control. Ahead of me a rocky prow swung to left and right, rose suddenly high in the air for a second like a wave over my head, and then plunged down below my horizon.

Horizon? There was no longer a horizon. I was in the wings of a theatre cluttered up with bits of scenery. Vertical, oblique, horizontal, all of plane geometry was awhirl. A hundred transversal valleys were muddled in a jumble of perspectives. Whenever I seemed about to take my bearings a new eruption would swing me round in a circle or send me tumbling wing over wing and I would have to try all over again to get clear of all this rubbish. Two ideas came into my mind. One was a discovery: for the first time I understood the cause of certain accidents in the mountains when no fog was present to explain them. For a single second, in a waltzing landscape like this, the flyer had been unable to distinguish between vertical mountainsides and horizontal planes. The other idea was a fixation: The sea is flat: I shall not hook anything out at sea.

I banked—or should I use that word to indicate a vague and stubborn jockeying through the east-west valleys? Still nothing pathetic to report. I was wrestling with chaos, was wearing myself out in a battle with chaos, struggling to keep in the air a gigantic house of cards that kept collapsing despite all I could do. Scarcely the faintest twinge of fear went through me when one of the walls of my prison rose suddenly like a tidal wave over my head. My heart hardly skipped a beat when I was tripped up by one of the whirling eddies of air that the sharp ridge darted into my ship. If I felt anything unmistakably in the haze of confused feelings and notions that came over me each time one of these powder magazines blew up, it was a feeling of respect. I respected that sharp-toothed ridge. I respected that peak. I respected that dome. I respected that transversal valley opening out into my valley and about to toss me God knew how violently as soon as its torrent of wind flowed into the one on which I was being borne along.

What I was struggling against, I discovered, was not the wind but the ridge itself, the crest, the rocky peak. Despite my distance from it, it was the wall of rock I was fighting with. By some trick of invisible prolongation, by the play of a secret set of muscles, this was what was pummeling me. It was against this that I was butting my head. Before me on the right I recognized the peak of Salamanca, a perfect cone which, I knew, dominated the sea. It cheered me to think I was about to escape out to sea. But first I should have to wrestle with the gale off that peak, try to avoid its down-crushing blow. The peak of Salamanca was a giant. I was filled with respect for the peak of Salamanca.

There had been granted me one second of respite. Two seconds. Something was collecting itself into a knot, coiling itself up, growing taut. I sat amazed. I opened astonished eyes. My whole plane seemed to be shivering, spreading outward, swelling up. Horizontal and stationary it was, yet lifted before I knew it fifteen hundred feet straight into the air in a kind of apotheosis. I who for forty minutes had not been able to climb higher than two hundred feet off the ground was suddenly able to look down on the enemy. The plane quivered as if in boiling water. I could see the wide waters of the ocean. The valley opened out into this ocean, this salvation.—And at that very moment, without any warning whatever, half a mile from Salamanca, I was suddenly struck straight in the midriff by the gale off that peak and sent hurtling out to sea.

There I was, throttle wide open, facing the coast. At right angles to the coast and facing it. A lot had happened in a single minute. In the first place, I had not flown out to sea. I had been spat out to sea by a monstrous cough, vomited out of my valley as from the mouth of a howitzer. When, what seemed to me instantly, I banked in order to put myself where I wanted to be in respect of the coast-line, I saw that the coast-line was a mere blur, a characterless strip of blue; and I was five miles out to sea. The mountain range stood up like a crenelated fortress against the pure sky while the cyclone crushed me down to the surface of the waters. How hard that wind was blowing I found out as soon as I tried to climb, as soon as I became conscious of my disastrous mistake: throttle wide open, engines running at my maximum, which was one hundred and fifty miles an hour, my plane hanging sixty feet over the water, I was unable to budge. When a wind like this one attacks a tropical forest it swirls through the branches like a flame, twists them into corkscrews, and uproots giant trees as if they were radishes. Here, bounding off the mountain range, it was leveling out to sea.

Hanging on with all the power in my engines, face to the coast, face to that wind where each gap in the teeth of the range sent forth a stream of air like a long reptile, I felt as if I were clinging to the tip of a monstrous whip that was cracking over the sea.

In this latitude the South American continent is narrow and the Andes are not far from the Atlantic. I was struggling not merely against the whirling winds that blew off the east-coast range, but more likely also against a whole sky blown down upon me off the peaks of the Andean chain. For the first time in four years of airline flying I began to worry about the strength of my wings. Also, I was fearful of bumping the sea—not because of the down currents which, at sea level, would necessarily provide me with a horizontal air mattress, but because of the helplessly acrobatic positions in which this wind was buffeting me. Each time that I was tossed I became afraid that I might be unable to straighten out. Besides, there was a chance that I should find myself out of fuel and simply drown. I kept expecting the gasoline pumps to stop priming, and indeed the plane was so violently shaken up that in the half-filled tanks as well as in the gas lines the gasoline was sloshing round, not coming through, and the engines, instead of their steady roar, were sputtering in a sort of dot-and-dash series of uncertain growls.

I hung on, meanwhile, to the controls of my heavy transport plane, my attention monopolized by the physical struggle and my mind occupied by the very simplest thoughts. I was feeling practically nothing as I stared down at the imprint made by the wind on the sea. I saw a series of great white puddles, each perhaps eight hundred yards in extent. They were running towards me at a speed of one hundred and fifty miles an hour where the downsurging windspouts broke against the surface of the sea in a succession of horizontal explosions. The sea was white and it was green—white with the whiteness of crushed sugar and green in puddles the color of emeralds. In this tumult one wave was indistinguishable from another. Torrents of air were pouring down upon the sea. The winds were sweeping past in giant gusts as when, before the autumn harvests, they blow a great flowing change of color over a wheatfield. Now and again the water went incongruously transparent between the white pools, and I could see a green and black seabottom. And then the great glass of the sea would be shattered anew into a thousand glittering fragments.

It seemed hopeless. In twenty minutes of struggle I had not moved forward a hundred yards. What was more, with flying as hard as it was out here five miles from the coast, I wondered how I could possibly buck the winds along the shore, assuming I was able to fight my way in. I was a perfect target for the enemy there on shore. Fear, however, was out of the question. I was incapable of thinking. I was emptied of everything except the vision of a very simple act. I must straighten out. Straighten out. Straighten out.

There were moments of respite, nevertheless. I dare say those moments themselves were equal to the worst storms I had hitherto met, but by comparison with the cyclone they were moments of relaxation. The urgency of fighting off the wind was not quite so great. And I could tell when these intervals were coming. It was not I who moved towards those zones of relative calm, those almost green oases clearly painted on the sea, but they that flowed towards me. I could read clearly in the waters the advertisement of a habitable province. And with each interval of repose the power to feel and to think was restored to me. Then, in those moments, I began to feel I was doomed. Then was the time that little by little I began to tremble for myself. So much so that each time I saw the unfurling of a new wave of the white offensive I was seized by a brief spasm of panic which lasted until the exact instant when, on the edge of that bubbling cauldron, I bumped into the invisible wall of wind. That restored me to numbness again.

Up! I wanted to be higher up. The next time I saw one of those green zones of calm it seemed to me deeper than before and I began to be hopeful of getting out. If I could climb high enough, I thought, I would find other currents in which I could make some headway. I took advantage of the truce to essay a swift climb. It was hard. The enemy had not weakened. Three hundred feet. Six hundred feet. If I could get up to three thousand feet I was safe, I said to myself. But there on the horizon I saw again that white pack unleashed in my direction. I gave it up. I did not want them at my throat again; I did not want to be caught off balance. But it was too late. The first blow sent me rolling over and over and the sky became a slippery dome on which I could not find a footing.

One has a pair of hands and they obey. How are one's orders transmitted to one's hands?

I had made a discovery that horrified me: my hands were numb. My hands were dead. They sent me no message. Probably they had been numb a long time and I had not noticed it. The pity was that I had noticed it, had raised the question. That was serious.

Lashed by the wind, the wings of the plane had been dragging and jerking at the cables by which they were controlled from the wheel, and the wheel in my hands had not ceased jerking a single second. I had been gripping the wheel with all my might for forty minutes, fearful lest the strain snap the cables. So desperate had been my grip that now I could not feel my hands.

What a discovery! My hands were not my own. I looked at them and decided to lift a finger: it obeyed me. I looked away and issued the same order: now I could not feel whether the finger had obeyed or not. No message had reached me. I thought: "Suppose my hands were to open: how would I know it?" I swung my head round and looked again: my hands were still locked round the wheel. Nevertheless, I was afraid. How can a man tell the difference between the sight of a hand opening and the decision to open that hand, when there is no longer an exchange of sensations between the hand and the brain? How can one tell the difference between an image and an act of the will? Better stop thinking of the picture of open hands. Hands live a life of their own. Better not offer them this monstrous temptation. And I began to chant a silly litany which went on uninterruptedly until this flight was over. A single thought. A single image. A single phrase tirelessly chanted over and over again: "I shut my hands. I shut my hands. I shut my hands." All of me was condensed into that phrase and for me the white sea, the whirling eddies, the saw-toothed range ceased to exist. There was only "I shut my hands." There was no danger, no cyclone, no land unattained. Somewhere there was a pair of rubber hands which, once they let go the wheel, could not possibly come alive in time to recover from the tumbling drop into the sea.

I had no thoughts. I had no feelings except the feeling of being emptied out. My strength was draining out of me and so was my impulse to go on fighting. The engines continued their dot-and-dash sputterings, their little crashing noises that were like the intermittent cracklings of a ripping canvas. Whenever they were silent longer than a second I felt as if a heart had stopped beating. There! That's the end. No, they've started up again.

The thermometer on the wing, I happened to see, stood at twenty below zero, but I was bathed in sweat from head to foot. My face was running with perspiration. What a dance! Later I was to discover that my storage batteries had been jerked out of their steel flanges and hurtled up through the roof of the plane. I did not know then, either, that the ribs on my wings had come unglued and that certain of my steel cables had been sawed down to the last thread. And I continued to feel strength and will oozing out of me. Any minute now I should be overcome by the indifference born of utter weariness and by the mortal yearning to take my rest.

What can I say about this? Nothing. My shoulders ached. Very painfully. As if I had been carrying too many sacks too heavy for me. I leaned forward. Through a green transparency I saw sea-bottom so close that I could make out all the details. Then the wind's hand brushed the picture away.

In an hour and twenty minutes I had succeeded in climbing to nine hundred feet. A little to the south—that is, on my left—I could see a long trail on the surface of the sea, a sort of blue stream. I decided to let myself drift as far down as that stream. Here where I was, facing west, I was as good as motionless, unable either to advance or retreat. If I could reach that blue pathway, which must be lying in the shelter of something not the cyclone, I might be able to move in slowly to the coast. So I let myself drift to the left. I had the feeling, meanwhile, that the wind's violence had perhaps slackened.

It took me an hour to cover the five miles to shore. There in the shelter of a long cliff I was able to finish my journey south. Thereafter I succeeded in keeping enough altitude to fly inland to the field that was my destination. I was able to stay up at nine hundred feet. It was very stormy, but nothing like the cyclone I had come out of. That was over.

On the ground I saw a platoon of soldiers. They had been sent down to watch for me. I landed nearby and we were a whole hour getting the plane into the hangar. I climbed out of the cockpit and walked off. There was nothing to say. I was very sleepy. I kept moving my fingers, but they stayed numb. I could not collect my thoughts enough to decide whether or not I had been afraid. Had I been afraid? I couldn't say. I had witnessed a strange sight. What strange sight? I couldn't say. The sky was blue and the sea was white. I felt I ought to tell someone about it since I was back from so far away! But I had no grip on what I had been through. "Imagine a white sea . . . very white . . . whiter still." You cannot convey things to people by piling up adjectives, by stammering.

You cannot convey anything because there is nothing to convey. My shoulders were aching. My insides felt as if they had been crushed in by a terrible weight. You cannot make drama out of that, or out of the cone-shaped peak of Salamanca. That peak was charged like a powder magazine; but if I said so people would laugh. I would myself. I respected the peak of Salamanca. That is my story. And it is not a story.

There is nothing dramatic in the world, nothing pathetic, except in human relations. The day after I landed I might get emotional, might dress up my adventure by imagining that I who was alive and walking on earth was living through the hell of a cyclone. But that would be cheating, for the man who fought tooth and nail against that cyclone had nothing in common with the fortunate man alive the next day. He was far too busy.

I came away with very little booty indeed, with no more than this meagre discovery, this contribution: How can one tell an act of the will from a simple image when there is no transmission of sensation?

I could perhaps succeed in upsetting you if I told you some story of a child unjustly punished. As it is, I have involved you in a cyclone, probably without upsetting you in the least. This is no novel experience for any of us. Every week men sit comfortably at the cinema and look on at the bombardment of some Shanghai or other, some Guernica, and marvel without a trace of horror at the long fringes of ash and soot that twist their slow way into the sky from those man-made volcanoes. Yet we all know that together with the grain in the granaries, with the heritage of generations of men, with the treasures of families, it is the burning flesh of children and their elders that, dissipated in smoke, is slowly fertilizing those black cumuli.

The physical drama itself cannot touch us until someone points out its spiritual sense.

from The Spirit of St. Louis

by Charles A. Lindbergh

Just five years after he learned to fly, Charles Lindbergh (1902–1974) in 1927 became the first person to fly solo across the Atlantic Ocean. During the 33-hour trip, Lindbergh filled his time in part by recalling other adventures that had fueled his passion for flight and led to his ocean crossing.

A winter on the mail, or a flight across the ocean—which involves the greater danger? From October through March—those are the worst months—each pilot makes about a hundred and twenty flights between St. Louis and Chicago. That totals close to thirty thousand miles, or about ten times the distance from New York to Paris. Well, I'd rather fly ten miles over Missouri and Illinois than one mile over this ice pack—or would I? How about that storm northeast of Peoria, last December?

There had been plenty of ceiling when I took my DH off from the mail field. The lights of the city formed a horizon as soon as I cleared the trees' dark masses. But a half hour's flight left me skimming two hundred feet over the ground, brushing the bottom of clouds with my wings, searching through thickening snow for lights of the next village. I'd held on to the last dim glow behind until I could see another on ahead. Then, I found myself circling the center of a small city, my lower wing tips less than a hundred feet above its street lamps. The blizzard had shut off all trace of lights beyond. I can still see the path I followed in my bank. There's the corner drug store, with a flat-fronted restaurant three doors away. Two cars are parked against the curb, hazed by snowflakes. There's the church, below me, with its black steeple merging into night. There's the vaguely outlined street, lined with yarded houses. There, the filling station. Again, the drug store and restaurant. A dozen men and boys have run out onto the sidewalk to look up, hands shielding their eyes against the snow.

I was like a moth circling its flame—blinded to more distant objects, unable to break away. Suppose my engine had stopped then, over those stores and houses – – – Yes, I'd as soon land on the ice pack.

I'd found my way through to Chicago that night. The heavy snow blew over enough for me to break away from my circle of the city, and pick up farmhouse lights. I'd held my course partly by instrument, partly by glowing windows, partly by lines of street lamps, until I saw the Maywood beacon flash.

On our mail route, the pilots expect forced landings. We don't average a hundred hours between them. There was the time my throttle controls vibrated apart, a few miles north of Springfield—engine running perfectly one moment, barely turning over the next. I was no higher than I am now. Fortunately there was a clover field ahead which I could reach with a shallow bank. I sideslipped in over trees, and stalled down onto rain-soaked ground. The wheels plowed ruts ten inches deep in places; but the tail was heavy enough to keep my plane from nosing over.

On another flight, the metal tip of my propeller ripped off from its wooden blade. I'd been daydreaming along at 1100 feet. Daydreaming – – – good Lord, that's what I'm doing now! I'm almost 10 degrees off course. I shake myself vigorously, skid the *Spirit of St. Louis* back into position, and rub circulation through my cheeks. There's a big gap below in the ice field. As I stare at it, my mind wanders back to the mail route. All of a sudden, the DH's engine had started vibrating so violently that I thought it would jerk itself out of the plane before I could cut my switches. I avoided a crack-up that time by stalling into a twelve-acre field and ground looping just short of the fence corner.

Every month included incidents such as these. Yes, a winter on the air mail holds fully as much danger as a flight across the ocean. Whirlwind engines aren't like our old Liberties. They average thousands of hours between failures. The controls in the *Spirit of St. Louis* are new and carefully designed. There'll be no breakage of a throttle rod. And my propeller blades are made of metal, not of wood. They have no screwed-on tips to throw.

But I didn't start on this flight to Paris because of its relative safety. I used that argument only to bolster my decision, and to convince people that the hazard wasn't too great. I'm not bound to carry the night mail. I'm not bound to be in aviation at all. I'm here only because I love the sky and flying more than anything else on earth. Of course there's danger; but a certain amount of danger is essential to the quality of life. I don't believe in taking foolish chances; but nothing can be accomplished without taking any chance at all.

When I was a child on our Minnesota farm, I spent hours lying on my back in high timothy and redtop, hidden from passersby, watching white cumulus clouds drift overhead, staring into the sky. It was a different world up there. You had to be flat on your back, screened in by grass stalks, to live in it. Those clouds, how far away were they? Nearer than the neighbor's house, untouchable as the moon—unless you had an airplane. How wonderful it would be, I'd thought, if I had an airplane—wings with which I could fly up to the clouds and explore their caves and canyons—wings like that hawk circling above me. Then, I would ride on the wind and be part of the sky, and acorns and bits of twigs would stop pressing into my skin. The question of danger didn't enter my dreams.

One day I was playing upstairs in our house on the riverbank. The sound of a distant engine drifted in through an open window. Automobiles had been going past on the road quite often that summer. I noticed it vaguely, and went on sorting the stones my mother and I had collected from the creek bed. None of them compared to the heart-shaped agate I'd found at the edge of a pool the week before—purple crystals outlined by stripes of red and white. Suddenly I sat up straight and listened. No automobile engine made that noise. It was approaching too fast. It was on the wrong side of the house! Stones scattered over the floor. I ran to the window and climbed out onto the tarry roof. It was an airplane!

Flying upriver below higher branches of trees, a biplane was less than two hundred yards away—a frail, complicated structure, with the pilot sitting out in front between struts and wires. I watched it fly quickly out of sight, and then rushed downstairs to tell my mother.

There had been a notice in the *Transcript*, my mother said, about an aviator who had come to our town. She'd forgotten to tell me about it. He was carrying passengers from a field over on the east side of the river. But rides were unbelievably expensive. He charged a dollar for every minute in the air! And anyone who went up took his life in his hands—suppose the engine stopped, or a wing fell off, or something else went wrong.

I was so greatly impressed by the cost and danger that I pushed aside my desire to go up in a plane. But I used to imagine myself with wings on which I could swoop down off our roof into the valley, soaring through air from one river bank to the other, over stones of the rapids, above log jams, above the tops of trees and fences. I thought often of men who really flew. From grown-up conversations, I heard and remembered the names of the Wright brothers, and Glen Curtiss, and Lincoln Beachey—they'd found a way to fly in spite of cost and danger.

As I grew older, I learned that danger was a part of life not always to be shunned. It often surrounded the things you liked most to do. It was dangerous to climb a tree, to swim down rapids in the river, to go hunting with a gun, to ride a horse, to drive my father's automobile. You could be killed as quickly on a farm as in an airplane. I had felt death brush past several times on our farm, and it was not as terrifying as I at first imagined.

I never felt safer, and never came closer to being killed than when a gangplow turned over behind my tractor. It was on one of those May days "when leaves on the oak trees are as big as squirrels' ears," and it was "time to plant corn." I was behind with plowing on the western forty, and working late into evening to catch up. It was an old field, with only a few stones left to hook a plowshare. The furrow lay straight behind, seven inches deep. I had just tripped the plow-lift and started to turn at the field's end when bright steel flashed by my head and thudded heavily on ground. The lift mechanism had jammed, upsetting the entire gangplow. If I hadn't turned my tractor at the moment I pulled the trip-lever, I would have been crushed on the seat. As it was, the share missed my head by less than six inches.

No, farm life isn't as safe as it's cracked up to be.

I center the earth-inductor compass needle, and drop down closer to the ice field.

When I was eleven years old, I learned to drive my father's Ford car, and at twelve I chauffeured him around the country. That car had seemed terribly dangerous at first. You could get your arm broken cranking the engine. You could skid off an embankment. You might collide with someone at any intersection. The Minneapolis paper carried stories about auto accidents each day. But as my driving experience advanced from a hundred miles to a thousand, and from one thousand to several, my confidence increased. There were foils against danger— judgment and skill. If you clasped your thumb and fingers on the same side of the crank handle, a backfiring engine wouldn't break your bones. If you adjusted speed to road conditions, skids and collisions could be avoided. Twenty miles an hour had seemed an excessive speed when I started driving. A decade later, sixty was safe enough on a clear stretch of pavement. I learned that danger is relative, and that inexperience can be a magnifying glass.

A drink of water would be good. I reach for my canteen. No, I'm not thirsty enough now. I've allowed only one quart for the flight, and I'll need it more tomorrow. The instruments? All readings are normal. I drain a few drops of gasoline from the Lunkenheimer sediment bulb—no sign of dirt or water. Fumes drift through the fuselage, and drift away.

When I was a sophomore at the University of Wisconsin, I decided to give up my course in mechanical engineering, and learn to fly. One of my closer friends, an upperclassman, tried to persuade me not to leave my studies. He said a pilot's life averaged only a few hours in the air, and cited wartime figures to prove his point. Why, he asked, did I want to enter so dangerous a profession? I argued that flying in peacetime was safer than flying in war, and that accidents could be reduced by care and judgment. He shrugged his shoulders and said it was far too dangerous anyway, but that my future was my own.

My friend was captain of the rifle team, and spoke in terms I understood. He was one of the initiated. He knew how to value danger. Hadn't we shot twenty-five-cent pieces out of each other's fingers at a range of fifty feet? His statement impressed me, but I'd grown tired of the endless indoor hours of university life. I longed for open earth and sky. The fascination of aircraft had mounted to form an irresistible force in my mind. Was a life of flying to be renounced because it shouldered danger? I chose a school in Nebraska, and enrolled for a course in the spring.

I'd never been near enough to a plane to touch it before entering the doors of the Nebraska Aircraft Corporation's factory. I can still smell the odor of dope that permeated each breath, like ether in a hospital's corridors. I can still see the brightly painted fuselages on the floor, still marvel at the compactness of the Hispano-Suiza engine which turned the force of a hundred and fifty horses through its little shaft of steel.

Ray Page, the Corporation's president, took my check for tuition and welcomed me to his school. On April 9, 1922, at the age of twenty, I made my first flight. The plane had been hauled out from the factory the day before, wings stacked and padded carefully in a big truck, fuselage trailing behind, tail high and foremost. I stood on the air field all morning, watching riggers attach wings and "hook up" ailerons, flippers, and rudder; watching mechanics strain in fuel, drain the sediment bulb, tune up the engine; watching the engineer test cable tautness with his fingers and measure wing droop with his knowing eye.

Behind every movement, word, and detail, one felt the strength of life, the presence of death. There was pride in man's conquest of the air. There was the realization that he took life in hand to fly, that in each bolt and wire and wooden strut death lay imprisoned like the bottled genie—waiting for an angled grain or loosened nut to let it out. The rigger wound his copper wire with a surgeon's care. The mechanic sat listening to his engine and watching his gages as a doctor would search for a weakness in the human heart—sign of richness, blowing valve, or leaned-out mixture? An error meant a ship might crash; a man might die. I stood aside and watched the engine tested, watched the plane taxi out, take off, and spiral up through sky. I'd be on the next flight, if this test showed nothing wrong. I'd be a part of those wings, now no larger than a bird's, black against the clouds toward which they climbed.

How clearly I remember that first flight—I've lived through it again and again. Otto Timm was the pilot.

"*CONTACT!*"

The mechanic throws his leg and body backward as his arms jerk the propeller down.

"*BOOSTER!*"

There's a deep cough – – – vicious spitting. – – – The mechanic regains his balance – – – takes his place by the wing tip. Miraculously his fingers haven't been chopped off by that now invisible blade. The cylinders bark out their power – – – merge into a deep and constant roar. I am belted down in the front cockpit, goggles and leather helmet strapped tight on my head. Beside me is a younger boy, one of the workmen from the factory. He, too, has never flown before.

The roar grows louder. Wings begin to tremble. The engine's power shakes up my legs from the floor boards, beats down on my head from the slipstream, starts a flying wire vibrating. I twist about to look back at the pilot. His eyes study the instruments—no trace of a smile on his face. This is a serious business, flying.

The engine quiets. The pilot nods. A mechanic from each side ducks in and unchocks a wheel. We taxi downwind, bumping over sod clumps, to the end of the field. A burst of engine – – – the tail swings around into wind. There are seconds of calm while the pilot glances a last time at temperature of water, pressures of oil and air; checks again the direction of wind and clearness of field; makes a last slight adjustment to his goggles.

Now! – – – The roar becomes deafening – – – the plane lurches forward through a hollow in the ground – – – the tail rises – – – the axle clatters over bumps – – – trees rush toward us – – – the clatter stops – – – the ground recedes – – – we are resting on the air – – – Up, past riggers and mechanics – – – over treetops – – – across a ravine, like a hawk – – – The ground unfolds – – – we bank – – – it tilts against a wing – – – a hidden, topsy-turvy stage with height to draw its curtain.

Trees become bushes; barns, toys; cows turn into rabbits as we climb. I lose all conscious connection with the past. I live only in the moment in this strange, unmortal space, crowded with beauty, pierced with danger. The horizon retreats, and veils itself in haze. The great, squared fields of Nebraska become patchwork on a planet's disk. All the country around Lincoln lies like a relief map below—its lake, its raveled bend of river, its capitol, its offices and suburbs—a culture of men adhering to the medium of earth.

The world tilts again—another bank – – – we tighten in a spiral – – – My head is heavy – – – the seat presses hard against me – – – I become conscious of my body's weight, of the strength it takes to lift an arm – – – Fields curve around a wing tip – – – gravity is playing tag with space – – – Landing wires loosen—vibrate with the air. How can those routed wooden spars, how can that matchwork skeleton of ribs withstand such pressure? Those slender flying wires, hardly larger than an eagle's tendon—how can they bind fuselage to wings? On the farm, we used more metal to tie a wagon to a horse!

Why can't I keep the compass needle centered? I skid the Spirit of St. Louis *back onto course again.*

• • •

We made that flight at Lincoln five years ago last month. I was a novice then. But the novice has the poet's eye. He sees and feels where the expert's senses have been calloused by experience. I have found that contact tends to dull appreciation, and that in the detail of the familiar one loses awareness of the strange. First impressions have a clarity of line and color which experience may forget and not regain.

Now, to me, cows are no longer rabbits; house and barn, no longer toys. Altitude has become a calculated distance, instead of empty space through which to fall. I look down a mile on some farmer's dwelling much as I would view that same dwelling a horizontal mile away. I can read the contour of a hillside that to the beginner's eye looks flat. I can translate the secret textures and the shadings of the ground. Tricks of wind and storm and mountains are to me an open book. But I have never realized air or aircraft, never seen the earth below so clearly, as in those early days of flight.

I was the Nebraska Aircraft Corporation's only student that spring. Ira Biffle was my instructor—a dark-haired, face-creased man of the world and the sky. He'd soloed a lot of flyers for the Signal Corps during the war. But:

"Slim, you'd better watch your step," the factory workmen warned me. "The Army didn't have 'em any tougher."

Biff was impatient, quick, and picturesque of tongue, but not as hard-boiled as his reputation. We got along together well enough. But he'd lost the love of his art, and I found it hard to get time in the air. When rain was falling or wind blew hard, of course, flying was out of the question for a new student. On such days, I rode my motorcycle to the factory and spent hours watching the craftsmen show their skills. A would-be aviator had to learn how to care for his plane in the field. Tail skids and shock absorbers broke, ribs snapped, and wing covering ripped all too easily. Spark plugs needed cleaning out each week, and exhaust valves warped with regularity. You had to know how to lockstitch, how to bind the ends of rubber rope, how to lap a propeller hub to its shaft. There were hundreds of details you had to learn; for as a barnstorming pilot, you were often your own helper, rigger, and mechanic.

But on mornings of calm, clear weather, I felt it was my right to receive the instruction I had paid for. And Biffle was often nowhere to be found. "The air's too turbulent at midday, Slim," he'd tell me when he arrived at the factory, later. "Meet me at the flying field when it smooths out this afternoon."

Around five o'clock, I'd park my motorcycle next the fence line, lie down under a wing, and watch the wind sock spin its tale of air—whipping, wilting, filling with the gusts. Sometimes Biff would come out with his roadster in time to make a half-dozen take-offs and landings before dusk. But often he didn't come at all. "Slim, it was just too rough," he might tell me the next morning, in his high-pitched voice, as he leaned against the Fokker's gold-varnished fuselage. "Let's try at sunrise tomorrow—that's the smoothest time of day."

Then the factory workmen who overheard would smile. "*Sunrise?*" they'd say later. "Ha, Biff *never* starts work before eleven. He's a damn good pilot," they'd usually continue, "but he's been different since Turk Gardner spun in. Biff took it hard. He knew Turk was good, too. They'd always been close friends."

Wherever aviation people gathered, talk of crashes arose. And yet the safety of flying had steadily increased. I could look forward to some nine hundred hours in the air as the average pilot's lifetime, I was told. I learned that most people thought of aviators as strange and daring men, hardly a human breed—men who had nerves of steel and supernatural senses; men who were wild with drink and women, and who placed no value on their lives. But of the aviators at Lincoln there was none who didn't want to live. The pilot I admired most had already spent more than two thousand hours in the air. He may not have held onto life as tightly, but he valued it as highly as anyone I knew. He didn't drink, and he didn't smoke. He flew for the love of flying. And above that, he flew to make enough money to marry his fiancée.

In factory and on flying field, I often worked with the boy who shared the cockpit with me on my first flight. He was four years younger than I, but our interest in aviation bridged the gap of time.

Bud Gurney came from the sandhills of Nebraska, and he'd been hired by the Corporation a few months before I arrived at the school. He swept floors, lock-stitched wings, and acted as general handy man— anything to get a job, especially around aircraft.

Bud kept me posted on factory current events. He knew the character of each employee, sieved off their gossip from their facts. "You can trust Saully anywhere," he said. "He's *really* a good mechanic. But I don't know why Page keeps on paying N – – –. He's just a great big bluff. Watch out for him, Slim. He'll send you off to find a left-handed monkey wrench, or to get a quart of stagger."

The Spirit of St. Louis *has a tendency to gain altitude when I'm not watching carefully. I push the stabilizer adjustment forward a single notch, to change pressure on the stick.*

It was Bud Gurney who warned me that the Corporation's training plane was being sold:

"Ray Page is making a deal with Bahl, Slim. I think he's the best flyer around Lincoln. But you'd better solo pretty soon or you won't have any plane to pilot."

"They can put dual controls in that silver job," I replied. "It's all ready to assemble."

"You're a week behind time. Page sold the silver job too."

I'd received about eight hours of flying instruction when Biff made it clear that his obligations as a teacher were fulfilled. Business, he said, was calling him away from Lincoln. "You can get up and down all right, as long as the air's not too rough. But you'll have to get Page to okay it, Slim, before I can turn you loose."

I lost no time getting to the factory and into the president's office. But Ray Page showed neither the confidence of his instructor nor the enthusiasm of his flying school's catalogue. "There isn't any question about your ability to fly," he said, after congratulating me. "But you understand we can't just turn an expensive airplane over to a student. Couldn't you put up a bond to cover our loss if you crack up?"

I didn't have enough money for a bond; and I knew that even if I soloed, there wouldn't be a pilot's job waiting for me. Owners of aircraft wanted experienced pilots, men with hundreds of hours of flying to their credit. They were like Ray Page. They weren't going to trust their lives or their machines to a newly graduated student. No, there were other steps that would have to be made between graduation and a pilot's job. Maybe I could get Bahl to take me with him, barnstorming.

Erold Bahl was a different type of pilot. Serious, mild-mannered, slender, there was no showmanship about him. He flew with his cap turned backward and in ordinary business clothes. He never wore an aviator's helmet and breeches like the rest of us. I waited until I found a chance to talk to him alone in one corner of the factory.

"You don't need somebody to help when you're out barnstorming, do you?" I asked. "I'd be glad to pay my own expenses – – – "

"I don't need any help where I'm going – – – " He started out to say no, in his soft but definite way. Then, hesitating a moment as he looked at me, he continued, "But if you want to go along badly enough to pay your own expenses, I'll take you."

We left on our first barnstorming trip in May. I kept the plane wiped clean, pulled through the propeller, and canvassed the crowds for passengers.

"You know, Slim," Bahl told me, after the first few days, "you're working hard, and you're making me extra money. From now on, I'm going to pay your expenses."

I felt secure flying with Bahl. He'd take off in weather that would keep most pilots on the ground; but he handled his plane perfectly, and he never did any silly stunts. "I think aviation can be safe," he told me. "And I intend to make it that way." Bahl believed that safety lay in judgment. He followed no frozen set of rules. I once suggested that we might draw a bigger crowd if I stood out on one of the wings while we flew over town. "You can climb out of the cockpit if you want to," he said, "but watch how you step on the spars, and don't go farther than the inner-bay strut the first time." Those simple instructions gave me my start as a wing walker.

After the trip with Bahl, my finances were getting low. I began working on odd jobs at the factory, at a wage of fifteen dollars every
Saturday. And I left my twenty-dollar-a-month boarding house for a
room I rented at two dollars and a quarter a week. I had several hundred dollars in the bank at home, accumulated slowly over many years;
but I was determined to hold as much of it as I could in reserve for the
day when I'd want to buy a plane of my own.

That June—it will be five years ago next month—a parachute maker
came to Lincoln to demonstrate his product. His name was Charlie
Harden. I watched him strap on his harness and helmet, climb into the
cockpit and, minutes later, a black dot, fall off the wing two thousand
feet above our field. At almost the same instant, a white streak behind
him flowered out into the delicate, wavering muslin of a parachute—a
few gossamer yards grasping onto air and suspending below them,
with invisible threads, a human life, a man who by stitches, cloth, and
cord, had made himself a god of the sky for those immortal moments.

I stood fascinated while he drifted down, swinging with the wind, a
part of it, the 'chute's skirt weaving with its eddies, lightly, gracefully,
until he struck the ground and all that fragile beauty wilted around
him into a pile of earth-stained, wrinkled cloth.

A day or two later, when I decided that I too must pass through the
experience of a parachute jump, life rose to a higher level, to a sort of
exhilarated calmness. The thought of crawling out onto the wing,
through a hurricane of wind, clinging on to struts and wires hundreds
of feet above the earth, and then giving up even that tenuous hold of
safety and of substance, left in me a feeling of anticipation mixed with
dread, of confidence restrained by caution, of courage salted through
with fear. How tightly should one hold on to life? How loosely give it
rein? What gain was there for such a risk? I would have no pay in
money for hurling my body into space. There would be no crowd to
watch and applaud my landing. Nor was there any scientific objective
to be gained. No, there was a deeper reason for wanting to jump, a
desire I could not explain. It was the quality that led me into aviation

in the first place, when safer and more profitable occupations were at hand, and against the advice of most of my friends. It was a love of the air and sky and flying, the lure of adventure, the appreciation of beauty. It lay beyond the descriptive words of men—where immortality is touched through danger, where life meets death on equal plane; where man is more than man, and existence both supreme and valueless at the same instant.

My search for the parachute maker ended in a corner of the factory where wing coverings were made. He and his young wife were busily engaged with sewing machine and shears, cutting and stitching the long, triangular strips of a new parachute. Folds and piles of white muslin lay all about them.

"You want to jump?" They both eyed me keenly.

"I'd like to make a double jump," I said.

"A double jump! You want to do a double jump the *first* time?" The tone was disapproving—I had to think fast. Why *did* I want to make a double jump the first time?

"I want to see what it's like – – – I want to learn how to do it – – – I—I might want to buy a parachute." (Yes, I might even become a parachute jumper myself. Maybe that was the best way to get out on barnstorming trips and really learn to fly.) "I've read about the multiple jumps you make. It isn't more dangerous with two 'chutes than with one, is it?"

Charlie Harden's handbills said that he had used as many as ten parachutes in one descent, and claimed the utmost reliability for the products he made and sold. My questioning of his parachutes' safety, and the prospect of a sale, had the effect I was after.

"It's not the danger. I just never knew anybody want to start with a double jump. All right; if Page will give you a plane, I'll let you use my 'chutes."

"How much does a parachute cost?" I asked.

"A hundred and twenty-five dollars for the twenty-eight-foot type. But if you really want to buy one, you can have it for a hundred dollars cash—harness, bag, and all."

• • •

Is that a small boat on ahead? No, of course not—just a shadow on a chunk of ice.

I watched with amazement the transition of my daydream into the reality of me, my mind, my body, in the front cockpit of an airplane climbing up through empty space into which I was to throw myself against the instincts of a thousand generations. The stiff, double-canvas straps of the harness dug into my legs and pressed down on my hip-bones. The big parachute bag lay awkwardly out on the right wing, its top lashed to the inner-bay strut's steel fitting. To the uninitiated eye, it might have contained a bushel of potatoes. It was a long way out along that panel, but you had to be sure the parachute would clear the plane's tail surfaces as you jumped. How secure the cockpit of the airplane seemed! How strong wings, struts, and wires had become, now that I was giving up their citadel of safety for cords and cloth!

The sun was low in the west, the sky clear, the air smooth. The day's puffy wind had dropped. The plane's nose mounted high on the horizon, climbing. I looked down at the group of minute figures on the field—the president of the Corporation, the parachute maker and his wife, Bud Gurney, and a half dozen passersby who had stopped to watch us prepare the 'chutes. How carefully that preparation had been made—just to think about it gave me confidence. We'd stretched the parachutes out full length on grass, their shroud lines running straight from skirt to ring. The canopies were packed in free, accordion folds. Each reversing turn of cord was separated by a paper sheet. Each lip of cloth was laid to grab the wind. Tangle?—there was no chance for those lines to tangle; once loosed, the 'chute must unfold, string out, billow on the air.

Those parachutes had been used before, time and time again, and they'd always brought their human freight to earth in safety. I should have confidence in them. I *must* have confidence in them, for I'm to jump when we reach two thousand feet. But it's hard to see safety inside that dirt-smeared canvas sack bulging on the wing. My heart races. My throat is dry. Minutes are long.

The nose drops, the wing lowers, the plane banks toward the field. The nose dips, rises, dips again. That's my signal. I look back. The pilot nods. Thank God, the waiting time is over! Unbuckle the belt – – – get a firm hold on center-section struts – – – rise in cockpit – – – leg over side – – – lean into the slipstream's blast – – – Air wedges between my lips, rushes down my sleeves, presses against the forward motion of my arm – – – A too-long strap on my helmet whips my throat – – –

The pilot throttles back a little more; that's better – – – Careful of the wing – – – I must keep my feet on the narrow walk next the fuselage – – – Now, out along the spar – – – Give up the safety of center-section struts – – – Nothing but wires to hold onto – – – their slenderness gives no substance to the hand's grip, no confidence to flesh leaning over space – – – Heels off nose ribs – – – follow the spar with soles – – – fabric dents with a touch. The blast of air drops down – – – that's the slipstream's edge – – – I reach the inner-bay strut – – – Remember to hang on at top or bottom—never at the center, lest it snap.

The pilot opens his throttle. We've been losing altitude too fast – – – Pressure of air builds up again – – – I sink down on the wing—buttocks on spar—legs dangling on top of patchwork fields – – – I unsnap a parachute hook from the landing wire - - snap it onto my harness – – – now the other – – – The parachute bag shifts forward on the wing – – – I look back – – – the pilot nods – – – I let myself down on drift and flying wires – – – they bite into my fingers – – – Nothing but space—terrible—beautiful – – – swinging free beneath the wing.

Now I *must* jump. It's impossible to get back on the plane. The flying field—I'd forgotten about it crawling out—is more than a mile ahead. It's too soon to jump. I'll have to wait till the pilot cuts his engine—that's to be the signal. I dangle under the varnished, yellow wing panel. Two ropes from my harness run up above my head and disappear into the parachute bag. A bowknot holds the bag's canvas lips together. It's like the knot I tied this morning on each boot. It's all that holds me to the plane. Eyes dry in wind. Clothes flutter against skin. I slant tailward over space, leaning on the turbulence of air.

The roar of the engine dies – – – the nose drops slightly – – – Now!
– – – no hesitation – – – I force my hand to reach up and pull the
bow's end – – – Tightness of harness disappears – – – the wing recedes
– – – white cloth streaks out above me – – – I'm attached to nothing
– – – I turn in space – – – I lose the sense of time – – – My body is
tense in a sky which seems to have no place for tenseness – – –

Harness tightens on legs—on waist. My head goes down – – – muscles
strain against it – – – tilt it back – – – The canopy is pear-shaped above
me – – – It opens round and wide – – – There's the plane, circling – – –
There's the field, below – – – I swing lazily, safely on the air. The sun is
almost setting. Clouds have reddened in the west.

But there's a second jump to make. I must leave plenty of altitude.
The ground has already risen—fields are larger. I reach over my head
for the knife-rope; a pull, and it will cut the line lashing the second
'chute to the first. I glance at the earth – – – back at the 'chute – – –
and—*yank* – – – The white canopy ascends – – – I'm again detached
from old relationships with space and time – – – I wait – – – I turn
– – – but my body is less tense – – – I have experience – – – I know
what to expect – – – The harness will tighten – – – and – – – But why
doesn't it tighten? – – – It didn't take so long before – – – Air rushes past
– – – my body tenses – – – turns – – – falls – – – good God – – –

The harness jerks me upright – – – My parachute blooms white – – –
Earth and sky come back to place – – – I'm controlled by gravity once
more; I'd never realized the security of its oriented pressure. "Mother
Earth" had been only a figure of speech to me before, a tongue's lightly
tossed expression. Now, in a sense, she holds me as the arms of a
mother hold a frightened child. I have disobeyed her laws, strayed too
far, and yet I find a welcome on return.

Now, danger is behind. There are no more parachutes to open. And
the ground is still several hundred feet below. I swing gently, the white
canopy above me rippling, indenting, refilling with the air. I have a
small camera in my pocket; I pull it out and photograph my 'chute's
silhouette against the sky. There's still a little time to practice gliding.
You must learn how to glide a parachute so you can miss trees and

buildings. I reach up and take two groups of shroud lines in my hands – – – Pull – – – The skirt drops – – – the big canopy deforms and slips ahead – – – I swoop down – – – let go the shroud lines – – – cords burn across my palm – – – I swing up the other side – – – The ground is rising – – – must stop the swing – – – Pull down on top lines – – – glide the 'chute back overhead – – – too much – – – the other lines – – – too much again – – – no more time – – – I'm going to miss the flying field – – – I'll land on the golf course – – – so fast, these last few yards – – – Sod rushes up – – – I brace to meet it – – – It clumps against my feet – – – I crumple sidewise – – – thigh and shoulder hit – – – earth presses hard against me – – – I feel its security—its strength.

Harden, Gurney, and two strangers come running up. Page is a little way behind.

"Slim! That was *some* jump!"

"Did you get much of a jerk?" Harden asks, out of breath.

"Not too bad," I reply, trying to appear calm.

"I sure didn't like the way that second 'chute came out," he continues. "I was afraid the break-cord was too light—but it's all we had. Well, it turned out all right. That's the longest fall I've ever seen one of my 'chutes take."

I learned later that Harden's usual procedure was to tie the vent of the second 'chute to the shroud ring of the first with a piece of twine. The idea was that the 'chute would string out its full length before the twine snapped; then it would leave the plane in the best possible position for a quick opening. But he'd forgotten to put twine in his pocket, and a hunt around the field produced only a piece of old white string. He used that, doubled two or three times, but it apparently broke during the packing. When I pulled the knife-rope, the second parachute came free in a wad, and several hundred feet of air were required to straighten it out.

"Slim, that was just grocery string," Bud told me as we rode back to Lincoln. "It was so rotten you could pull it apart with your finger. I cut off a piece to try."

How soundly I slept that night—as I always have after a jump! I simply passed out of mortal existence a few seconds after my head hit its pillow; and when I became conscious again, the sun had risen. There wasn't a dream in memory.

I push up, with legs and elbow, enough to shift my rubber seat-cushion an inch forward. Even this slight movement turns the Spirit of St. Louis *eight degrees off course.*

I believe parachute jumping had an effect on my dreams as well as on my sleep. At infrequent intervals through life I had dreamt of falling off some high roof or precipice. I'd felt terror and sickening fear as my body sank helplessly toward ground. It wasn't like that in a real parachute jump, I discovered. Real falling didn't bring horror to your mind or sickness to your belly. Such sensations stayed behind with the plane, as though they were too cowardly to make the final plunge. Strangely enough, I've never fallen in my dreams since I actually fell through air. That factual experience seems to have removed completely some illogical, subconscious dread.

Life changed after that jump. I noticed it in the attitude of those who came to help gather up my 'chute—in Harden's acceptance of me as a brother parachutist, in Page's realization that I'd done what he didn't dare to do. I'd stepped suddenly to the highest level of daring—a level above even that which airplane pilots could attain.

"Hi, Slim! Did you do it?"

"What was it like?"

The next morning I was giving information to the same experts who had previously been teaching me—I'd left my role of apprentice far behind. Saully might scrape his con-rod bearings to a thousandth of an inch, but I could tell him how it felt to pull the bowknot, to glide the canopy, to simmer down through air on a muslin bolt.

Science, freedom, beauty, adventure: what more could you ask of life? Aviation combined all the elements I loved. There was science in each curve of an airfoil, in each angle between strut and wire, in the gap of a spark plug or the color of the exhaust flame. There was freedom in the unlimited horizon, on the open fields where one landed. A pilot was surrounded by beauty of earth and sky. He brushed treetops with the birds, leapt valleys and rivers, explored the cloud canyons he had gazed at as a child. Adventure lay in each puff of wind.

I began to feel that I lived on a higher plane than the skeptics of the ground; one that was richer because of its very association with the element of danger they dreaded, because it was freer of the earth to which they were bound. In flying, I tasted a wine of the gods of which they could know nothing. Who valued life more highly, the aviators who spent it on the art they loved, or these misers who doled it out like pennies through their antlike days? I decided that if I could fly for ten years before I was killed in a crash, it would be a worthwhile trade for an ordinary lifetime.

acknowledgments

Many people made this anthology.

At Thunder's Mouth Press and Avalon Publishing Group:
Neil Ortenberg and Susan Reich offered vital support and expertise.
Dan O'Connor and Ghadah Alrawi also were indispensable.

At Balliett & Fitzgerald Inc.:
Sue Canavan created the book's look. Maria Fernandez oversaw production with tremendous grace and skill. Paul Paddock and Carol Petino helped with production. Margot Abel and Donna Stonecipher proofread copy with care.

At the Writing Company:
Shawneric Hachey gathered books, permissions, facts and photographs; he also scanned and proofread copy. Meghan Murphy gathered and checked facts, contributed ideas and helped in many other ways. John Bishop, Nate Hardcastle, Mark Klimek and Taylor Smith also helped with the book.

At various publishing companies and literary agencies, many people supported this project.

Finally, we are grateful to all of the writers whose work appears in this book.

b i b l i o g r a p h y

The selections used in this anthology were taken from the editions listed below. In some cases, other editions may be easier to find. Hard to find or out-of-print titles often can be acquired through inter-library loan services or through Internet booksellers.

Amis, Martin. *The Information*. New York: Harmony Books, 1995.

Baldwin, Sherman. *Ironclaw: A Navy Carrier Pilot's Gulf War Experience*. New York: William Morrow, 1996.

Buck, Rinker. *Flight of Passage*. New York: Crown Publishers, 1996.

Collins, Michael. *Carrying the Fire: An Astronaut's Journeys*. New York: Farrar, Straus & Giroux, 1974.

Dahl, Roald. *Going Solo*. New York: Penguin Books, 1986.

Gann, Ernest K. *Fate is the Hunter*. New York: Simon & Schuster, 1986.

Harrison, Marshall. *A Lonely Kind of War*. Novato, CA: Presidio Press, 1989.

Lindbergh, Charles A. *The Spirit of St. Louis*. New York: Scribner, 1998.

Lishman, William. *Father Goose*. New York: Crown Publishers, 1996.

Markham, Beryl. *West With the Night*. San Francisco: North Point Press, 1983.

McEwan, Ian. *Enduring Love*. New York: Nan A. Talese, 1998.

Rankin, William H. *The Man Who Rode the Thunder*. Englewood Cliffs, NJ: Prentice-Hall, 1960.

Reporting World War II: Part 1, American Journalism, 1938-1944. New York: Library of America, 1995, (for "The Price of Fire" by Martha Gellhorn).

Saint-Exupéry, Antoine de. *Wind, Sand and Stars*. San Diego: Harcourt Brace Jovanovich, 1984.

Taylor, Sir Gordon. *The Sky Beyond*. New York: Doubleday, 1991.

Wolfe, Thomas. *The Right Stuff*. New York: Farrar, Straus & Giroux, 1983.

about the editors

David Fisher has written more than 40 books, which have sold millions of copies. His books include the number one bestsellers *Gracie* (with George Burns) and *The Umpire Strikes Back* (with Ron Luciano), as well as the best-selling *Been There, Done That* (with Eddie Fisher). William Garvey, a contributing editor of *Flying* magazine, writes regularly for *Smithsonian Air and Space* and other aviation publications. He holds a commercial pilot rating.

Clint Willis is series editor of Adrenaline Books. His other anthologies for the series include *Epic: Stories of Survival from the World's Highest Peaks; Rough Water: Stories of Survival from the Sea*, and *The War: Stories of Life and Death from World War II*.

adrenaline™

**More exciting titles from
Adrenaline Books
edited by Clint Willis**

WILD: Stories of Survival from the World's Most Dangerous Places

The wilderness—forest, desert, glacier, jungle—has inspired some of the past century's best writers, from Edward Abbey and Jack London to Norman Maclean and Jon Krakauer. *Wild* contains 14 selections of their finest work, for people who love the wilderness and readers who love great writing. Also includes selections by Barry Lopez, James Dickey, David Roberts, Bill Bryson and Joe Kane.
$16.95 ($26 Canada), 368 pages

ICE: Stories of Survival from Polar Exploration

The Arctic and Antarctica have been the sites of many of this century's most gripping adventure stories. *Ice* features 15 of the best and most exciting accounts by the greatest explorers and observers of the polar regions—from Robert Scott, Ernest Shackleton and Richard E. Byrd to Barry Lopez, Nancy Mitford and Beryl Bainbridge.
$16.95 ($26 Canada), 384 pages

All **Adrenaline Books** are available at your neighborhood bookstore, or via the Internet. To order directly from the publisher please call Publishers Group West at (800) 788-3123.

For more information on Adrenaline titles, visit thewritingcompany.com

(adrenaline)™

CLIMB: Stories of Survival From Rock, Snow and Ice
Edited by Clint Willis

The third entry in Adrenaline Books' unique climbing trilogy, this collection focuses on the most exciting descriptions of the hardest climbing in the world. From the cliffs of Yosemite to the windswept towers of Patagonia to the high peaks of Alaska and the Himalayas, *Climb* offers more than a dozen classic accounts.

Shackleton's Forgotten Men: The Untold Tale of an Antarctic Tragedy
By Lennard Bickel, foreword by Rt.Hon.Lord Shackleton, K.C., P.C., O.B.E.

The drama of Shackleton's Antarctic survival story overshadowed a near-simultaneous expedition that the explorer launched—but did not lead—to lay support depots across the Great Ross Ice Shelf in preparation for the Shackleton party. Now Lennard Bickel tells the tragic story of these forgotten heroes in a thrilling account that illuminates Shackleton's legend and recounts the courage and endurance of these men who served the great explorer so well.

RESCUE: Stories of Survival from Land and Sea
Edited by Dorcas Miller, Series Editor Clint Willis

Some of the world's best adventure writing tells stories of people in trouble and the people who come to their aid. *Rescue* mines that rich literature for accounts from mountain ledges, sea-going vessels, New Hampshire trails, North African desert wastes, the Greenland Ice Cap and the real Wild West. It includes work by some of the world's best writers, from John Hersey and Antoine de St. Exupéry to Spike Walker and Pete Sinclair.